"If you have been looking to move your person
level and raise your standards to the stars, then
may seem to have been written specifically witl
-*Martin Gollery, CEO, Sierra Success Technologies, Associate D..*,
Nevada Center for Bioinformatics

"*Today is Your Day to Win* is a special book geared toward self reflection
and growth. It should be on every leader's night stand. For what we think
about most we become. This book will guide everyone to higher level of
success and personal accomplishment."
-*Mark J. Miller, MS, ATC, V.P. Operations, Merritt Athletic Clubs*

"*Today is Your Day to Win* is chock full of swift kicks to the
whatchamacallit to remind you that you have what it takes to reach the next
level of personal and professional excellence. Take the plunge! Mike, this
book is a winner!!!"
-*Todd L. Shuler, President and CEO, ThoughtBulb, Inc.*

"*Today is Your Day to Win* is a fascinating and inspiring manual that will
bring immense joy to your life. Even as a personal success coach myself, I
gain brilliant strategies that I use in my own daily life... All thanks to Mike
Brescia."
-*Ted Hebert, CEO, TRH International & Creator of "Passionate &
Fearless Sales Method"*

"*Today is Your Day to Win* is the most remarkable demonstration of the
power of the human spirit. An enormous source of strength, wisdom and
encouragement, I couldn't do without it."
- *Dr. Clint Jones, President, Success Consultants Limited*

"So many motivational tactics do not have the ingredients for getting senior
executives to take action - They don't offer motives that are relative.
'Today Is Your Day To Win' by Mike Brescia gives thought provoking
reflections that resonate with senior executives or those who seriously want
to be."
-*Louis P. Kasman, CMC/APR/CBC, President, Marketing/Management
Associates, LLC*

"*Today is Your Day to Win* should have been published 250 years ago. Too
bad that Mike wasn't able to do just that, because our world would be a
much finer place. "
-*David L. Kirchner, President, Basin & Range Hydrogeologists, Inc.*

"*Today is Your Day to Win,* like a certain cereal, is the breakfast of champions: Read, Think and Repeat!"
-David G. Phillips, Pres. and CEO Custom, Development Solutions (CDS)

"Like a well-balanced diet, Mike's words feed and enhance every aspect of our professional and personal lives. We apply his techniques daily and pay them forward to clients and colleagues."
Matt Dutra, President & Chief Creative, Rubic Design

"*Today is Your Day to Win* is that much needed wake up call that just seems to show up when you need it - on time and on target. It expands your focus when the pressures of the day tend to constrict it."
-John K. Goyak, CEO, JG&A, Inc., Developer of GamePlanTM, A Powerful Strategic Planning Capability

"As a quality leader and mother of a child with learning disabilities, I am continually looking for "lessons learned" to share with my organization and children. *Today is Your Day to Win* is THE TOOL I am using both at work and at home. It is inspiring, positive, proactive...a MUST read for any lifelong learner!"
-Sharon Horne-Ellstrom, Director of Quality, Concept2Bakers

"*Today is Your Day to Win* bridges the gap between extraordinary learning skills and taking massive positive action. This book is like a friend who takes a no-nonsense approach...a straight shooter with an aim to win!"
-Jon Ensor, National Accounts Manager, UrologyTech LLC

"*Today is Your Day to Win* has changed the destiny of my life and the path that my company will follow forever (a blueprint)-superbly done and well-constructed. I can only see good things coming."
-Michael A. Riberal, North Star Financial Services

"*Today is Your Day to Win* not only motivates, excites and inspires you, it works! I would passionately recommend this book to everyone searching for their winning path." *-Sheryl L. Draschil, CEO, Corporate Image Inc. Author of "I Need You: The Ultimate Relationship Guide"*

"I have been fortunate enough to spend the last 34 years as a public school principal. One of my most critical jobs has always been helping teachers find new ways to reach children. *Today is Your Day to Win* is a fantastic source of fuel to lights my teachers' fires. I'm ready for *Today is Your Day to Win #2.*" *-Ivan Kershner, Assistant Principal, Palmetto Middle School, Williamston, SC*

Foreword

When I heard that Mike Brescia was releasing a new book, I was excited and immediately got a copy.

Here's why.

I've been reading Mike's wisdom for over 18 months now in his *Your Day To Win* Ezine and not a day goes by that I don't glean a life changing gem from his writings.

I've had the opportunity over the last 5 years to interview the most successful people in the world today, Tony Robbins, Robert Allen, Mark Victor Hansen, Les Brown, Jim Rohn and dozens of others, so I know something good when I see it. And Mike Brescia has something good within these pages. Real good.

Wherever you are in your life, you can open a page of *Today Is Your Day To Win* and you'll get inspired, motivated, and be moved to greater action and purpose.

This is very rare in books today.

Today Is Your Day To Win is the kind of book you want to leave next to your bed and the kind of book that you'll want to tell your friends about.

You're about to enter an excursion into excellence.

As you turn the pages, you'll be turning the pages of your new life.

Read and apply.

Enjoy!

Mike Litman
#1 Best-Selling Co-Author, *Conversations With Millionaires*

This is dedicated to you, Grampa.
I love you and miss you.
Thanks for all the lessons.

Today Is Your Day To Win

Mike Brescia

How to use this book

What you are about to read has changed the lives of thousands around the world. And it can change your life.

"Today Is Your Day To Win" will send you on a path of introspection, self-discovery, inner joy, self satisfaction, massive action, and with some "lucky bounces" thrown in, outer success that few ever attain.

But I'll warn you now…

If you read a few stories and get sucked in, wanting to read a bunch of them all at once, STOP! Don't do it.

Most people believe that if a little is good, then a lot *must* be better. Sometimes that's true. Most times it's not.

The "more is better" belief system makes for overindulgence, addictions, lack of appreciation and many other habit patterns that can squash a person's unlimited potential and turn their life into hell on earth.

Used correctly Today Is Your Day To Win' is an inspiring action guide to a better life.

And like life, this book is meant to be lived one day at a time, <u>not</u> all at once. If you follow this one simple instruction, it will be impossible for you not to be changed dramatically.

So I must ask that you refrain from getting caught up in the enthusiasm that each story stirs up and plow through the book in just a few days or weeks.

One Fast Session per day. Monday through Friday. That's it.

And DO what each session says to do. Don't fear, you can do it. Nothing you'll be asked to do in 'Today Is Your Day To Win' is beyond your ability...IF you take it one day at a time. Soon you will find that inner and outer success is not impossible.

You'll see that it's probable...IF you'll just follow a few simple instructions.

Again, don't worry.

Each Fast Session is designed to motivate you and challenge you and push you like no book you've ever read. With these daily calls to action, you'll find that you're quickly able to make small changes... changes that produce HUGE results.

At the time of this writing, over 70,000 people all over the world receive only a couple of these sessions per week via email, and it's changing their lives. I get dozens of letters every single day from people across the globe expressing their appreciation for what these simple yet inspiring sessions have done for them...

Spaced repetition of positive, empowering, hope-filled thoughts is the key to replacing bad habits with good ones.

If you read a number of sessions all at once... if you zoom through the book, nothing will have changed for you because it can't last. Soon you will be back to the same old ways of feeling and acting.

Read one session per day five days per week and reflect on each day's session throughout your day. Focus only on that day's session. Every single one is important. Over the course of four and a half months, you'll have finished the book and will have been exposed to amazing information in the most powerful way... repetitiously over time.

By then, no doubt, you'll have taken massive actions, learned valuable life lessons, witnessed your small daily achievements growing into large important accomplishments and felt the satisfaction of doing the best you are capable of...

Then, you should look back to where you were four months ago. If you do what is in these pages, you should not be able to recognize who you were before.

That is my dream for you, my new wonderful friend.

I know, as you read and work through the following pages, that your belief in yourself will grow and grow and grow. Because of my experience with people all over the world using 'Your Day To Win,' I absolutely know that if you move through this book with purpose and persistence, you will be able to do, be and have anything you can dream.

At the end of each day's session, you'll find 'Today's Empowering Beliefs'. To get the most out of these, print them on 3x5 cards and read them with emotion, shaking your head up and down as you read them. It also helps to instill these powerful beliefs if you say to yourself, "YES!" or "THAT'S RIGHT!" or "ABSOLUTELY!" as you read them – all the while shaking your head up and down. Do this short activity three times per day, once when you arise in the morning, once at lunch time and once before you retire for the evening. This does take a few minutes per day, but isn't your happiness and success in life worth a few minutes? Deep inside you know it is.

Limit your reading of your 3x5's to 10-15 cards. Any more than this and you'll be overwhelmed. The rule of thumb is to find empowering beliefs that you don't currently have, where your attitudes and actions are opposite to the statements.

Many people take these statements and type them into their copy of our visual success conditioning software, Think Right Now! for Windows, letting the software help to imprint them into their subconscious minds.

To learn more about the software, go to
http://www.thinkrightnow.com/trnwindows.htm

Follow these simple directions, and I'm confident that 'Today Is Your Day To Win' will be the most important personal development book you've ever had the good fortune to own.

Your partner in success,

Mike Brescia

TABLE OF CONTENTS

FROM THE BENCH TO THE PLAYING FIELD

TODAY'S EMPOWERING QUOTE

"I have brought myself by long meditation to the conviction that a human being with a settled purpose must accomplish it, and that nothing can resist a will which will stake even existence upon its fulfillment."
    -Benjamin Disraeli

TODAY'S EMPOWERING QUESTION

"What am I willing to give up in order to reach my objective?"

TODAY'S FAST SESSION

OK, OK. I give in. Since I've had so many requests about how I went from a real bum to being able to write to tens of thousands of friends all over the world, here's the story. It's... interesting.

Up until early 1987 I regularly used to beg the gods for an answer to the question of why I couldn't get myself to do what I needed to do to get my simple goals met. Why was I so lazy and miserable? I was just... a bum.

I got fired from countless jobs. I flunked out of college. And then got fired some more.

Finally, after reading some very popular books on selling and motivation over and over...

...I continued to fail, not making one single solitary thin dime in my commissioned sales job for close to TWO more years. If it weren't for friends and then my trusty Ford Econoline van, I literally would've been living "on" the street.

One day, during this period, while sitting in my van, a man walked up and started talking to me. He was brilliant. He went on to tell the story of when he, as an announcer, covered the World Series back in the late 60's. He had all the names; he knew stats like it was yesterday. His voice was clearly that of a broadcaster. But the thing that was most incredible was...

...He was pushing a shopping cart, which carried all his earthly possessions.

He was homeless, too. Living on the street. I couldn't believe it.

He told me that he just got sick of the daily challenges. One problem after another. He literally became unable to function in any capacity. Very quickly he had lost everything. At the end, it was by choice.

Sadly, I could identify with THIS guy more than anyone I had met in a while. I was very low, but fortunately, I hadn't quite reached that level...

...Yet.

I did want to get off the "street" and stop being a bum. So I found this great bookstore around Hermosa Beach that had comfy chairs, and I started spending a lot of time there. Ultimately, I had gotten very familiar with a number of self-help change methods, including NLP, self-talk and Accelerated Learning techniques. Like I said, I had a lot of time on my hands.

I soon came back to Upstate New York, got a menial job and started to create my own Superlearning tapes with three cheap, borrowed tape players. Only instead of learning a language or factual data at lightning speeds, I figured I'd teach myself new attitudes and instruct myself to do things that sent tremors of fear through me... actions that could change me from a loser to someone I'd be proud to be.

So from every sales, biography, motivation, NLP and don't worry, be happy book I could find, I pulled out all the lessons, the beliefs and the attitudes of life's top performers. I turned them into self-instructions, and recorded them onto tapes with very specific baroque music passages playing in the background.

It was quite a setup. I was desperate and willing to do anything. I couldn't be getting fired more from any more $5.00 an hour jobs.

In what seemed like just a few days, I began to feel differences. In my new job, I started working lots of hours putting coin-operated TVs together and installing them. Soon, I was making telephone calls to prospective customers, large travel plazas with big restaurants.

These early TV boxes were downright ugly, but I was able to convince the presidents of nearly every one of these huge corporations to let us tear up their nice dining rooms to put these things in. It was wild. I mean, I just got in a frenzy of conviction before each call.

The more I listened to my tapes while I slept, the more fanatical I got about reading and learning. Among my recorded self-instructions were ones that told me I loved learning and that I was the greatest salesman in the world. Ha!! I put in that the more I succeeded, the more success I wanted. Talk about a vicious cycle, huh?

Well, soon I had exhausted the company's inventory of TV's. And since the revenue each one made wasn't that high, the company had no money to buy the parts to build hundreds more. Even though it proved to be a dead end job, it felt good not being fired.

So I left to start selling hearing instruments. I just got scary good. In an industry where 20-25% closing ratios were typical, I was selling 95%. In just about 4 months, that self-instruction about being the greatest salesman in the world was eerily coming true... at least in that industry. Soon I was going seven days a week. Missing a sale was just not an option.

I continued to listen to my tapes and develop new ones. Considering where I came from to where I was now, I figured that anything was possible. I researched and made tapes for everything from diet practices to anxiety. I had gone from being scared of everything to feeling like I couldn't fail.

I used to use double negatives when I spoke. "I didn't do nothing" was a famous line. This drove people around me crazy. So I researched communication and public speaking and made an accelerated success tape.

Whenever I wanted to eliminate a block, get good at something, or feel better about myself, I looked for the top professionals, researched their findings, uncovered lots of conflicting data, found what made sense and made a tape in the accelerated learning format.

I've found there wasn't anything that I couldn't literally install into or rip out of my mind. And with the right thoughts and instructions, you could create an endless loop of success, each good outcome fueling in you the desire to keep the positive change and to improve even more.

In short, that's the early part of the story that leads me to today, getting to talk to you.

I hope this answered a few questions and inspired you to believe that no matter what you're going through right now, you are truly magnificent. All you have to do is release your blocks and embrace your unlimited potential. There's enormous power within you. It might be buried, but it's there.

I know, I know.

If that seems a little beyond what your belief system currently allows you to accept, I understand. That's OK. Keep reading and repeating your self instructions.

You'll become a believer soon enough.

TODAY'S WINNING BELIEFS

-- Every success I achieve fuels in me the desire for more
-- I can achieve anything that I can imagine
-- I have the ability to visualize every aspect of my success
-- My ability is greater than any challenge I could face

YOU ARE HERE TO ENRICH THE WORLD

TODAY'S EMPOWERING QUOTE

"You are not here merely to make a living. You are here in order to enable the world to live more amply, with greater vision, with a finer spirit of hope and achievement. You are here to enrich the world, and you impoverish yourself if you forget that errand."
  - Woodrow Wilson, 28th President of the United States

TODAY'S EMPOWERING QUESTION

"What can I do to best help the largest number of people?
Why should I?"

TODAY'S FAST SESSION

A lot of people ask me how I got into such a unique profession, how this form of communication got started, how our products got their start.

As we all regularly should, toward the end of 1996, I asked myself the question, what do I want to do with the rest of my life?

For me, it wasn't unlike the situation that Tom Hanks' character in the 1999 movie, 'The Green Mile' was faced with.

To see the similarity, you need some background:

The bulk of the story takes place in 1935, during the Depression, in a southern maximum-security prison. Paul Edgecomb (Tom Hanks) is the head guard on death row... the last mile.

John Coffey is a new prisoner convicted of raping and murdering two young girls - sisters. He was sentenced to die in the electric chair.

The thing is, he was innocent.

John wasn't retarded, but if his IQ were measured on a standard test today, it would probably be very low. He was black, nearly 7 feet tall, and easily weighed over 300 pounds. His muscles had muscles.

10

He was found sitting on a small riverbank with both girls in his arms, screaming over and over, "I tried, but I couldn't take it back."

So he didn't exactly get a fair trial.

But what made the story so incredible was John's special gift...

He had the ability to heal other people. He performed literal miracles. He would take a person's infection or disease into his own body and then eliminate it by opening his mouth, and what looked sort of like black flies would fly out by the thousands and dissipate. He even brought a mouse, 'Mr. Jingles,' back from the dead.

The process completely exhausted him temporarily, but the person (or mouse) would be completely healed.

When he was found with the girls, he was trying to tell people that he tried to bring the girls back to life, but he "couldn't take it back."

Learning of John Coffey's gifts, benefiting from them personally and witnessing other healings, Paul Edgecomb went into John's cell a couple days before his scheduled execution and had the following dialog:

"John, tell me what you want me to do... you want me to take you out of here... just let you run away and see how far you can get?"

John replied, "Why would you do such a foolish thing?"

Paul answered, "On the day of my judgment, when I stand before God, and he asks me why did I kill one of his true miracles, what am I going to say? That it was my job?"

John answered back, "You tell God, the Father, that it was a kindness that you done... I know you're hurtin' and worryin'. I can feel it on ya. But you ought to quit on it now. I want it to be over and done with. I do. I'm tired, boss. I'm tired of bein' on the road, lonely as a sparrow in the rain. I'm tired of not having anybody to be with to tell me where we's goin' to, comin' from or why."

He continued, "Mostly I'm tired of people being ugly to each other. I'm tired of all the pain I'm feeling in the world. There's too much of it. It's like pieces of glass in my head all the time. Can you understand?"

Paul could do nothing to change this.

So it was done... and he had to live with the execution of John Coffey for the rest of his life.

I felt that I was faced with a similar question.

A decade after I created the first audiotapes that changed me and changed what I was able to manifest in my life, I ultimately recognized it as a tool that could potentially help millions change their destinies in so many ways.

So ten years after my own metamorphosis, the work began.

And 6 years later, thinkrightnow.com is the most popular self-help product site on the planet.

Why?

Because the products work.

In working with people all over the world, I believe more firmly than ever in the ability in each of us to create the lives we want and enrich the world in the process, as President Wilson said.

John Coffey quit. Circumstances made it nearly impossible for his life to improve or for him to use his gifts to help those who needed them the most.

But that isn't you. And that isn't me. You may hide from your choices, seeing them as something scary, but they don't have to be. Practically all your daily decisions can have tremendous power to transform you and your life into something truly spectacular. There are millions of people alive who are living dream lives...

You can be one of them, no matter how old or young you are.

My purpose now is to empower others so that they can create a continual process of growth in the world. It's working.

Remember, everything you do will ring in eternity. When you have a bad day, it could affect people for many centuries to come.

So you owe it not only to yourself, but also to the future of your family, your friends and the entire human race to grow and share all your gifts.

Maybe your gifts and skills are modest, but to hide them, to not develop and share them, whatever they are would be a great tragedy.

Six years ago, I wondered how I could live with myself if I didn't do what I knew would improve the lives of so many.

I knew I couldn't.

Take time to reflect today and every day on what your life could mean expanded out over the decades and centuries.

No matter how much or how little time on earth you have left, you can be a great contributor and potentially a catalyst for positive change around you... and thus around the world, possibly for centuries to come.

So when you are ever tempted to feel bored or uninspired, chew on that for a while.

It should get your juices flowing.

TODAY'S WINNING BELIEFS

-- I'm making the most of my life now and every day.
-- I am committed to living my life with passion
-- I'm using my unique gifts to enrich myself and others
-- I'm making myself worth more each and every day
-- I believe in the future of the human race
-- I bring out the best in others

SUCCESS IS SIMPLE

TODAY'S EMPOWERING QUOTE

"The mind is like the stomach. It is not how much you put into it that counts, but how much it digests."
   --A.J. Nock

TODAY'S EMPOWERING QUESTION

"What can I do to ensure that this will stick in my mind?"

TODAY'S FAST SESSION

As statistics show, most of what is written in the world's greatest self-help and how-to books goes unread by the buyers. And the material that is read is typically not used.

Most people just aren't self-disciplined enough to take a bit, study it, master it then move on to the next level. That's why universities are so valuable and so expensive... they do it right.

They give you a little bit, test you and then give you some more - building on your knowledge after you've learned the easier stuff.

That's why these letters always end with some affirmations so that you can have something to use to program your mind. That's also why books like 'Chicken Soup for the Soul' have helped so many millions, because, as I counseled people as they bought those books from my store, the stories are meant to be read one per day...

Just enough to be not too fast. Any more than that and the lesson in the story is missed, being plowed over by the next one.

These sessions are meant to be read the same way...

...Just one a day.

That is the best way to get the most out of them.

Benjamin Franklin, one of the world's greatest scholars, politicians and inventors, made a list of 13 virtues that he valued but did not possess. What Ben did was work on only one virtue at a time, noting when he messed up, and when he succeeded in using the virtue. He made turning himself into a person who possessed that virtue his mission and did not worry about any of the other 12 until he had mastered the first one.

Ultimately, he conquered them all.

And he will forever be remembered as one of the greatest men who ever lived. Man, this is simple! And so sad...

...Because so many people go to their graves never conquering even one of their major hurdles in life, settling for mediocrity.

Let me ask you, was Ben Franklin's growth plan so complicated that you or... well, practically anyone else couldn't use it?

Couldn't even someone with no common sense or potential for any more than pushing a broom eight hours a day go after just one goal at a time with passion?

Success isn't complicated, is it?

The average person wants to believe it is so that their failures can be explained away, their weaknesses can be hidden and their poor decisions justified.

As you read through the rest of these sessions, keep in mind how simple it is to follow them and easy it is to use them to achieve massive success and peace of mind.

Not one thing you'll be asked to do is beyond your ability to do it. Practically anything you desire is within your grasp.

Just look at the individual tasks and go to it, one tiny step at a time.

TODAY'S WINNING BELIEFS

-- I work on one area of my life at a time
-- I master easy jobs before I move on to harder things
-- I am a fast learner
-- Mastery and I are one

WHAT'S LOVE GOT TO DO WITH IT?

TODAY'S EMPOWERING QUOTE

"Praise is well, compliment is well, but affection-that is the last and most precious reward that any man can win, whether by character or achievement."
 --Mark Twain

TODAY'S EMPOWERING QUESTION

"What do I love about _____(name of person)?"

TODAY'S FAST SESSION

When I train a sales person, the first thing I try to find out about them is how they view their customers and other people in general. Pretty quickly I can tell with good accuracy if they're going to make it or not.

My first lesson always starts with love.

You can't sell effectively, whether it's a product or an idea, if you hold contempt and dislike for other people, or simply if your own best interests come first. In fact, it's difficult to get through each day without abundant feelings of love or just sincerely good opinions about other people flowing through your veins.

When I started in the sales world, I failed for a few YEARS. I just wanted to make money—it was all about myself. Well, that must've come through in my voice and actions, because I couldn't give my products away.

But I read a book, "The Greatest Salesman in the World," and it helped to change my life. That was my introduction to affirmations. The first scroll, which was to be read three times/day for a month was about "greeting this day with love in my heart." My sales went crazy!

I began looking at everyone as a friend, not as a paycheck. I changed every view I had about other people. And they responded...

Not just in sales, but in all areas. Where I had enemies, they became friends. Where I was laughed at, I was admired.

To give you just the tiniest of glimpses of what Og Mandino writes and what I read, one passage reads...

"...And how will I speak? I will laud my enemies and they will become friends; I will encourage my friends and they will become brothers. Always will I look for reasons to applaud; never will I scratch for excuses to gossip. When I am tempted to criticize, I will bite my tongue; when I am moved to praise, I will shout from the roofs.

Toward the end of that scroll it is affirmed...

"... If I have no other qualities, I can succeed with love alone. Without it I will fail though I possess all the knowledge and skills in the world."

Imagine soaking your consciousness with that and many other thoughts like it three times a day for 30 straight days.

Think about this...

Who do you buy products and ideas from? Those you trust and love (or like), right? Most people are more likely to listen to their cousin about a stock tip over a 40-year stock-investing guru, if they don't know him or her.

That's what familiarity and trust does.

When you look at someone for the first time, do you look for things to judge, criticize or distrust; or do you see things you can admire, compliment and feel good about?

No matter what, you'll find what you're looking for...

If you habitually look for bad, you'll find it--even if you have to manufacture it.

But when you train yourself to unconsciously look for good, you'll find that, too.

Deep in your heart, you know I'm right. You know it.

But in your daily actions, it's difficult to implement it. That's why Og Mandino's books always ended with scrolls, vows or success memorandums that had to be read every day. Og understood that his teachings would not benefit anyone if they were read once and put on the bookshelf to be forgotten.

The unseen power of love will escape you if you just read this and say, "Wow, that's right. I'm going to do it."

You've got to install this and any other empowering beliefs in your mind daily if they're to make a dent in those habits of yours so they can start affecting your feelings and actions.

Get this in your head and you will be miles ahead of where you were this morning.

Condition your mind with positive empowering new beliefs and success producing attitudes, and your destiny will change.

TODAY'S WINNING BELIEFS

-- I've dissolved the criticism habit
-- I look for the good in others and they respond to me
-- I love other people and they love me back
-- I greet this day with love in my heart
-- I look for things to like in others and I find them
-- My love is creating opportunities for me today

WHAT ARE *YOUR* ASPIRATIONS?

TODAY'S EMPOWERING QUOTE

"There is no shame in having fallen. Nor any shame in being born into a lowly estate. There is only shame in not struggling to rise. And also shame for not wishing to attain the better. Or not dreaming about it and praying for it."
 --Samuel Amalu

TODAY'S EMPOWERING QUESTION

"How did those people get there? How did they become that way? Was everything given to them, was it genetics, or a loving mother? Or was it planning and dedication that got them to where they are, to be who they are?"

TODAY'S FAST SESSION

The people who have a number of possessions or "status" that didn't earn it are known as being "born with a silver spoon in their mouth"... or state lottery winners.

But statistics reveal that the average rich person that doesn't have to work for what they get doesn't know how to keep it, or anything else in their lives - and becomes the type that just can't make anything work.

They get trained to live their lives with their hands out to Mommy and Daddy. If that sounds a bit hard to believe, read 'The Millionaire Next Door.'

Whether you're wealthy or not, giving your kids everything creates social and financial cripples.

Most follow-up research on Lottery winners shows the same thing. Within a short time, it's all gone.   They didn't EARN it, never learned responsibility with money, so they're helpless against every expensive temptation there is. So even if you win, you lose.

My possibly unpopular opinion is this: Stop blowing your money on lottery tickets. Figure out how much you spend on them and that expensive daily gourmet cappuccino, and put exactly that much in a money market fund

20

every week or two and become rich the proven way - slowly. Surely. But how do you start to get the discipline to be able to do something like that? To achieve any worthwhile objective?

Goals.

The average person has no long-term goals. And the word creates a lot of confusion.

Most think a goal is a goal when it's something like: You want to be rich; want a screen star body; win a gold medal; get an advanced college degree; in short, to desire something really huge.

The trouble with big goals is not that you're dreaming out of your league-- it's that very few set goals in such a way that they ever get accomplished. Like everything, there's right and wrong ways to do it. You can buy books, and go to seminars to learn how. I did. But honestly, it boils down to a few simple steps and some things you can do to ensure that you'll stick it out and be there at the end with your hands raised high.

The first mistake everyone usually makes is getting excited about having something - prompted by an external source, a commercial maybe. Wrong way to start.

I know I sound like a broken record, but setting and achieving goals is not REALLY about what you get as much as it is what you become during the process of attaining your goal. When you ARE more, you'll get more automatically now and in the future.

A natural by-product.

What you need to do first is look at an area of your life that's causing you some trouble. You are in pain about it. Emotional, physical, whatever.

Choose an area that gives you a big one of these "pains." I mean, why go after something you really don't want badly, right? Getting rid of a gnawing pain that you've had for a while is a great way. Getting rid of the fabricated pain that a commercial stirred up and then proposed to cure is often the wrong way...

The "I'm a sheep" way. Baaaaa!

Take your pain and look at it. What does it cost you to have the problem or lack? Write down the physical costs, emotional, mental, social, spiritual, financial. Spread it out for 1, 2, 5 and 20 years. Feel it. Get by yourself and do this, because you just might need a few tissues during this process. Take your time.

It's been a long time that you haven't had this "goal" so a little time spent doing this is an investment. Trust me.

This will give you determination you didn't think you had. Let me tell you. You have it...

You just have to find this pain and then keep it handy.

When you have that, you'll have a base for the setting of a goal - a goal that inspires you to keep going... to reach down deep.

Do this exercise and you'll begin to see the power of starting out intelligently instead of letting others control your goals for you.

TODAY'S WINNING BELIEFS

-- I set goals based on my real needs and desires
-- Today I'm setting my sights on defining what I want
-- I'm willing to put the effort in to achieve my goals
-- I enjoy the process of setting and reaching worthwhile goals
-- I set goals the right way

THOSE WHO KNOW ARE WHERE TO GO

TODAY'S EMPOWERING QUOTE

"Listen to everything a man has to say about what he knows, but don't let him advise you about what he doesn't know. And usually he doesn't know too much about what's best for you."
   -Barney Balaban

TODAY'S EMPOWERING QUESTION

"Whose advice have I been listening to? Has it helped? Where can I get the most helpful information and feedback?"

TODAY'S FAST SESSION

Doesn't it seem like everywhere you turn someone is willing to tell you how to get rid of your problems... whether they know what they're talking about or not? The danger is when you start to listen to it. You'll usually find that your advisor/critics rarely, if ever, follow their own advice.

I was recently watching the NY Yankees play the NY Mets, when a commercial came on that starred Mike Piazza, the catcher for the Mets. He's having a rough season so far.

In the commercial, here's Mike standing on the street. A guy in a truck asks Mike, "How deep is right field?" Mike says, "About 330 feet." Then the guy asks, "How deep is center field?" Mike says, "About 410 feet." So the guy says to Mike, "Hit it to right field!"

The game announcers remarked that those kinds of interactions happen all the time between players and fans.

Here's an important question: Who are you listening to?

Do you take advice and criticism from people who have no business giving it out? Is it usually helpful?

Now don't get me wrong. Criticism delivered properly is healthy, course correcting feedback... if you seek to learn.

Too often though, critics have other agendas. And they couldn't take their own advice if their lives depended on it.

The problem with hearing unwanted or unwarranted criticism is that it often isn't put in a constructive way, so instead of getting, "You know I read that walking just 20-30 minutes a day can help you lose x # of pounds. Have you tried that?" you usually hear, "You are fat. You better start exercising."

This from a person who probably only puts on a pair of sweat pants to sleep in.

Here are a few bad examples of well meaning but potentially costly advice.

-You should get into XYZ stock. It's been climbing for a year.
-I take Supercalifragilistic weight loss pills and I lost 13 pounds. You ought to try it, too. A doctor made it.
-I quit smoking cold turkey. That's the only way that works.
-Don't let it get to you. What you need is a drink.
-Vegetarian? How do you get protein? You have to eat meat.

When I was failing at selling, everyone had advice. The trouble was, the people giving it were the furthest thing from professionals.

So in addition to reading books, listening to tapes and going to seminars, I set up an evaluation system that told me with absolute accuracy if I was doing a good job that day.

I graded my performance each day on about 30 different factors. Everything from number of calls, how I greeted someone, my facial expressions, question structure, listening with empathy, concern for their problems instead of mine, answering questions, building value, etc. It was an extremely thorough, honest assessment.

After each appointment, I pulled out my sheet and filled in the grades for each factor. It took 1-2 minutes, and was brutally honest at telling me where I needed to improve. Many salespeople who knew me asked me how I turned it all around so fast. I didn't offer it. They asked first. When I'd tell them what I did, they couldn't believe something so simple could work so well.

And every single one of those salespeople continued on their mediocre ways. Many left the sales profession all together.

Imagine that. They had a world record holder willing to share a critical idea, yet they continued listening to their equally inept co-workers instead. Very few people want constructive criticism, even if it's just from themselves.

So I have two tiny little suggestions...

One, don't give advice. People don't want it. They don't use it. And they'll get sick of hearing it. If you must, be a sounding board instead. When people hear themselves out loud, they often get the answer they were looking for without outside advice. It's hard enough to change yourself. Changing others is fifty times more difficult.

And two, don't let critics ruin your mood. Not even for a minute. If someone comes along and gives you their two cents and you find yourself feeling powerless, make a mental note, "This is what I get when I let just anyone mess with my esteem and confidence."

Listen to yourself and to people who have overcome the same challenges that you're working on. That's it. Talk to people about your challenges, but unless they've overcome the same thing, be careful about taking their suggestions.

It could be very costly to your emotional, physical and financial health.

TODAY'S WINNING BELIEFS

-- I seek out advice from the appropriate places
-- I check out all options when I make important decisions
-- I'm good at evaluating the value of advice
-- I'm in solid control of my own self-esteem
-- I am honest with myself in areas that need improvement

DEVELOP YOUR TALENTS

TODAY'S EMPOWERING QUOTE

'All of us do not have equal talent, but all of us should have an equal opportunity to develop our talents.'
    -John F. Kennedy

TODAY'S EMPOWERING QUESTION

How much more work would it be to do this task as well as I can versus as quickly as I can? What value would it be to me to do it as well as I can?

TODAY'S FAST SESSION

In our back yard, about 15 feet from the house is a large, gorgeous maple tree.

In the summer, it's home to a number of birds.

Last year, at the end of a long branch, which extends to within 7 feet of our upstairs bathroom window, some robins built a nest where they lived all summer until the weather got too cold.

Both our cats just lay in the windowsill for hours all summer watching the birds come and go less than 7 feet from their window perch.

Now keep in mind that this winter was absolutely brutal.

14 feet of snow. The wind that blew like no winter that I can ever recall. Never as often and as hard as this year, it seemed. It was just miserable from mid October until April.

Yet this bird's nest, sitting on a long branch wide open to the chilling, hammering winds and cold that snaps electrical wires like tooth picks, stayed right there.

Every day, I'd look out at this nest and there it was, gripping that branch...

And I've got to believe that the robins that built the nest were no smarter or more skilled in nest building than any of the robins in my neighbors' trees.

They simply didn't want their home to fall apart no matter what. So they build it to withstand the worst possible conditions.

No short cuts.

No excuses.

Tell me, what if you were to take every little task you do today, and do your absolute best?

What if you were to mow the lawn as well as you could today?

What if you gave your all to every customer or prospective customer?

How much more effort would it take to be the best husband, wife or significant other than you normally put in?

What would it really take to avoid eating beyond being comfortably full?

To finish your homework and then study for another 30 minutes for good measure?

You know, the difference between failure, moderate success, an OK marriage, an undistinguished career and a raging success in any one of those areas is usually miniscule.

It's not that much more work.

Often it's hardly any real effort at all.

Every single day I get emails from people who have given up hope of ever being really happy and satisfied in life. "I'm beyond help." "I'm happy that you're doing this work for other people... Too bad it can't help me."

They read the emails. They may even buy the tapes, and either don't listen to them as prescribed, or when changes do begin either with positive progress or with negative tension created by the rapid changes happening, they quit because the change is uncomfortable at first.

"Whoa! That's not me! Who am I kidding? Better slow down."

The bottom line is, change is always wanted on some level but hardly ever completely enjoyable at first.

If there is one thing that you MUST beat into your head every day like a mantra is that success at anything is simple.

GOD, it's so simple!

It's just a matter of repetition of little thoughts and little actions.

For example, to allow yourself to do shoddy work once and then again is to create momentum. A third time is like an avalanche...

Hard to stop it. The fourth time is virtually guaranteed.

When the brownies or chips and soda make it into the shopping cart every week, that's it.

Run past that aisle. Achieve a little success. Get a little momentum going the other way.

When the sitcom wins out consistently over the homework or baseball practice in the back yard, then you are creating a rotten habit, which develops a character.

Done long enough, and that becomes who you are...

But thank God that with just a little effort we can change those things by making only slight direction changes.

The nest in my back yard is now housing a new family of robins who didn't have to do a thing. They just moved in. All the work was done already. They just hung a few pictures, threw out a "Welcome" mat and called it home.

And once you change the momentum of any downward slide you may be in, it's deceptively simple to stop the slide, make a few right decisions and your entire destiny can change.

If I was to get in my truck right now and drive due west for just four days, I'd be in North Bend, Oregon.

But if I was pointing only about 5 degrees to the south, in the same four days I'd end up in Los Angeles, California... about 960 miles away.

Now hold your thumb and fore finger about an eighth of an inch apart.

Go ahead. Do it.

You see, most of the time the difference between horrible, devastating failure and massive, glorious success is only that far apart.

In the next four days, will you have chosen to stay on course?

Keep reminding yourself of how important each hour and each decision is. Do that every hour today, and I guarantee that no matter what doesn't go right, you won't be too terribly bothered by it.

Isn't THAT the direction you wanted to go in today?

TODAY'S WINNING BELIEFS

-- I'm keeping on course today
-- Today is my day to succeed
-- I'm making all the right decisions now
-- I enjoy each of my victories no matter how small
-- I'm doing things right the first time today

LOVE MAKES THE WORLD GO ROUND

TODAY'S EMPOWERING QUOTE

"All you need is love."
  -John Lennon/Paul McCartney

TODAY'S EMPOWERING QUESTION

"How would it feel to do something special for (name a person) who can't or won't do anything in return?"

TODAY'S FAST SESSION

We've all experienced what it feels like to help someone who needed it, haven't we? It feels great.

When I say someone who needed it, it's easy to picture victims of tragedies, accidents or those who are ill.

But the truth is...

We all have needs. Little ones and big ones. Every day.

And if we only give of ourselves, whether it be time, money or good feelings and a smile ONLY when those we are giving to are dying, mourning or destitute, then a couple dynamics start and/or continue.

One is that the world you live in, your community and your immediate environment becomes or stays one of individuals who are only looking out for themselves. A perfect example is what happens with most teenagers who are now spreading their wings and getting new privileges never before enjoyed. Feelings of "I don't have to..." and "You can't make me..." are devastating to every facet of society, including the person carrying these beliefs.

Being only or primarily "self-centered" is what makes people take things that aren't theirs. It causes hazing over or "forgetting" the truth even though there are certain bad consequences to others. This sick mentality of hiding the truth to escape a potential punishment is facilitated in our homes, our schools and in our jobs. When honesty is only offered up when it won't hurt, then there is no learning, no growing and we ALL get hurt by it.

I'm convinced that honesty and compassion may be the most important virtues that a person could possess.

The knowledge that, "We got away with that one!" doesn't help—it hurts.

It teaches us to look for short-cuts to the reward by cheating.

It prevents us from doing something nice for someone else "just because." It makes us believe that "winning" and "getting mine" are the only things that count.

Legendary coach John Wooden's philosophy is that doing our best is the most important thing. And because that was the goal, not winning, his UCLA basketball teams did win 10 national championships in 12 years.

What's this got to do with "All you need is love"?

-Love is doing what's best for all.

-Love is believing that you get more by giving more, not hoarding what little you've got.

-Love is knowing that you've got incredible talents (you do!) and using them for a larger good.

-Love is seeing the good in others and helping it shine.

-Love is feeling the fear and doing it anyway.

-Love is continuing to learn and compassionately helping others to learn, too.

In the weeks that have followed since September 11th, we've all seen what love is.

Here's the challenge... Keep it in mind always. Every time we:

-Cheat and try to find justification
-Lie to protect ourselves or others
-Yell insults to others in the name of "just being honest"
-Ignore someone who needs assistance

...every time we do these things, we teach ourselves to do it again. We teach those around us to do them.

And we become something we despise in others.

It's awfully hard to have high self-esteem and feel worthy of success then, isn't it? It's not hard to wonder why most people don't achieve more in life, huh? We don't think we're worth it. Not after all we've done "to" others instead of "for" others.

We've all got it in us. I've seen it. You've seen it. But we only occasionally show brief glimmers of it.

Show more today.

Do your best. Help someone before they ask. Tell the truth. Teach what you know. Earn your rewards and you'll get more than you think.

Just give it a try.

Don't worry about what reactions you do or don't get from anyone else. The most important thing is that YOU know you're doing right and showing love in all that you do.

Give all your passion in everything you do today and I'll bet you'll sleep better tonight than you have in a long, long time.

TODAY'S WINNING BELIEFS

-- I have unlimited capacity to love
-- I am a shining example of love in action
-- Love is growing and expanding in my life
-- Others are naturally drawn to me
-- I am worthy of love and praise

GOOD THINGS WILL COME TO ME WHEN I...

TODAY'S EMPOWERING QUOTE

"The best preparation for good work tomorrow is good work today."
--Elbert Hubbard

TODAY'S EMPOWERING QUESTION

"What can I do now that will prepare me for tomorrow?"

TODAY'S FAST SESSION

Often the most frustrating thing that any of us feel on a regular basis is to want something really bad, and not be able to get it right away.

Yes, it's frustrating. But it's usually not realistic, is it?

The challenge that we face is that advertisers want us to get motivated to buy their products immediately. But if you have limitations of one sort or another, like... you don't have a space to park a 50 foot yacht, or simply no money, then you're not going to be able to buy this thing. And it's not just products, is it? Many people see someone else with some personal trait or a job they want and they get jealous.

They want it, too... NOW!

It's getting so that it's increasingly rare to find people who are truly willing to put in the requisite time necessary to get the traits or items they want. Our world today is trying to teach us that we must get what we want immediately; that it's our right. And that's why so many of us are jealous, smoke or drink, are overweight, use drugs, etc.

Listen up.

It's your right, all right.

It's your right to have the same opportunity to work for what you want. You have to sacrifice to reach your dreams just like every other person who ever lived, who reached the same kinds of ambitions.

Today MUST be the day that puts you on, or keeps you on, the road to attaining what you want. Remember, God helps those who help themselves.

Many days don't afford us the time to push certain things forward, it's true. For example, if you're traveling and you use that as an excuse to not eat right and to not exercise, then you probably won't do it even when it's more convenient.

Life is NOT like school.

In school, you can trick yourself into thinking you're doing great if you cram for exams and get decent scores. It is possible to get fairly good grades for a while that way.

But you don't learn it. You're likely to just remember it until the exam is over... maybe.

That's why new college graduates often find it difficult to find a decent paying job. Companies like successful work experience. In college, you can fool the system and yourself. In the professional world and in most other areas of life, it's a lot tougher. Almost impossible.

Real life is truly like a farm.

On the farm, you must move the rocks, buy seeds and all the other stuff, plant the seeds, buy and maintain the equipment, pull weeds, keep the pests away, water the crops, buy and sell the animals, feed them, nurse the sick ones back to health, fertilize, etc. And you need to keep up with it all everyday...

Or you won't have a crop at the end of the season.

Life is like this, too. Just like a farm, you can't "cram" in life. Don't be fooled. Don't believe the lies that others want you to believe. You want to believe it. I know you do. But think.

The people who have the things you want earned them. And don't believe they just got lucky. Luck takes work.

Put the effort in today and you'll get luckier and luckier. Will it be immediately? Probably not.

Beat this into your head... Anything worth having takes time to get it.

When I'm tempted to believe that I should have something (before I've earned it), I think of my grandparents.

They owned a farm.

And I realize that life can be long and that I can't put tomorrow before today.

Then I look at my goal, put my shoulder down and keep going...

With a smile on my face.

TODAY'S WINNING BELIEFS

-- I've dissolved and released all jealousy from my heart
-- I receive all my rewards at the appropriate times
-- I'm at peace with my responsibilities
-- I'm preparing myself for tomorrow today

WHAT'S GRATITUDE WORTH?

TODAY'S EMPOWERING QUOTE

"I was complaining that I had no shoes till I met a man who had no feet
-Confucius

TODAY'S FAST SESSION

Alright! Let's go!

Let's take stock of ourselves, shall we?

What do we have? Legs? I wouldn't take any amount of money for mine. How about you?

How about your arms? Would you sell them? Your eyes? Would you take even a million dollars for them? Well then certainly your brain. After all those times that you cursed it for forgetting something and called yourself a stupid you-know-what?

Would you take a million for it?

Didn't think so.

Did you know that scientists and doctors have studied many thousands of people under hypnosis and have found that we have virtually perfect memories? People who have had electronic stimulation to parts of their brains have shown the same thing.

When stimulated, people have been literally "brought back" to days and moments in their lives and they remembered every thought, word, look, step, everything. Just as if they were in the moment again. Even 30+ years later.

That's astonishing, isn't it?

But to get more out of it and yourself on a daily basis, you have to be in the right state of mind. Hypnosis is simply a state of alert relaxation. In that state, photographic memory can occur.

Let's make a commitment together. Let's commit to keeping a watchful eye on our states of mind. Every moment.

How else can we possibly do the things that we want to do today and in our tomorrows?

If you say and think those woe-is-me thoughts every second of the day, you're going to get sub-par or no performance at all. You're absolutely killing your chances of success and happiness…

And with a magnificent brain like yours, that is a tragedy.

So write down on a 3x5 card two statements:

1- "What is great about right now?"
2- "What am I thankful for right now?"

Calm down... there's something. You just need to find it. Even if you're an extreme optimist, do this. Tomorrow might provide you with some challenges that you don't normally have and you need weapons, too.

What could be good/great? After we come up with our laundry list, look at each one and feel it. Is this a made-up list? A fake, a fraud? Well, let me ask you what all those disempowering worrying thoughts you've had over the years and decades that didn't amount to anything are? The truth? The way it really is?

Hey, the truth is what you believe it to be. And I contend that we should bend our beliefs towards what is USEFUL-not just the way something seems to be on the surface.

What could be great? What could you be grateful for?

Oh… nothing?

Keep this thought in mind, "And this too shall pass." Life goes on. And there's never a better time to practice leveling our moods than NOW. This is not a dress rehearsal. Today IS practice for tomorrow.

Let's go...

Your physical health - tens of thousands didn't wake up today.

Your significant other - your soul mate

Your best friend – your confidant

Your boss - many don't even have a boss (or a job) to curse

Your co-workers/teammates - can't do it without them

Your children

Parents - make up with them. If you don't, ultimately, you'll wish you did.

Cousins/Nieces/Nephews/In-laws

Your country – and the freedoms it provides to you

Hey, stop reading and start writing... yes, that means you, too. These are my ideas. What are yours?

Your neighbors

Your favorite TV shows

Your pets

The habit you just gave up, the weight you just lost

Any other accomplishment - no matter how small

Your new car/house/clothes/furniture

Your education, degree

Your future prospects/next month/next year (imagining can help you feel good now)

Your new hair cut/weekly massage

Your chance to learn something right now and what it will mean to you in the future

Your chance to rise above the problem and how that will make you feel

All the people at the end of the phone who are waiting to serve your needs

Mike Brescia - yeah, me. I'm here for you, too.

Wow, you sure have a lot to be in a good mood about. Now don't just read this and say, "Hey that's neat. I feel pretty good." You need to do it now...

The magic is in the doing.

Do you want to feel good today, but not be quickly able to get back here? Nothing lasting will happen unless you get out the pencil, write it down and feel it.

And when you have a moment or a day when things aren't going well, remember that your state of mind DICTATES what you'll do next and the way you do it.

When you need to, just pull out your sheet of paper with all the things you can feel good about, and before you know it, you will feel better.

Maybe not great, but better IS going in the right direction... Isn't it?

And when you *feel* good, you are more likely to *do* good.

TODAY'S WINNING BELIEFS

-- I'm grateful for all that I have
-- I have so much to be thankful for in my life
-- I can feel great any time I want simply by remembering my blessings
-- I quickly let go of negative thoughts when they threaten to overtake me
-- My mind is a powerful tool that I have at my disposal any time I want

ASK QUESTIONS!

TODAY'S EMPOWERING QUOTE

"Better be wise by the misfortunes of others than by your own."
  --Aesop

TODAY'S EMPOWERING QUESTION

"What additional information do I need to make a wise and informed decision here?"

TODAY'S FAST SESSION

How many of us try like heck to get ALL the appropriate information we need before we try to accomplish something really big (or even small things)?

A few years ago, I invested some money into something and I didn't bother to tell my accountant about it. I didn't want him to talk me out of it.

Now I'm the first one to admit that accountants don't always make the best investment counselors. My wife's a CPA, so I'm not picking on them. I just wanted to be a big boy and make this decision on my own. Big ego, you know.

The short story is I lost over $30,000 and a bunch of tax benefits due to my wanting to feel like a smart guy. That was one big hurt that I keep in mind when I feel like charging off without consulting my advisors, reading books, doing more research, etc.

It doesn't matter how fast you're going if you're going in the wrong direction, does it?

It's embarrassing and costly to when the only thing you can say is, "But I thought..."

No, you didn't.

Questions are the answer.

If you don't routinely ask yourself questions like today's empowering question, you'll be sorry soon enough.

Most failed pursuits began and flopped because no one had the presence of mind to ask, "What could go wrong if I go ahead with this action?" Being positive and confident in your abilities is good. Being uninformed, especially due to ego or pride is bad.

And potentially VERY costly.

Trust me.

Keep asking yourself wise questions and learn from other's mistakes AND successes and you'll toast more victories and mourn fewer defeats.

TODAY'S WINNING BELIEFS

-- I always ask the right questions at the right time
-- The right answers come to me by asking good questions
-- I am guided toward my highest good by the answers to my questions
-- I trust my intuitions

HUMOR IS MAGIC

TODAY'S EMPOWERING QUOTE

"Men will confess to treason, murder, arson, false teeth, or a wig. How many of them will own up to a lack of humor?"
--Frank Moore Colby

TODAY'S EMPOWERING QUESTION

"How many things can I notice today that are truly funny?"

TODAY'S FAST SESSION

It probably goes without saying but humor is in the eye of the beholder. Not everything is funny to all people.

But...

Why are so many people (you and I included) so serious about so many things? ... all the time?

Lighten up!

My wife tells me regularly that aside from my incredible wit and stunning good looks, it's my sense of humor that that made her love me. She is one smooooooth talker!

By taking ourselves too seriously, at any time, we literally close off parts of our brain so that it can only produce chemicals in our bodies that make us feel bad. If someone has teased, laughed at, or talked badly about you, you have choices about how to act.

It may not SEEM like you have choices, because your emotions are probably on autopilot most of the time.

Stimulus -> Response.

No pause, just instantly think the worst, the chemicals surge and→ Bingo! - Irrational reaction.

What happened to Evolution? :-)

Our mental programming has been made up not only of the words you hear. Your emotions, prejudices, and surroundings get mixed into the soup, too. Your moods - your states of mind - are a HUGE factor.

If someone was laughing at you for doing something ridiculous, and you were in a playful mood... let's say you've had a fairly good day, then you would be pretty likely to brush it off and maybe join in the laughter.

But if you had a particularly tough day and your mood wasn't so good (or if you've already been too self-centered for too long), that same laughter could feel like ridicule... and your reaction could be vastly different, couldn't it?

It's these kinds of patterns over a lifetime that make people stuffy, no fun, vengeful and even suicidal. [Remember Columbine?]

Or...

These situations could be "used" to develop your sense of humor, and take your life in a completely different direction.

Humor is a big factor in everyone's life. Really big...

And your habitual moods play a giant role in what you consider to be funny or stupid... harmless or cruel... interesting or frightening.

Want to help yourself develop that sense of humor that can be so critical in making your moods supportive of your big life goals?

Then take the statements below, put them on index cards and read them three times per day. Morning, noon and just before you close your eyes at night.

TODAY'S WINNING BELIEFS

-- It's easy for me to see the humor in each situation
-- I smile at people I meet and they smile back
-- My moods are even regardless of what is happening around me

DON'T WORRY… JUST SMILE

TODAY'S EMPOWERING QUOTE

"Good humor is tonic for the mind and body. It is the best antidote for anxiety and depression. It is a business asset. It attracts and keeps friends. It lightens human burdens. It is the direct route to serenity and contentment."
    --Grenville Kleiser

TODAY'S EMPOWERING QUESTION

"What tense situation can I look back on and laugh about?"

TODAY'S FAST SESSION

In continuing our previous discussion on humor, how it can help us, and what the lack of it can do, today's question is a terrific clue about the value of humor.

In asking it of yourself, you HAVE to get an answer. You'll find an answer in a memory of something that really got your furnace hot. When you think about it now, it not only doesn't get you mad but it probably seems funny or at least neutral.

We often let our emotions control us, thinking the worst without pausing first...

The act of worrying, for example, is a major illness today as, of course, it has probably been since the dawn of mankind. I say illness not to give you one more excuse for not taking ownership of your own actions, but to highlight the misery it can cause.

Boy do people love to worry, huh?

We get all worked up about things that haven't happened yet, but "probably will" ...and rarely ever do.

Let me make a point here.

Being PREPARED for the worst is not worrying.   That's productive. Heading off problems is valuable.

Worrying is thinking about a negative outcome and not letting it go. Losing sleep over it. Not having any humor about it or about anything else until what you're fretting about has passed.

In sports, who usually wins - the team that's loose and care-free or the team that's tight and worried about making mistakes?

It's been estimated that ninety nine percent of all the things that most of us worry about never actually occur. And in those rare times that what we're worrying about does happen, we say, "See, I knew it!" Most of us live "problem centered" lives and defend it as being realistic.

People with a developed sense of humor rarely worry about things that they don't have control over. It's insane to bother yourself over things you can't affect, isn't it?

Come on now, be honest!

Also, don't you envy those people who can crack just the right joke at just the right moment? Those who can break the tension with the right words ...almost on cue? I don't mean tasteless jokes. I'm talking about good, clean, witty humor.

Don't they make us feel good just being around them?

State enhancers is what they are...

Having a great sense of humor makes you popular. It keeps your blood pressure lower. It helps you sell better. It can help you worry less and do better work every minute of every day. It has also proven to be able to heal the sick...

Even when the sick have cancer and other serious diseases.

The world is small. We've all heard those stories by now, haven't we?

Let's develop our own humor muscles... today. Right now.

On a piece of paper, write a big **W** (For "Worry") in the middle. Use up the whole sheet. And in the place where you work or where you spend a lot of time, tape this sheet on the wall.

That's your trigger...

When you're in the middle of a big fat worry - no matter how seemingly unimportant it might be - look at your **W** and ask yourself, "What can I find to laugh at in this situation?" or, "What is funny about this?" or, "How can I look at this and stay optimistic and light?"

That's the great thing about questions. They're free. You can ask yourself any question you want. No tolls. Just ask the right ones and you'll be miles ahead and on the right road.

And guess what? You'll feel better. And if you put that **W** on your wall and make this questioning a daily habit, it will become automatic, and you'll get all those benefits I just listed and lots more.

Dozens and dozens more.

If you think that putting a big **W** on your wall is juvenile, what is worrying and fretting over things that usually never happen?

Point made? Good.

Black markers make nice **W**'s, don't you think?

TODAY'S WINNING BELIEFS

-- I have a great sense of humor
-- I look for and find the humor in all situations
-- I release all tension and worry from my mind and body
-- Tension and worry has left me now
-- My sense of humor puts others at ease

DO IT — NOW!!!

TODAY'S EMPOWERING QUOTE

"Putting off a hard thing makes it impossible"
--George Horace Lorimar

TODAY'S EMPOWERING QUESTION

"What's the one thing I've been putting off that, if I did it, I would feel the weight of the world lifted from me?"

TODAY'S FAST SESSION

You have things that you've been putting off, don't you?

Is there a secret that keeps it from happening? I've heard a rather idiotic suggestion of putting off putting it off. But somehow I don't think that'll work for most.

Procrastination is a habit. My wife will be the first one to tell you that I procrastinate a lot.

...But in my opinion, there is a right way and a wrong way to do it. OK, I'll tell you the right way.

I put off unimportant things. Now I don't consider obligations to other people that are counting on you to be unimportant. THAT'S important. Cleaning up after yourself is important. Cleaning the garage can wait. That's just my opinion, you see.

In the years since I "woke up," I've seen co-workers, bosses, employees and vendors' employees take short cuts, not do things they said they were going to do, put important things off -- and it affects other people dramatically.

Their reputation gets ruined. No one trusts them any more. And even worse, their lives will be mere shells of what they could be...

...Because putting important things off is a habit. A rotten, stinking, dirty, selfish and self-sabotaging habit.

What? You think it's alright to commit to someone that you'll do something and then blow them off? Five-year-olds do that. Not responsible adults.

And not you... not if you have any desire to have a happy productive life.

I learned years ago that all I had to do most times was just show up with my game face on and I'd win. When I was selling one to one every day, I made sure that the most important things got done and worked on my to do list in order of importance, not in order of how much fun the tasks were. And I earned at least double and often ten times what my stunned co-workers and competitors earned.

That's what I mean by there's a right way to procrastinate. Don't put too much on your plate. If you don't, when someone gets on your case about not doing such and such a thing, you can truly say you were too busy.

After all, you have to have SOME free time, right?

Is this hard?

Not if you look at the benefits of doing the most important thing, instead of the things you're "missing out" on.

What's more important to you - what you GET right now, or what you BECOME in your life?

Want to make breaking this stinking, insidious habit easy? Good.

Then take the statements below, put them on index cards and read them three times per day. Morning, noon and just before you close your eyes at night.

When you actually believe them, you'll act upon them and you'll have given yourself choices in life that few will ever have.

TODAY'S WINNING BELIEFS

-- I love doing the most productive thing possible at every given moment
-- I have plenty of time to do the things I want to do
-- I get everything done on time
-- I see time as a precious gift and I use it well

THERE'S A CLOWN IN ALL OF US

TODAY'S EMPOWERING QUOTE

"Make one person happy each day, and in forty years you will have made 14,600 human beings happy for a little time, at least."
  -Charley Willey

TODAY'S EMPOWERING QUESTION

"Who can I make smile right now?"

TODAY'S FAST SESSION

A couple days ago, I called my wife at work. One of her co-workers answered the phone. Now, I like to clown around...a lot.

Do you remember those guys who did the Budweiser commercials that asked each other, "Wazzuuup?" Well, remember the other Bud commercial with the "uncool" guys who ask, "What are you doing?" in the nerdiest way possible?

Well, the woman who picked up the phone, I've only met once for about 5 minutes. After she said hello, I didn't identify myself at all. I just said, "What are you DOING!?" in the uncool way. She said, "Who is this?" Again I asked, "What are YOU doing?!"

All I heard was hysterical laughing and another woman in the background saying, "Is that Mike?"

Later, my wife told me that my "victim" was talking about it throughout the day... about how funny it was.

Now, I know it was only silliness, even mindless. But don't we all need a little of that in our days? Oh, a lot? I'm for that.

I remember in my book store, if a customer asked for a specific book, and if I was close enough to it, I would do a little soft shoe (with fake top hat and cane) over to the shelf it was on, grab it and dance back over to the customer, presenting it to them with a bow.

That used to floor people!

I had the biggest business of its kind in the world at the time. And I think that giving people a little humor and entertainment was part of it.

Hey, like it or not, we are all 'state' inducers.

Whenever we have an interaction with someone, even if it's just a hello, we leave them with a definite feeling.

What do you think people feel about us when we're walking around with a sour puss on?

No one wants to be around that.

Do you?

Do you go out and search for the complainers? If you do, notice the topic of your typical conversations. Are they usually centered on what's wrong, who said what rotten thing, what someone had the gall to ask you to do? In short, whining sessions?

Look, you are what you think. You get back what you put out. If you put out cheerfulness, then that's how people will treat you back.

Did you ever hear the centuries-old story about the old man who sat next to the road and greeted people who entered and exited just outside his small village?

When travelers came in, often they would ask what kind of people were in the town. The man responded by asking them what the people were like in the town they just left. If the traveler said the people were terrific, the man told them that he'd find the people in this town were much the same.

If the traveler said the other town had horrible people in it, the man said that they'd find the people here much the same.

It kind of goes right along with another Your Day To Win that talked about running from your problems. The thing is, you bring yourself with you wherever you go. And since you are what you think, the only way for you to escape your problems is to change your attitudes.

If you understand that you induce states of mind in the people that you meet all day, it brings it right to the front of your consciousness, doesn't it? People respond to you whether you like it or not.

To my way of thinking, it's better to bring a smile than a frown or pity or disdain. Better than nothing either. What the heck! It doesn't cost anything at all.

Just one person a day that you make smile will do something amazing for them and...

...inside of you.

Try this easy exercise. I think you'll find it shocking.

Smile for 60 seconds straight. Just sit there and smile. Don't do anything else. Take the next minute. C'mon, you have another minute! Just sit and smile for one minute.

I'll wait...

Isn't it amazing?!

Don't you immediately sense an actual physical feeling inside you the very second you start to smile? You did, huh? Another thing you'll notice is, you can't do this exercise without getting all kinds of great pictures in your head, remembering fun times, etc.

The physiology of this is quite extraordinary. It's wired into us. When we smile, we are literally programmed to feel good.

If you thought that you had to first feel great to smile, you couldn't be more mistaken. Smile first and you'll feel great.

It's impossible to feel down when we are smiling. If you're still doubting it, try it. Just try to get into a rotten mood with a big dumb silly grin on your face.

You literally can't do it.

Now imagine what you'll be doing for other people if you make it your mission to make at least one person smile per day. The feelings that you're feeling right now as you're sitting there grinning is exactly what you'll be doing for everyone that you make smile...

It's kind of nice to think that you can do that for people any time you want, isn't it?

And another question… what will those people think of you?

If you're up to the assignment, go make 'em smile!

Do it everyday and your life will change.

TODAY'S WINNING BELIEFS

-- I induce positive happy states in the people I meet
-- I've released all frustration and anxiety from my mind
-- I enjoy making people smile and laugh
-- I forget problems when I'm smiling and I smile a lot
-- I have a sunny disposition

LIVE YOUR PURPOSE, EVERYDAY

TODAY'S EMPOWERING QUOTE

"Success is the progressive realization of a worthy ideal."
 --Earl Nightingale

TODAY'S EMPOWERING QUESTION

"How did I get so lucky to be blessed with
 another day to live my life's purpose?"

TODAY'S FAST SESSION

You know, it's ridiculous.

I watch NBA basketball VERY infrequently, because it's clear that these highly paid babies have no idea what success is. They think it's getting a big contract. They hear the crowd roar when they hit a basket and they think that's success. The next day, this multi-millionaire might pout and score only 3 points.

So, feeling full of themselves like they are some kind of gods, they yell at the coaches and they don't listen. They yell at the referees. Fight with the fans if someone says something they don't like.

They should all watch Michael Jordan highlight footage if they want to see what success is. Day after day, year after year, he performed at a level no one else could have demanded of anyone. He held himself to a higher standard. His definition of success was related to "what I need to do right now"—not about what he had done in the past.

Have you ever lost weight because an event was coming up and then put it right back on afterwards... for say, a wedding? Perhaps even your own?

Why? For pictures?

Don't you realize that everyone who sees you after that event is going to see your stomach hanging out - today? Maybe you should just have those pictures of the "thin you" blown up and paste them to the front and back of you so you can remind everyone what you "used" to look like.

Questions:

-- In the NFL or college, does anyone remember who has the rushing record for a game? Most remember Walter Payton for a career, though.
-- How about the most home runs in a Major League game? No? Hank Aaron quickly comes to mind for most, when talking about the lifetime record.
-- Most hits in a game? Me neither. But Pete Rose is who most remember as the all-time hitting champ.
-- What about how good-looking you were 20, 30, 50 lbs. ago?

It's hard to even remember your "glory days" when today is a mess isn't it? It kind of makes you laugh when someone tells you that life is too short, doesn't it? You can't even remember the "good old days" very clearly, can you?

They lose their impact over time.

Long term success isn't measured that way, is it? Anyone can succeed for a day or even a month. But ultimately, it's who you ARE that decides whether you'll suck it up today and make the right choices or whether you'll "put off" the right choices.

You can't reach success unless you can define it.

I like Earl Nightingale's definition because it asks you to reach inside and give your love today, your energy today, your best today. It asks you to put forth effort today and tomorrow. Yet it lets you feel joy NOW, not at some time in the future.

Stop putting off being happy. Decide. Isn't life a bit too short to be crying over your lost opportunities and mistakes?

Just say yes. Do something important now, follow through and finish it. Do it now. That's it. Get up, and...

Keep a smile on your face while you're doing it. You just MIGHT start to enjoy yourself.

TODAY'S WINNING BELIEFS

-- I am successful
-- Success and I are one
-- My road to success is progressive and worthwhile
-- Today is my day to win

GOT A HUGE GOAL? HERE'S HOW TO REACH IT!

TODAY'S EMPOWERING QUOTE

'Live Now / Die Later'
  -tattoo on Carmelo Anthony's right bicep
    All-American Basketball Player
    (2003 National Champion Syracuse Orangemen)

TODAY'S EMPOWERING QUESTION

What can I do today that I have been dreaming
about for a long time?

TODAY'S FAST SESSION

You know them instantly when you meet them.

You want to be near them.

You want to be like them.

You know the type...

Always smiling. Hard worker. Optimistic. Assured.

And they win... a lot.

Carmelo Anthony, only 18 years old, is that person.

This past April, as a freshman, he led our hometown Syracuse Orangemen
to the NCAA men's national basketball championship.

He routinely did the impossible.

Showing skills reserved only for those 'touched by the hand of God.'

All with a smile that lit up the entire Carrier Dome.

He made us all forget about the whipping winds and the 14+ feet of snow
we were hammered with this winter. It didn't matter.

Because we got to witness someone special.

Sure, he has natural skills, but it's a LOT more than that.

He works like no one else.

He's as coachable as they come...

He listens closely, learns from every mistake, practices every day like he's playing for the NBA title.

And he's only eighteen.

Most people want to believe this kind of talent gets inserted at birth.

Most want to believe that they just don't have it.

It absolves them from responsibilities for their failures.

And it's true that few people are born with the physical ability to play sports at the highest levels or the ability to tolerate the kind of stress endured by presidents of huge corporations.

But what most people forget is that to become great at anything, you've got to get single minded.

If you want greatness, or heck, forget about greatness for a minute...

If you want to get past this next challenge, to succeed at getting rid of the habit that has you by the throat...

...then work on that one thing only. Sure, fulfill your daily responsibilities.

But when it comes to reaching this one top goal, make it absolutely, positively a must. Look at this goal like it's the most important thing in your life.

If you do this, I guarantee you of one thing...

...that if you DON'T make it all the way, you'll most certainly come closer than you ever have before.

And in the process of the reaching and the straining, you'll be growing.

Becoming more capable.

Becoming the person other people want to be like.

Because even if you reach your big goal, it's possible to lose it all in the future, to go back to your old ways.

Right?

But if you put all of yourself, and I mean ALL of yourself into your reaching, learning everything you can along the way, then not only will you most likely succeed now, but you'll be able to do more in the future.

How do you think highly skilled people in any field got so good? Were they born with all that knowledge and skills?

Give me a break!

It's called work. I know that's a dirty word to most people...

But if you want to get to that place and be that person you imagine when you close your eyes, then honest effort is the only way.

But don't be so glum...

Carmelo Anthony wasn't even considered an elite recruit as a high school junior. No. But during his senior year, he blew up... working like a maniac, that year building massively on the skills he already had developed through intensely practicing the same things day in-day out.

And because of it, he just barely passed his college entrance exams.

And those people who love to look down on those with lesser vocabularies, grades or looks... those things are nice.

But you don't have to know everything to reach your goals and to be successful in this life of yours. You can't be all things. It's impossible.

You just have to do what you must to get where you want to go.

If your goals aren't huge now, that's fine. Reach the small ones. Build your confidence. And go from there.

The tallest buildings start with many sub-floors under the ground.

So, if that's where you are starting from, know that you can still get where you want to go... one step at a time.

The time for living is now.

So what are you going to do?

TODAY'S WINNING BELIEFS

-- I am working hard to reach my biggest goal now
-- I learn something valuable every day in pursuing my goal
-- I am becoming more today than I was yesterday
-- I love reaching for and achieving challenging goals
-- I can do it... I know I can

CHANGE YOUR VIEW, CHANGE YOUR LIFE

TODAY'S EMPOWERING QUOTE

"Should one look through a red glass at a while lily, he would seem to see a red lily. But there would be no red lily. So it is with humanity's problems. They consist of false mental pictures."
   --M.D. Garbrick

TODAY'S EMPOWERING QUESTION

  "Is this problem a problem, or am I looking
  at it the wrong way? Is it something better?"

TODAY'S FAST SESSION

Ya know, it's all in how you look at it.

How many people out there are sick of hearing that?

Are you usually the one saying it to people?

Most all "problems" you experience lie in how you look at things. It makes the difference in everything you do.

EVERYTHING.

You know, when I was growing up and even well into adulthood, I was rarely happy about anything for long. It would never last. I always wished I were with a different group of people...never felt like I said the right things. I always just wanted to be where I was on the way to. The trip was always dreaded. I wanted to be someone else.

I never felt good enough.

Did you notice that, of all those things I just mentioned, none of them were "real?" They were all in my head. Just emotions...

Just emotions? Only thoughts?

Could it be thoughts are real?

Oh, they're as real as the chair you are sitting in now! I didn't understand that myself for so long.

And most people go to their graves NEVER being able to control what they think about and how.

But once I became educated to the power of thoughts, absolutely everything in my life changed. My problems weren't problems anymore. They became challenges. I had heard all that before, as I'm sure you have. But when it finally sunk in and I saw for myself how our thoughts can make us and break us, I was never the same.

So everything I did, I did better.

I hope you don't have to go through what I did before you finally "get it." But the day you do, and I want THIS day to be a turning point for you... the day you do, the big weight on your back will shrink to the size of a pea.

Proper perspective is highly underrated.

Here's something that you can do now, later today, tomorrow and for the rest of your days.

Whenever you think you have a "problem," look at it.

Is it a problem or just a challenge? At those times (and "those times" can number in the hundreds each day) your goal must be to ask yourself this question: Isn't this just another challenge that I will most certainly meet?

Ask yourself that question constantly. I say constantly because that's how fast challenges can come sometimes. Isn't that right?

Like a hail storm.

"Yeah, but you don't understand. This person in my life, they're the problem! My kids, they're the problem! It's my landlord. It's my boss. I can't do anything about it! I can't help it!"

Bull!

And the only time you're going to be able to change even the most horrible situations, is if you say "Bull," too.

They are challenges. That is what they are.

Just because you don't see it that way right now, doesn't change the fact that they are challenges. They are tests... tests for you to pass or fail. If you pass, you get to grow. If you fail, you get to feel depressed and have more of the same crap.

That's what life is. And that truth, that fact, isn't to be despondent about.

It's to look at from all sides with a clear glass around it so you can see the truth.

There is nothing that can happen to you that is bigger than you. You can get through anything.

Look at Christopher Reeve, if you need some real perspective. The guy played Superman! Now he can't move a single muscle in his body. But he's authored two books and is giving other people hope that they can overcome their mostly smaller challenges than his.

If you are to live a life of purpose... If you want to reach some truly amazing goals in life, you must view your roadblocks for what they are... stepping stones. And the awareness that when you're starting to get upset about something, you need perspective - fast!

You don't have to be able to jump over them. Crawl if you must, but get over them... and move on. To expect life to be problem free and to put off happiness until it is, is crazy.

Trust me, I know.

Choose to be happy today. Don't worry about tomorrow. Prepare for it, but don't obsess. Just get through today's challenges.

And smile. Things aren't always going to go the way you want. There most certainly will be periods where nothing seems to go right.

Accept that as a given.

So when the events don't unfold as you want them to, you'll be able to think clearly and quickly decide what you should do next without wasting precious seconds mourning...

Because your next decision could be the very one that takes your "challenge" and turns it into victory.

TODAY'S WINNING BELIEFS

-- I see today's problems as challenges
-- I see roadblocks as stepping-stones
-- My challenges help me grow and learn
-- I appreciate my challenges for their value to me
-- I dissolve all problems from my life

CREATE *YOUR* VICTORY LOG

TODAY'S EMPOWERING QUOTE

"Think of yourself as on the threshold of unparalleled success. A whole clear, glorious life lies before you. Achieve! Achieve!"
--Andrew Carnegie

TODAYS FAST SESSION

Even though you don't want to live in the past, it can be an invaluable tool to you.

Throughout our lives, every single one of us have had times where we did something great, or at least really good... someone gave us an approving glance, a promotion, a new client. Perhaps we dated someone hot! Wedding day, giving birth, scoring a touchdown, winning a medal. You simply helped someone out that needed it. These events made you feel good.

A very effective way to put yourself into a great mood any time you want, especially at times where exceptional performance is needed NOW is to create...

YOUR VICTORY LOG.

A victory log is merely a sheet of paper that you have nearby any time you need to be reminded of past successes of ANY kind. By reminding yourself about your successes, by pulling out that little sheet, you'll often be able to go on and reach down and grab your greatest performance ever even from the depths of despair. Often times, you just need to be able to REMEMBER that you can do it, when your thinking is really cloudy.

If you get depressed, pull out your Victory Log and you'll feel a whole lot better. I absolutely guarantee it.

Yes, this is simple. That's why it works.

Do you think that the doers – the real winners in life - are that much different than you? Mostly, with exceptional people, they just keep their victories just below their consciousness, so that magical confidence is right there when they need it.

So PLEASE, PLEASE, PLEASE do this exercise.

Don't put it off. If now isn't good, do it later today. It's easy. It's fun. And you'll feel great about yourself when you're done.

And... you'll have it forever.

What a great gift to yourself.

PLEASE TAKE A FEW MINUTES AND DO THIS!!!! This silly little sheet of paper can pull you out of the deepest hole faster than anything you've ever seen.

Here's how. In the areas listed below we want to create a big list of even the tiniest successes. I often look at my list when I'm feeling not up to a task. Hey, no one can be at their best all the time.

Write down just a few words to jog the memory so that when you look at it, you'll know. Many people type these out afterwards. Go back to as far as you can remember. Even kindergarten is fair game.

Learning - tests, quizzes, semester averages, awards, scholarships, I.Q., diploma. Include all grades and college.

The opposite sex - dated a "hottie," got the glance in the mall, had a particularly romantic night/week/month, had 'em all after you, summer camp, phone call, poems, cards, got whistled at. Go back as far as you need to.

Sports (even backyard sports) - touchdowns, hits, baskets, goals, blocks, double plays, great shots. Include board games and cards, too.

Work - promotions, sales, raises, pats on the back, contests, trips, saved money for the company, teamwork, great days, winning, solving a problem, saving a life, got elected, a finalist for the job, made the big sale, got the listing.

Personal – convinced someone to a new way of thinking, landscaping, painting, art, cleaning the house, new clothes, great dinners, children in plays or sports, losing weight, eliminating a bad habit, building/fixing something, tuning up the car, new car day, new home, getting a letter/notification, made dinner, helped a friend.

Social - kept your temper, you were elegant, gave a great speech, the party was a success.

Health - cholesterol is down, stopped smoking, lost weight, ran 100 yards/one mile/three miles, climbed the mountain, changed your diet, walked by the chips in the store, etc.

Do this for every area of your life. I have one for kicking a 50 yard field goal. Don't you believe I'll ever forget it. Not when NFL kickers have missed 30 yarders to lose games!! But even the small ones like walking by the potato chips today. That's a victory and shouldn't be discounted. Because you were strong just then, and deserve recognition. No one else is likely to do it, so you MUST.

Don't think little things are not important. They're everything -- everything.

Watch during sporting events, when a player makes a mistake and the other team scores as a result. Momentum shifts.

Why?

Because after mistakes they begin focusing on what went wrong... instantly.

And the team that scored is focused on their scoring. They're pumped up. Confidence rises.

You need that confidence, too, to do your best every day and every minute.

So focus on what you've done right, and you'll develop it.

How can you do this?

Your Victory Log... the fastest way in the world to build your confidence and increase your skills.

TODAY'S WINNING BELIEFS

-- I keep my Victory Log with me at all times
-- When I look at my Victory Log I feel powerful
-- I have many victories to power my determination
-- My victories give me confidence
-- I have many little victories every day
-- I give myself pats on the back when I do something well

WHAT GOALS REALLY DO

TODAY'S EMPOWERING QUOTE

'Goals give you more than a reason to get up in the morning; they are an incentive to keep you going all day. Goals tend to tap the deeper resources and draw the best out of life.'
    - Harvey Mackay

TODAY'S EMPOWERING QUESTION

What have I done for the last hour? What do I plan on doing this next hour? Why?

TODAY'S FAST SESSION

My dad used to tell me stories about the day every year that the auto manufacturers introduced their new linc of cars and trucks.

That day, people would flock to the dealerships. It looked like the county fair at the local car lots. Dealers sold more cars that day than the whole month before.

There wasn't anything like that excitement, I've been told.

Today, new models hardly get noticed. At least not the way they used to.

Why?

Because there is so much more trying to grab our attention today.

Because billions of dollars have been spent by companies in all the world's industries studying what makes us buy or not buy things. Learning how to target us more effectively.

I mean, at every turn everything we could ever want, as a consumer, is being promoted to us... "GET ME!" "ALL YOUR FRIENDS HAVE ME." "YOU DESERVE TO HAVE ME NOW!"

The marketing noise is deafening.

And it works.

It makes us want what's being sold... right now.

In fact, it makes us want to have EVERYTHING now.

"Why does THAT person get to have that car, those clothes, that girl friend, that job, that grade, those sneakers when I'm stuck with less."

"I deserve to have it now."

"Let's steal that money, that bottle, that shirt, that car, his girl friend."

"Life's not fair."

Yeah, life's not always fair. But that's life.

Oh, I know, life's too short to work so hard to be thin, to be financially secure, to follow rules, to get good grades, to...

Too often, depression and anxiety is a result of false expectations of what life "should" be.

Did you ever hear of the saying, "If you always do what you've always done, you'll always get what you've always gotten?"

So my dear, dear friend, in the areas of life that you want to change, you need concrete goals or you'll always get the usual crap.

Look at today's quote again.

Gives me chills.
.
Did you ever meet anyone who lost 50 pounds or more unless they had the goal to do so?

No goal... no achievement.

How about building a multi-million dollar company without some clear daily and long-term goals?

Does anyone get straight A's without the goal to do so first?

Let me be as clear about this as I can be...

You can get along, get some halfway decent grades, maybe rise up in your company just by showing up, get married, have kids and have a fairly average life without clear goals.

I mean, if you're typical you've gotten where you are now without setting and achieving any REALLY challenging benchmarks for yourself in any area of life. If you're typical and honest with yourself, you'll likely agree.

And while this discussion isn't meant to be the final word on goals, I think you can see now that committing to a clearly defined goal is critical to getting what you really want.

Especially with all of life's distractions, and the constant pressures to believe that our successes must happen NOW.

Look at today's quote again now.

Want energy? Set some goals in any area of life you want.

And this time, commit to it like you've never committed to anything before.

This process will give you such a charge it will astound you.

Truly depressed? Then set a really challenging goal and work like you've never worked for anything else before.

Make reaching this goal the most important thing.

And I know this sounds too simple.

Look, life isn't as complicated as it feels sometime.

My life sucked in every way until I was nearly 25 years old.

I got fired from a lot of minimum wage jobs and had to live in a 9 year old van as a result.

And it didn't turn around until I got super focused on one thing... keeping a job. When I focused on that almost exclusively, suddenly I started to get really good at it.

I didn't get fired either.

Well, many huge goals later, and my web site is the biggest of its kind in the world. More big goals and 'Your Day To Win' is the biggest ezine of it's kind. And there are many other incredible things going on here that will ultimately change millions of people's lives.

And none of them would have ever come about without a committed focus to mastering one thing, then mastering another one thing, then...

Now, that does lead to some imbalance at times.

But in all honesty, the most successful, wealthy, well known and yes, happiest people who ever lived totally mastered just a few things. That mastery in just a few areas of life gave them freedoms and joy that few people will ever know.

Why?

Because few people want to work hard enough to master anything.

Most don't understand the implications of earning what they get.

Most don't understand, until it's often too late, that things that come too easy or that were dishonestly gained never stay around long.

What? You thought your bad luck was just bad luck?

Not bad luck. Bad beliefs. Bad actions.

And it doesn't matter how big the gains are...

90% of all million+ dollar lottery winners blow it all very quickly and spend the rest of their lives bitter and with nothing...

But not you.

You're going to set a big goal right now, take concrete steps toward reaching it and make decisions that will support you on your path to success.

And this will all start to make sense.

Don't read this and forget about it.

Do something now or your chance will be lost.

All right! There's hope for you!

TODAY'S WINNING BELIEFS

-- My goals are increasing my passion for life
-- I feel exhilarated by my goals
-- I am growing by leaps and bounds today
-- I'm truly happy to be alive
-- I can get through any hardship, no matter what it is
-- My skills and confidence are growing today

HOCUS POCUS... IT'S ALL IN YOUR FOCUS

TODAY'S EMPOWERING QUOTE

"Objects we ardently pursue bring little happiness when gained; most of our pleasures come from unexpected sources."
   --Herbert Spencer

TODAY'S EMPOWERING QUESTION

"What can I notice right now that makes me smile?"

TODAY'S FAST SESSION

I probably get more questions about the plain desire to be happy than anything else. Most people are miserable, generally.

And yes, it's horrible, but also avoidable.

I know... I was one of the biggest perpetrators of stinkin' thinkin' you've ever met. But that simple, yet profound, shift, when it comes over you - actually when you make it your objective to change it - just puts a different shading on how you see nearly every hour of your life...

Now, I'm NOT an advocate of ignoring huge challenges raining down on you like hail. Look 'em straight on, and be honest with yourself. Everything you experience has a value to you, whether you believe it or not.

Problems are always opportunities. They can make you stronger. But if you don't train your brain to view them as opportunities, then they make you weaker. And if you don't watch out, you can drop down to a level where everything makes you frightened and nervous.

Take heart. Your competitors/opponents rarely make it through all their own problems. So you are blessed every day with many chances to get further ahead. If you live in a setting where you don't think you compete, you're wrong...

You do compete... if not with someone else, then with yourself to keep your moods regulated so that you can perform and respond to situations properly. You have forces that are in your daily environment constantly working on ruining your moods and wrecking your performance and your motivation. The daily news, other people... if you're an established debater, life's a constant battle waiting to happen.

Your moods are primarily the result of what you focus on.

When I was in commissioned sales, in my car on the way to appointments I would chant out loud, "I now command my subconscious mind to give me the strength, the humor, the brevity, the love, the persuasiveness... whatever it takes to get (name) to like me and to see the value of my product and to buy it today!" I did this for up to 15 minutes straight... before every call... for years.

And I closed around 95% of my appointments. Ask any salesperson you know or meet if it's possible to close 95% of their calls.

They'll say it's impossible.

In my industry, it was impossible too, but I did it.

Why?

Because when I walked in the door after chanting my mantra for 15 minutes, every fiber of my being was focused on helping this other person. No other thoughts entered my mind. I would not allow them to deter my focus. When you're in front of someone who seems to be completely tuned into what you need and want, you almost instantly like him or her...

And we buy from and are persuaded easier by people we like.

That practice helped me become the top sales executive in the world in that industry.

Big lesson coming up...

Put that same kind of focus on looking for things to lighten your mental load, to make you smile, to help you appreciate the little things that other people do (not just for you). If you do, you'll feel awesome. I promise.

It's impossible to fail at this.

Keep today's empowering question in your mind all day. You'll get answers. And you'll feel cleansed. Lighter. Loved.

Guaranteed.

TODAY'S WINNING BELIEFS

-- Today I'm focusing on what's good
-- I transcend problems
-- I am solution oriented now
-- I'm helping other people feel good about themselves today
-- I allow myself to feel unbounded joy now

YOU ARE NOT HERE TO BE SERVED...

TODAY'S EMPOWERING QUOTE

"Success is about who you are, not what you have. Successful people work to discover their talents, to develop those talents, and then to use those talents to benefit others as well as themselves."
   -Tom Morris

TODAY'S EMPOWERING QUESTION

"If I concentrate on getting good at _____, what could I be like in a year? What could my whole life look like?"

TODAY'S FAST SESSION

When you go from being a self-centered, lazy, depressed person like I was for over 20 years, to someone who lives 180 degrees in the opposite direction, you find it happens by changing your definition of what life means.

We are all given different gifts and have different interests. If you are trying to start a business, for example, and you're doing it only because you want to make a lot of money, you'll probably fail. If you answer a biz-op ad in a magazine and the one you choose is mostly because of a low investment, you'll probably fail again.

The only way you'll ever feel great inside your own skin and become successful at anything, especially in business, is if you decide to become of service to others. Period.

Watch others closely. You'll find, as I have, that one of the biggest problems we humans have with one another is the lack of a desire to help out, to give a hand to someone who needs it. People who never jump in to help clean up or offer their help are universally despised.

Recently, I saw a movie I hadn't seen in years that is the epitome of what life's all about. The movie is 'Ground Hog Day.' Bill Murray plays an egotistical, selfish weatherman who travels to Western Pennsylvania every February 2nd to see if "Punxsutawney Phil" will see his shadow or not.

He and his crew have to stay overnight due to a snowstorm. And in a seemingly cruel twist of fate, he wakes up the next day to find it's February 2nd... again. This happens day after day after day. He's in groundhog hell imprisoned to relive the same day forever.

After a while he kills himself... only to be awakened at the same time each morning by his alarm clock playing Sonny & Cher. He kills himself again. Same result.

Everyone else is living as if it's Groundhog Day for the first time. He's the only one reliving it. The same people greet him at the same moment in the same place. The only difference is how he reacts.

He gets to see how he changes the outcome of the day for himself and everyone else...over and over.

Soon, he changes his tune and starts helping each person where they have a challenge; saves a kid from a fall, performs a Heimlich, fixes a flat tire, etc. He finds that he retains his skills from the "previous" day. So he learns about everyone's likes and dislikes, learns how to play piano, make ice sculptures and learns about the object of his affection.

Through trial and error, he works to make each "new day" a masterpiece. Each day, as it progresses, he learns that the way he viewed life was wrong... that he could have a great life if he just helped others.

People loved him... every day.

As the "days" went by, he learned about life. No lesson did he miss. All it took was awareness on his part.

Remember, at first it seemed like hell to him. Then as he grew in skill and in character, the woman he adored loved him back... even though she couldn't stand him before.

The first time I saw this movie, I missed the moral. I was too busy being entertained. It IS funny.

But just like in "real" life, as you're laughing and crying and living, there are lessons. If you don't notice them, you're doomed to never learn and will repeat the same mistakes... over and over.

Any problem you have has a solution. You just need to find it.

But you must look for it.

To begin, start taking an interest in other people instead of just yourself. Help out everywhere you can.

YOU WILL BE AMAZED.

As if by magic you'll learn faster, your relationships will improve, your job will be more fun, money will probably cease to be a problem... in short everything will be better for you.

Tomorrow your clock will wake you at the same time as yesterday.

Make that day and every day a masterpiece...

And be patient. Live just today. Tomorrow will come... tomorrow. Learn what you must to prepare for tomorrow.

You'll get what you want. But you must first become what you need to become in order to get it. Stop with the excuses.

Start today.

TODAY'S WINNING BELIEFS

-- I'm using today to learn, grow and make my life better
-- When I help other people they love me
-- I'm growing in skill and ability today
-- I let go of petty differences to focus on important lessons
-- My eyes are open to the lessons in life
-- I'm making today a masterpiece

SUCCESS BEGINS *AFTER* YOU FALL

TODAY'S EMPOWERING QUOTE

"Everyone has his superstitions. One of mine has always been when I started to go anywhere, or to do anything, never to turn back or to stop until the thing intended was accomplished."
  -Ulysses Grant, 18th President of the United States

TODAY'S EMPOWERING QUESTION

"Is that task really so big and bad that I can't get it done in a relatively short time? How will I feel when I'm done?"

TODAY'S FAST SESSION

Today's your day.

I'm convinced of it. It's your day. And today you're going to get up all your courage and just do what you've been aching to do.

Just before you begin taking the first actions in attacking your challenge, you might be shaking like a leaf. I don't know.

But it's at that moment, when you're feeling the most frightened that you'll be making your biggest strides. Because today, you're not going to back down. You're going to take a deep breath and go forward.

Are you guaranteed success? Will you reach your goal for sure? Will you absolutely get the outcome you're hoping for?

Not a chance...

But you'll prove to yourself and everyone that thinks that sometimes you're a dead person who just hasn't been buried yet, that you're alive and starting to kick.

People who know me well can tell you that I have failed at more things than I have succeeded at. But every time I get thrown for a loop, I immediately jump up. I ask myself what I should learn from it. And if I have to, I start completely over.

So many years after my "awakening," I'm still growing as fast as I ever have.

I remember my football coaches yelling at me after getting knocked down to "Get up! The play's not over yet!"

It's true...

In your own life, when you make a mistake or get laughed at, if your immediate response is to put your head down and start crying, you won't be able to see the next opportunity that's passing right in front of you, riding in the wake of your agony.

Get up!

I'm your coach now. Don't you dare give up. Not while I'm breathing will you ever again put your tail between your legs and turn away from what might be your greatest accomplishments. I won't accept that from you.

Not from you. You're too good.

Is that an odd way to describe your failure and humiliation?

Well, whenever you've succeeded at getting your way at just about anything, it's rarely been on the first try. Right? It's usually been after being told 'No' a few times, or screwing something up a bunch of times before finally getting it right.

Well, isn't that true?

Take that template for success and place it over everything you want to do. Everything.

When you think about some goal that seems quite a stretch for you, and the thought comes in that says, "I couldn't do that," stop and place your previous success template over it. Know that no matter how big it is, if you just "remember" that, while it might be difficult, you CAN do it. And you're already half way there.

Do this all day today. "I can do it" needs to be your mantra.

If you do, I promise you that your muscles will be stretched. Your mind will be stretched. And those goals that "looked" impossible will suddenly seem do-able.

It'll be like you've been given a new pair of eyes.

Don't just sit there...

Get up. Today's not over.

It's your day. Tomorrow may never come. Today is your whole life. Do what you fear today. You may never have another chance. Take your shot.

Oh heck. Take 20 shots.

And take them all today.

TODAY'S WINNING BELIEFS

-- I'm living this day as if it is my last
-- I'm really living today and it feels good
-- Today is my day
-- I appreciate my challenges, for they will make me great

VALUE YOUR TIME AND YOUR VALUE WILL RISE

TODAY'S EMPOWERING QUOTE

"Time ripens all things. No man is born wise."
   --Miguel De Cervantes

TODAY'S EMPOWERING QUESTION

"What can I do right this second that will change who and what I am a year from now; 4 years from now?"

TODAY'S FAST SESSION

It just drives me crazy to see people that are supposed to be busy doing something, but they're hiding out. Yeah, I'm like a former smoker who can't stand the smell anymore.

What I mean is I was the biggest procrastinator you've ever met, in my early years. I'd spend an hour trying to get out of half an hour's work. What a circus. My parents, teachers and employers weren't very amused. TV was big in my life.

What a shame. What an incredible limiter of life.

Today, I have a pact with myself. If I see a task that has to be done, I do it then, schedule it, or delegate it and make sure I follow up with the delegate.

Life has a way of loading more stuff on you as your responsibilities grow, so it's important now to become time wise.

Next month, or next year, when your skill at using time effectively is evaluated... or when you need to get something done fast, you'll have developed your ability-and you'll succeed. You'll be rewarded.

Isn't it amazing how, after a week or a month in preparation of a deadline, you're still working on it minutes before it's due? Why is that?

Poor planning... "Killing" time, hiding out.

If some thing you have planned is going to take a Herculean effort and may take a team, put the time into planning and delegating.

Don't you feel like a dog when you're hiding from a task? I know I did. I just felt like a criminal.

Want to feel like you deserve an award?

Want to feel like a hero?

Want to be admired by everyone?

Then watch yourself and how you use your time. If you catch yourself sitting around watching TV, shooting the bull or reading unimportant magazines or newspaper articles, stop immediately and do something that will make one of your ambitions come true.

That is what all effective people do.

You'll enjoy yourself once you get started...

That's the toughest part.

A year from now, you'll be a year older. Will you be any wiser? What are you here for exactly anyhow? What's your purpose? If you don't know, go to amazon.com, BN or borders.com and search for a book about developing a mission. Stephen Covey is a great person to read.

What if you're 80 years old? A mission can add a bunch of enjoyable years to your life. Why are you sticking around? Be productive.

The man across the street from us is 84 years old and his lawn looks like Disney World. It's his passion.

Get a degree. You've got the time. Be honest with yourself.

I learned an interesting technique a long time ago...

I talk to myself like I'm an advisor... to myself.

I tell me what to do, given the facts and situation. This way I can be less of a wimp when it comes to making tough choices with my time. Instead of immediately thinking I can't do a particular thing, I hear that voice that sounds like me but is much tougher than a person would normally be with themselves. Kind of like a drill sergeant in your own head.

All I can tell you is that it works. I rarely hear "I don't know..." for long before the sergeant comes in with, "It'll only take a minute. Get it done and you won't have to worry about it later." It always makes sense, so I do it just to shut me up!!

No matter what you may believe, you were born with tremendous ability. Use your own brain. It can help you do so many things that you can't imagine. You're NOT weak. You're strong.

You're NOT stupid. In many areas, you've got genius capabilities.

Pull it out of you.

You are worth it.

TODAY'S WINNING BELIEFS

-- Today I'm performing at my best
-- I love staying busy
-- When I see a new task, I do it, schedule it or delegate it
-- My time is valuable and I treat it that way

PURPOSE GIVES YOUR LIFE MEANING

TODAY'S EMPOWERING QUOTE

"Purpose is what gives life a meaning."
-Charles Henry Parkhurst, D.D.

TODAY'S EMPOWERING QUESTION

"What do I want the meaning and purpose of my life to be?"

TODAY'S FAST SESSION

Look at any person, past or present, who achieved truly great things. People you know. Behind their accomplishments you will undoubtedly find a passion and love for what they do.

That deep emotion can only be aroused by a compelling purpose...

...an idea about what their life is to stand for.

So few people ever take even a few minutes and think about their purpose. Hardly anyone ever asks himself or herself, "What am I here for?" I never asked myself that question until October 1996.

In building the largest business of its type in the world, I became a slave to it. Building that business was not my purpose. So I asked myself, "What would I really love to do if I didn't have to work to make a living?" The answer allowed me to be able to talk to tens of thousands of people every day.

And I love doing it...

Here's a great story about being led by a great purpose:

Back in the late 70's three white Canadians, two men and a woman, met and got to know a black teenage boy at a series of conferences held in New York City. They saw that he was very smart and enthusiastic, but were amazed that he couldn't even read. The school systems passed him through without regard to his future. His parents were both alcoholics. They couldn't run their own lives, let alone raise a family.

These three warm and loving people were skilled at buying and selling real estate, so they earned a very good living. They also had a lot of free time.

Something in their hearts made them want to help this boy succeed in life.

He had the mind and the desire, but no guidance. They were heartbroken with the thought that he could wind up in prison, like his brother. With the blessing of the boy's parents, they brought him to live with them, where they home-schooled him so that he might be able to go to college...

Soon after his arrival, at a used book sale, he bought his first book, "The Sixteenth Round," about a boxer named Rubin Carter, a former number one boxing contender, who had been unjustly accused and convicted of murder in 1966.

Being exposed to this story, the Canadians and the boy let a great mission guide them. They moved from Toronto to New Jersey to help Rubin win another trial, and went about trying to uncover new evidence that would prove his innocence. They had tremendous opposition to the gathering of their facts, but their determination and belief in Rubin's innocence kept them on course.

In 1988, through their persistence, and with the facts finally on the table, Rubin "Hurricane" Carter became a free man for the first time in twenty-two years.

Many had come before them in the fight to free Rubin. But only they had stuck it out to the end.

These three wonderful examples of love, passion and purpose helped Lesra Martin, the Brooklyn teenager, to ultimately gain a Masters Degree in Law. And together, those four people helped give Rubin Carter his life back.

Now I have some questions for you...

What could you achieve if you put in one tenth of the effort and energy they exercised to achieve your own outcomes? What does your life mean now? What will it have meant years from now?

You don't have to free the world.

You don't have to stop world hunger.

But unless you have a larger purpose in life and a larger purpose for today, you're open to all kinds of fears, worries...about small stuff. It's too easy to get depressed about stuff that doesn't mean anything in the big picture.

As Richard Carlson says, "It's all small stuff."

So start out small.

Make it your purpose to stay away from the refrigerator for the last 3 of your waking hours; to eat one raw vegetable today; to smoke one less cigarette today than yesterday; to send those e-mails; to make the call; to set a goal that will stretch you just a little bit.

And celebrate when you achieve it. Feel good about it.

Then tomorrow do it again... Make your days blocks of time where you're achieving 5-10 mini goals. And make sure you give yourself the credit you deserve. This will create tremendous momentum. Soon, you'll look forward to each day with an enthusiasm you thought couldn't possibly exist in you.

Lesra Martin couldn't read before he went to Canada...

Little by little he learned and built upon his knowledge. He was encouraged to keep learning. The little he learned each day built up and allowed him to read a single book. He then changed the course of many people's lives.

You CAN do the same.

What's today going to mean for you?

TODAY'S WINNING BELIEFS

-- I'm uncovering my larger purpose now
-- My purpose is bigger than myself
-- I'm giving incredible meaning to my life
-- Purpose and I are one
-- My purpose puts all things in perspective

IT'S A BEAUTIFUL DAY!

TODAY'S EMPOWERING QUOTE

"It's a beautiful day. Don't let it get away."
  --Bono

TODAY'S EMPOWERING QUESTION

"What beauty can I notice today, something I never noticed before?"

TODAY'S FAST SESSION

You hear other people say it and you've probably said it 1,000 times or more. "Life's too short."

What better reason to take each and EVERY day and live it out loud. Now, I hear this sentiment once in a while but rarely is it put in such a way where the message doesn't sound like a commercial for Mountain Dew.

What a gift life is. Another day. Wow.

Think about it. You are the sum total of ALL your days up until now. Every day has gone into creating you. When you're 70, 80, 90 what a horrible shame it would be if you were to look back and think, "I didn't do so many things I wanted to do. I was mad or scared half the time."

Use today to get where you want to go.

Maybe you're behind your pre-determined schedule. Perhaps you wanted to do more by now than you have.

That's not a problem.

You've got today. How lucky you are...

Don't even think about putting it off 'til tomorrow. Even if there's no PLACE to go or big goal you can work on today, you can do something else.

Look around. Things may be bustling, pushing, moving at cyber speed. But you can be alone in your thoughts and see whatever you want. That mountain is there just for you. "Awesome." Your mother's voice.

Beautiful. You may never hear it again. Your kids. Precious. Your friends. They love you. Enjoy it.

Is there crap? Huge difficult challenges? Sure, but you can learn from it. That's good, right? Just notice the good stuff right now.

What could possibly make today great? A bunch of stuff. And don't think that playing or lounging is the only way to celebrate YOUR day. What can you do?

--Do your best at work - Make today your crowning achievement.
--Recognize someone else - Put a smile on some faces.
--Find out about someone else - Someone on your "team." Be genuine.
--Take some time off if you need to - There might be some roses that need smelling.
--Call someone you haven't talked to in a while. Or pay 'em a visit.
--Meditate - With no goal in mind. Just notice your thoughts.
--Look in the mirror - You're a pretty cool person. Recognize it. It's true.
--Read a chapter - learning is your ticket to where ever you want to go.
--Look at your victory log - And do something today to add to it.
--Laugh - at yourself, others, cartoons, TV shows, commercials. Just laugh.

And I'm sure that you can think of more stuff. The important point is...

Today IS a beautiful day.

But if your perspective is screwed up, you won't see it.

Review the list above and add to it if you like. Review it regularly and your view will change. Guaranteed.

Don't make feeling good so hard. It's not. You don't have to be at Disney World to have a good day.

Today is God's gift to you. Appreciate the gift no matter what it is that you find yourself involved in. It was given in love.

Accept it with love.

TODAY'S WINNING BELIEFS

-- I'm making today my crowning achievement
-- Today is my day to excel
-- I am enjoying myself immensely right now
-- I love being me
-- Enjoyment and I are one
-- I appreciate this gift of a new day

BORROW SOMEONE ELSE'S BRAIN!

TODAY'S EMPOWERING QUOTE

"The body travels more easily than the mind, and until we have limbered up our imagination, we continue to think as though we had stayed home. We have not really budged a step until we take up residence in someone else's point of view."
   --John Erskine

TODAY'S EMPOWERING QUESTION

"How would (insert name) handle this situation?"

TODAY'S FAST SESSION

One of the things I hear most from people, and that I notice about myself, is that when you get an idea about going after some cool goal, often it's dismissed in a millisecond because you can't imagine taking the steps necessary to reach it. Imagining something that doesn't exist yet is a skill that very few people have...

But it just may be the single most important factor or skill in living a happy, contented, and productive life.

Usually, we don't get the outcomes we want simply because we can't imagine it. We aren't able to imagine saying the right thing or being confident no matter how much we prepared. We don't feel creative or successful, so that part of our mind stays hidden behind a brick wall. It's there, but we don't "let" it out. We "can't imagine it..."

Microwave ovens, disposable diapers, fax machines and email grew out of someone's mind. Forks had to be invented, too. All from the mind of a person. In fact, simply learning anything OLD requires imagination.

What you may not realize is that in just a few minutes a day, you can use your imagination for some other very interesting things... useful things. And if your ability to make real something that doesn't exist today is lacking, I have a new and simple tool for you. I'm amazed every time I do it.

It's literally a "no-brainer."

If you want to learn something or do something you've never done or done well, try this.

You can do this for absolutely anything, but let's say you're trying out for a play. Ask yourself who's done this before? Who's good at this? The simplest answer is to think of an actor you admire for their talent and range. My stepdaughter is going through this right now. So she chose Sarah Michelle Gellar, one of her favorite actresses.

What you do is this: When you need to perform at your best or if you need to get great ideas, replace your own head (or mind), figuratively speaking, with theirs. You imagine their head is put in the place of yours. Got the picture?

Once you've done that, ask yourself what they would do now.

-How would they stand?
-What would they think about their chances? What is their confidence level?
-What kind of look would they have on their face?
-How would they walk?
-What kind of pictures would they see in their mind's eye?
-What would they be imagining?
-What would they do? And after that, what? And on and on...

Sit down, close your eyes and imagine it. Have a piece of paper and a pencil next to you. Give yourself 5 minutes. Have all the questions above and more in your mind.

Become that person...

Studies have been done on this phenomenon and frequently found that at the exact moment the imagining exercise was being done by a person, others observed that person to be actually doing, saying or acting in the manner that they were imagining!!

School children who've never been good students have been transformed into 'A' students literally in minutes, just by imagining themselves as top students.

It's simple. You don't need training. But the more often you take these 5-10 minute "breaks," the faster you'll get the answers you want, the better you'll do your job or the better your grades will be.

Use it to improve your work performance and get that promotion and raise.

But if you're a gotta-have-it-now person, keep in mind that this will work and work quickly. But if you think that next week you'll be getting a raise, based on your great performance of the week before, success still demands that you continue to perform daily. Long-term rewards come in the long term.

So pack this one in your arsenal and pull it out whenever you need to effortlessly overachieve or when you're stuck. And if no one is there to pat you on the back, do it yourself. Or imagine someone you respect doing it.

Do this. It only takes 5 minutes. You just may get an idea that will revolutionize your entire life; and maybe everyone else's too!

Keep in mind that success is seldom complex. Just because this "seems" too simple to be effective, don't dismiss it. If your success and happiness are important to you, choose an area of life where you want to perform well and do this exercise.

5 minutes. How about right now?

TODAY'S WINNING BELIEFS

-- My imagination muscles are getting stronger today
-- I've dissolved all blocks to a vivid imagination
-- Great ideas are coming quickly and easily to me now
-- I imagine successful outcomes with ease
-- I use the success of others to develop my imagination

DO YOU HUSTLE OR HIDE?

TODAY'S EMPOWERING QUOTE

"It doesn't take talent to hustle."
  -H. Jackson Brown

TODAY'S EMPOWERING QUESTION

"How quickly and how well can I get this task done?"

TODAY'S FAST SESSION

Most of the time, I'll hallucinate, you're probably really busy. Going, going all day.

But how close are you getting to the big dreams?

You have fantasies about being able to wear some of those "skinny clothes" in your closet, don't you? Remember that friend of yours you had planned on calling? How about that group of leads that you wanted to work? What about that pile in the back yard that needs to be picked up and hauled away?

Man, life doesn't revolve around watching 'Friends' and staying for one more round of drinks. Is that really fulfilling? Do you look back on that with pride or a feeling of accomplishment? Will those happy-hour buddies really snub you if you left now? Are these people even supportive of your far off dreams?

The stars of 'Friends' make over a million per episode. How much do you make watching them? Get TIVO and you can watch them when you're too exhausted to do anything fun and rewarding.

I know what it's like to have no control over your desires...

AND what it's like to transcend them.

And it's even tougher to take sometimes, when you do everything you need to do and you still don't get your outcome. Damn frustrating, huh?

But here's a rule of thumb. If you're not done, keep going.

Does it seem odd to even think about working past 5:00? What about throwing in the exercise video at 10:00 at night?

What would happen if you missed your favorite show this week? What would really happen?

Shake up your routine.

Get out a piece of paper and write down just one goal. A medium-sized goal. Something you've been putting off. Put down the things you need to do to make it happen. Put a date that it absolutely will be done.

Again, make it a medium-sized task... something that would only take about 10-20 hours to complete. Make a schedule. Commit to it... and finish it.

When I did community hearing clinics, I made all of my own phone calls to set them up, took care of all the promotion... it was a lot of work.

But I was driven by one thing... not being second in the door.

If a competitor got there a week or a month ahead of me, it could mean thousands of dollars. I couldn't bear the thought of losing that much money because I couldn't get myself to pick up a 16-ounce telephone receiver to make two or three calls.

Look at your fears. Figure out what they're costing you.

If you don't ask that person out, you both may miss out forever.

If you don't practice, then you're not going to perform well.

Plug in your own situation. Do you want those results?

Listen to your inner voice. What's it saying when you're worried or having a panic attack... over a very routine thing for most people?

When you're stopped cold, notice what you're focusing on and what you're telling yourself.

I'll guarantee it's not, "Go for it!" You're most definitely NOT telling yourself that you can do the job... that's it's no big deal.

94

Look at the empowering beliefs below and commit them to memory. Say them over and over until you dream about them. Read them constantly.

Your circumstances won't change until your thoughts change. Pound that into your head.

You know, I must have watched the movies "Rocky" and "Rudy" 50 times each. Why? Because nothing changes until you change what you think about. And emotional stories about people who overcome huge odds can inspire you to do the same.

Whenever I'm feeling stuck I pull out my empowering questions or my affirmation cards or read/watch an empowering story.

It never ever fails to get me back on track and hopeful.

Do like the legendary basketball coach John Wooden says and "drink from good books." He reads something powerful and encouraging every single day.

And there was no better life coach than him.

Do you believe "what goes in must come out?"

Then act by what you believe and keep the positive flowing in every minute you can...

Set that goal...

And get hustling.

Do that and something good will always happen.

TODAY'S WINNING BELIEFS

-- I'm hustling to get important tasks done today
-- I do the things that make me happier, richer and wiser
-- I'm a self-starter
-- I'm motivated to achieve challenging tasks
-- I find it easy to keep focused on important things
-- I use failure to fuel in me the desire to do better
-- I finish what I start and I start a lot

MISTAKES: FRIEND OR FOE?

TODAY'S EMPOWERING QUOTE

"Life is very interesting, if you make mistakes."
 -Georges Carpentier

TODAY'S EMPOWERING QUESTION

"If I make a mistake during this task, what's the worst that could happen? What's the best?"

TODAY'S FAST SESSION

This is a sticky subject...

Fear of making a mistake is often the last thing you feel just before you start to do something really cool; and it stops most people dead in their tracks.

As usual, I'm not putting myself above this. I'll point out that for what is still more than half my life, I was dominated by fear. Fear of mistakes. Fear of looking like a fool. Fear of failure and success.

One of the most ludicrous situations I can recall where I was afraid of appearing stupid was in Junior High School. I was told by no less than a half dozen friends that a certain girl, who I did like very much, wanted me to ask her to the upcoming Saturday night dance. It was very obvious that she liked me.

I planned to ask her as soon as I could muster up the courage.

Well, I waited and waited...

Pretty soon, it's Friday afternoon. The last class of the day let out and everyone was making a mad dash for the buses to go home for the weekend. And she just "happened by" my locker.

Here was my chance...

A few seconds of small talk and I finally start, "Would you like to, um..."

And that was all I could get out. She waited for what seemed like a minute without me saying another word.

Thankfully, she helped my out, "...go to the dance?"

What a relief! I said, "Yes!"

"I'd love to," she said.

Happily, my fear of women subsided somewhat over the years, but it was just one more pattern that kept me from enjoying a normal part of life that we can all experience if we just stop being so "self" conscious.

Part of my growth was due to my new passion for reading self help books in my early twenties. Failure and poverty was starting to get old. I then started to learn what makes us humans tick. Common themes ran through many of these works.

One recurring and potent suggestion I recall as sticking out was simply doing what you fear.

How could this help?

Well, as simple as it sounds, if you do what you fear enough times, you'll find that there is nothing to fear. You'll become comfortable doing it. The thing you feared will soon become routine.

End of story.

I found out that girls didn't hold any special power over me. I learned that making mistakes actually gave me more opportunities to learn and gain proficiency... and that most mistakes weren't going to kill me.

But a HUGE lesson in life (and make a note of this because it's profound) I learned was that I could learn more from other people's mistakes than I even had time to make myself...

... if I paid attention.

I know. "Duh!"

But in the last 14 years, I have been able to succeed in business to a degree I never even dreamed of because my competitors (and most everyone else) don't do this.

If you keep your eyes open, each day can teach you dozens and even hundreds of important lessons that you CAN use.

Think about it. Do you need to get hit before you learn not to step in front of a moving vehicle?

Every second of every day provides you with lessons...

...If you have your eyes and ears open to them.

Watch and listen to other people. Pay attention to what causes the failure and success of others in even the most tiny of situations.

This little used but powerful habit can erase most of your fears, give you a feeling of power and put you in control of your emotions in just about any situation.

Watch. Listen. Learn.

Every minute.

Live life. Have fun. But take your blinders off. There's a lot going on around you every minute that can teach you about how to eliminate fear of making mistakes.

Mistakes are a part of life. Don't just accept that truth. Embrace it, and your life will be a whole lot happier and filled with accomplishment.

Remember, the people who are laughing at you as you're falling down are pointing at you to keep people from looking at them!

TODAY'S WINNING BELIEFS

-- Learning from mistakes and I are one
-- Mistakes are necessary to living a happy, successful life
-- I learn everything I can from each mistake
-- I see mistakes as part of what I need to learn fast

IF I ONLY HAD THE NERVE

TODAY'S EMPOWERING QUOTE

"For anyone on the downside of advantage but filled with courage, it's possible."
--Russell Crowe (accepting his Best Actor Oscar)

TODAY'S EMPOWERING QUESTION

"What can I think and do today that I have been too scared to even consider before?"

TODAY'S FAST SESSION

Before we begin, I want to thank everyone for your wonderful emails concerning my grandfather who, as many of you know, recently passed on to a very cool place. You warmed my heart and helped in the healing. Thank you.

Ready?

In Italy, when my grandfather was only 6 years old, he had to go to work to help support his family. He only went to school through the 7th grade. From there on it was full time work for him. In 1926, at 18 years old he came to the New World from the "Old Country" on a boat. He spoke not a word of English and had no money at all. Just a dream...

By the time he retired in 1969, he had over $50,000 USD saved, interest from investments and from selling his farm. The value of that money in today's dollars is over $240,000. Not bad for a guy that had absolutely nothing going for him, huh?

Why did I tell you this story?

Because it took courage to do all the things he did. And it took hard work, but he was always the first one to tell you that without the hard work and belief in his ability to get a job done, he couldn't have had the enormous joy he got from living.

Hey... you can do anything you want to do in your life if you'll enjoy right now for what you can, look forward with expectancy, use the gifts and tools you've been given and accept whatever bad cards you've been dealt. It's up to you to play them right.

So stop stewing and start doing! You can do great things. Believe!!

When he got the farm, he had to clear tree filled orchards so that he could grow corn and other crops. And he didn't own any buzz saws.

It was the hard way... by hand.

And the tree stumps?

Pulled out by huge horses and ropes. The same with the giant boulders that dotted the fields.

It's a sad thing to watch people become despondent with their lives. It's sad because there has never been a time when the human race has had it so good, especially in industrialized countries. Better tools, better education, better opportunities and better information to help take advantage of those opportunities.

Imagine how much harder it was to live decades ago and centuries ago. In many countries life is still the same as it was centuries ago.

So please, keep these things in mind, consider yourself lucky and start acting like you're lucky. Do what you fear enough and you will have developed courage...

...Almost as if by magic.

TODAY'S WINNING BELIEFS

-- Today I move ahead with courage
-- I can do it - I know I can
-- I use my fear and anger to fuel in me courage and determination
-- Courage and I are one
-- Feelings of fear are a trigger for me to feel courageous

YOU CAN'T FAKE CHARACTER

TODAY'S EMPOWERING QUOTE

"A man's reputation is the opinion people have of him, but his character is what he really is."
   --Jack Miner

TODAY'S EMPOWERING QUESTION

"What do I really want my life to be about?"

TODAY'S FAST SESSION

I'm glad you're here.

I've been training and helping people for what seems so long now that I forget sometimes that these letters go out to people in all situations... From multiple PhD's to night clerks at run down motels to people whose only computer is at the YMCA where they shower.

Regardless of where you are, do you really want to be there?

I mean, I used to work seven days a week constantly in pursuit of the dollar, and after some time I just stopped, caught my breath and said, "What do I want to do with my life? If I could do anything I wanted, what would it be?" Chasing money was unrewarding. I earned money but life was getting away. Friends were having fun experiences and I was working.

I know, you're thinking about the stories that I tell about my records and accomplishments. And they're true, but more than what you get from your achievements must be what you become.

It must be... or you're living a life without meaning.

Like you, I've known so many people who lie, cheat and steal and justify it with every ridiculous argument possible. "I'm no worse than anyone else," I hear. "So what", "I can't help it."

Does donating money or volunteering make you feel good? Super.

But in your life every day, what jazzes you? Figure it out and do more of it.

It comes down not to values, but character. You can value some pretty off the wall stuff... But character is like a classic suit. Everyone agrees on it. It's what people admire.

And you don't have to be wealthy or connected.

You just need a set of guiding principles. I'd recommend reading 'The 7 Habits of Highly Effective People.' If you're not a book reader, get the 6 tape program from Nightingale-Conant. And listen to it again and again. You can't imagine what you'll be exposed to. It's like God talking to you.

If you know what you stand for, if you don't feel hate or fear of everyone that's different than you then you're in a good place, so far.

If those characteristics don't describe you, then take a drive and spend some time alone and just be quiet. Ask yourself what it is that you want to spend the rest of your life doing.

What is your life to mean?

For me, it was helping people. As many of you know, I came from as far down as you could be without living behind bars. But it was a prison in my mind. I had nothing. No hope. I had failed so many times that it was just a foregone conclusion that life was going to be fast, wild and probably short...

And then I read 'Superlearning' and 'The Greatest Salesman in the World.' That led me to developing the first audio tapes that ultimately led to founding Think Right Now! International.

A 180 degree change almost overnight.

That's the type of question I'm asking you to ask yourself. What legacy do you want to leave?

If you ask you shall get an answer.

Take that answer and use it to guide your every day.

102

TODAY'S WINNING BELIEFS

-- I let the compass guide my actions today
-- I value my character as more important than any possession
-- I'm proud of who I am and who I'm becoming

YOU'LL SEE IT WHEN YOU BELIEVE IT

TODAY'S EMPOWERING QUOTE

"Doubts are more cruel than the worst of truths."
 -Moliere

TODAY'S EMPOWERING QUESTION

"What could I and should I be absolutely certain about?"

TODAY'S FAST SESSION

I talk a lot about momentum and belief in yourself... getting on a positive roll. Because if you believe that you can do something, you often miraculously get some otherworld ability to do it... even if you've never done it before. And if you fall down in your attempt, if you believe that the slip up was nothing more than a delay instead of a denial, then you'll get back up and keep going.

Sometimes, if the flame grows bright enough, even the very casual observer can notice a change in someone that switches from lack of belief to out and out passion for success.

If you're not a sports fan, read the rest of this letter and ignore the sports references. It's actually a discussion about our topic... BELIEF!

Last night I watched the NBA playoff game between the Milwaukee Bucks and the Philadelphia 76ers. The Bucks were up by 16 points! It was looking to be a blowout...

...But the 76ers never lost their belief. Their top scorer, Allen Iverson, was having possibly the worst scoring night of his life, but he was an animal on defense.

Their coach, Larry Brown, was imploring them to believe. Sure he talked X's and O's. I mean, they had to run plays. But he was jumping up and down on the court. Pleading with his team to keep up the pressure, to run down every loose ball, to make every pass as important as if it were the last one of the game.

Nothing but emotion.

He knew they could do it...

...as long as they didn't lose their faith.

He knew that they were as good as the other team. He didn't have to explain the basics of basketball. He knew his only job was to keep their heads in the game.

So did he get down on them when they made bad passes? Nope. He said, "C'mon. That's not like you. You can do this!"

They responded.

They started to believe. By the 4th quarter they had tied it up 63-63. The crowd was going crazy.

Momentum. It's nothing but emotion.

When things go right they tend to stay going right, don't they? But when things go wrong, the same rule applies, huh?

The interesting thing in the game was that as the emotion was exploding for the 76ers, the Bucks suddenly became doubters... missing shots, making bad passes, and worst of all, making stupid fouls out of anger. Their first half smiles turned into angry scowls. It was an incredible thing to watch. They had completely lost their belief in themselves.

It was an amazing display of momentum shift and a great example of how powerful a force it is in life.

Philadelphia responded to all those fouls the Bucks were making to hit 22 free throws in a row... and won 89-88.

A big lesson here is that you can have a lot of things going wrong and still get your outcome... if you don't give up.

Had the Bucks made just one more pass, or just one more basket, or if they had made just one less stupid foul out of frustration, they would have won.

When I was selling face to face every day, it was often at the last second, when I had emptied my mind and giving my prospect EVERY reason I could think of why they should get my solution that they finally said, "Well, all right. You sure do believe that you can help me. So I'll do it."

It's at that point in my life that I learned that I should never give up. Never, Never, Never. Ever.

If you can only take today...

...And get yourself to believe in your ability to do whatever it is you're doing a little faster, a little better, and with a little more enthusiasm, momentum will shift in your favor. Watch it work.

Soon YOU'LL go from the scowl to the winning smile.

Success and happiness always starts between your own two ears. Don't wait. Begin right now and throw that smile on, and keep thinking all day, I can. I can. I can.

Every hour. "I can."

Eating lunch. "I can."

Before you pick up the phone. "I can."

...And you will.

TODAY'S WINNING BELIEFS

-- I believe in myself, and it shows
-- My confidence is growing today
-- I've dissolved the habit of ever giving up
-- My resolve to win is strong now

WHAT WOULD THEY DO?

TODAY'S EMPOWERING QUOTE

"The principles you live by create the world you live in; if you change the principles you live by, you will change your world."
    -Blaine Lee

TODAY'S EMPOWERING QUESTION

What would (name of a successful person) think about this? What would they do in this situation? Then why don't I do that?

TODAY'S FAST SESSION

Picture in your mind someone who has already accomplished one or more of the very large goals or far off dreams you have.

This should be a real person.

You see, in pursuit of whatever place we think we want to be, there are many people, dozens... maybe millions of them who have succeeded before us.

And they hold clues.

"Well, of course," you say. "If I want to put a barn up, I have to learn how from someone who's built one before." "To be an accountant, I need go to school."

It's "common sense," as they say.

But when it comes to reaching some "dream" we've had for a long time, common sense isn't so common.

Think of a big dream you have. C'mon, you've got one...

Getting down to your ideal weight... Building a successful business... Coaching the school team to a winning season... Creating the love for math, reading or science in your students...

Have you had this dream (not quite a goal) maybe for years, even decades, and not followed through?

Why do you think that is?

Are you lazy? Stupid? Well maybe, but probably not.

The reason why most people don't reach their dreams and have trouble with self-control is that they don't have the same core level beliefs as people who've succeeded where you've failed.

Smokers typically believe that they will not die from it. Or they believe that the taste is good... Or that they truly "need" to smoke to handle the stress of the day. These false beliefs number in the hundreds, typically. Conversely, the typical life-long NON-smoker believes just the opposite to the core of their being.

Successful business builders have thousands of beliefs that differ from those who've never tried or who've failed repeatedly.

But this is rarely even considered...

Most people blame fate or lack of knowledge for their failures. 'How could what I believe be wrong?' is a typical bewildered question.

You give me any person who just failed at achieving some big wonderful goal that would have made a huge positive difference in their lives, and I guarantee there are hundreds or thousands of underlying beliefs that sealed their fate from the very beginning.

This is why "How-To" products fail 95+% of the time.

Want a funny example? O.K.

How many absolutely horrible web sites have you been on, even though there are literally dozens of terrific books written about web design and ecommerce? Good question, huh?

You see? Information alone doesn't matter.

Owning the mental factors that create the drive and the discipline is what matters. If you have that, it doesn't matter if you don't know WHAT to do. You'll go learn it, and you'll succeed.

If you've been in your field for 20 years, for example, and some hot shot comes in with only 2 years of experience and blows by you, it's your beliefs that have killed you. Your beliefs control your attitudes. And they dictate your emotions, which directly control your actions.

So if you routinely put important things off, do sub-par work, and generally have some areas of your life that just plain stink, then open up the closet and look at your assumptions.

A 30-second exercise to experience the power of belief:

Pick an area of life that isn't working for you at all. Health, weight, bad habits, relationships, career, financial, sports, school... you choose.

And grab a pen.

Have you planned out everything you need to do to reach your goal? Are you confident you'll absolutely reach it? When you make a mistake, do you often get down about it and get stalled? Do you believe you deserve success, even though there are millions of others who are just as deserving, but fail? Will factors outside your control dictate whether you'll succeed or not? If it would take many months or even years to achieve your goal, is that fine with you? Is following through on what you know are right decisions in this area somewhat difficult? There are literally hundreds more questions, but we'll stop there.

Now, imagine the MOST successful person you know of in that area of life.

Now, look at the questions again.

What do you imagine their answers would be for each of them?

The answers, most definitely, are completely opposite.

You see how disempowered, false beliefs hold you back?

Because this is such a foundational issue, when we create any new Think Right Now! behavior modification program, that is the first place we examine when comparing successful and unsuccessful people.

Sure, we look to past life experiences that may have helped to create the rotten programming, but traumas alone don't explain most future failure. Failures and trauma are often the fire that propels MANY people to great success and happiness.

It's not what happens to us that matters most. Life is a challenge no matter who you are. It's what we believe about what happens that decides our future... and our destiny.

If you want to learn more about belief systems, there are a number of good books on the subject. It's a fascinating and worthy subject for study.

If you want to alter the beliefs that are holding you back, then the best place I know of to help is at http://www.thinkrightnow.com

We've helped thousands of people change their automatic, unthinking responses with little or no effort at all. This has made even elusive success for so many easier that they ever dreamed possible.

Check out what some of our clients say about the process. It's pretty darn impressive.

TODAY'S WINNING BELIEFS

-- I absolutely believe that I can reach my biggest goals
-- I'm just as deserving of success as anyone else
-- I control my actions and my destiny
-- Right decisions are coming easily to me now
-- Answers are coming to me easily now
-- I can handle any situation that comes my way

SEEK AND YE SHALL FIND

TODAY'S EMPOWERING QUOTE

"The people who get on in this world are the people who get up and look for the circumstances they want, and, if they can't find them, make them."
  -George Bernard Shaw

TODAY'S EMPOWERING QUESTION

"How good am I going to feel when I (reach some outcome)?"

TODAY'S FAST SESSION

I just had a conversation with someone I've known my whole life. This man lost over $150,000 in the stock market in the last 20 months. He just kept watching it go down, down, down. Of course, he's been listening to a small town broker who doesn't know much.

It just breaks my heart to have watched this, because it was so avoidable. There is so much information in the world right at our fingertips that it's simply shocking to me that anyone would continue to blindly trust someone without getting more education on investing.

As people living in the 21st century, we've lost all excuses to getting beaten like that in most areas of life.

I mean if you want to lose weight, gain weight, stop a rotten habit, find your love, help your kids get better grades, be a great parent, make more money, etc., etc., etc. the How-To is out there. But you have to find it and then DO something.

When I had so screwed up my life that I was living in a vehicle, no one was betting on me to make it to my next birthday, let alone reach the top of the mountain. But it was by using the wealth of information that's available to us all that helped me salvage my life from certain destruction and put me on the right path.

Now I'd been imploring and begging this guy for the last 32 months to subscribe to investment journals and newsletters. Nope. Things were going just fine. Didn't need it. Market is going to turn around any time.

Now he's scared to put money into anything. That's what a lack of knowledge and fear will do to you.

It didn't take a genius to make money in the market for quite a long time. So after being lulled to sleep by the good times, he knows absolutely nothing more about successful investing than he did 10 years ago.

And investing is just one of many broad areas of life where you can easily succeed or fail based on just one more (or one less) bit of information.

Of course you still have to act on your knowledge. Because when it comes to the important decisions in life, motivation and belief aren't always enough. You must know what you're doing. There is no substitute for a good well drawn out plan based on solid principles.

Back to investing for a moment. Why doesn't Warren Buffett, the world's greatest investor, invest in high tech and internet stocks? Because as a whole, they don't have a long enough track record to have proven to be able to perform in many different economic environments. Hey, I worked for a large, well-funded "dot com" that doesn't exist anymore!

The bottom line is this...

If you want to learn something, you've got to learn it from the people who KNOW what you want to learn.

Don't cry about your relationships to people who have been married and divorced four times. Don't ask your next-door neighbor about their favorite stock. And don't take weight loss advice from someone who is 50 pounds overweight.

When I wanted to build my book business, for example, I called people from all over the country who had similar businesses. I called my largest supplier and asked them who their top distributors were. I then called about 20 of them. I picked their brains about everything I could possibly think of. This was a never-ending process for about 15 months.

And in less than 12 months, I had built the largest business of its kind in the world. Not because I'm so smart... but because I found out where the knowledge was and systematically proceeded to hunt it down.

Was it a lot of work? Whew!! But I don't regret it for a moment. It was part of the process of developing myself into the person I wanted to become.

It wasn't just a way to make money. The money is long gone. But the knowledge, the self-confidence and the incredible belief in my abilities stay with me even today. It's part of the foundation of who I am now.

It reminds me of what a body builder I used to work out with a number of years ago said about his methods and dedication to working out. He was not just big... he was perfectly proportioned as well.

He said, "I get to carry my trophy around with me forever."

Learn what you need to know to get what you want. It's the surest, fastest way. Then go about using what you've learned and YOU'LL get to carry YOUR trophy around with YOU forever, too.

TODAY'S WINNING BELIEFS

-- I'm growing & developing with each new day's experiences
-- I'm using my knowledge to help myself and others
-- My confidence in my abilities is growing daily now
-- When I need to know something, I get the knowledge
-- I stay current in the areas that are important to me
-- I'm worth the effort to build my skills and knowledge
-- I'm my own best friend and I act like it

WANT TO BE TRULY HAPPY?

TODAY'S EMPOWERING QUOTE

"One of the most amazing things ever said on this earth is Jesus' statement: "He that is greatest among you shall be your servant." Nobody has one chance in a billion of being thought really great after a century has passed except those who have been the servants of all. That strange realist from Bethlehem knew that."
>   -Harry Emerson Fosdick, D.D.

TODAY'S EMPOWERING QUESTION

"What can I do for someone today that will help them now?"

TODAY'S FAST SESSION

Yesterday, I got a real slap in the face.

The owner of an auto service business I had been going to for many YEARS, treated me more or less like a common criminal. I had forgotten my wallet, but I had my AMEX card (which he doesn't accept) in my pocket.

So, instead of letting me go home to get my wallet, he insisted that someone bring a form of payment before he would give me the keys to my car.

He said, "So you want me to chase you around to get paid?"

He actually said that to me. For $28. He knows me. I've been going there for years. I see him on the average of every two months.

This is an extreme example of not being able to see the forest for the trees.

Most of the sticky situations we all find ourselves in don't usually SEEM clear as to what we should do. But it probably is clear, if you are.

Look at today's quote again.

From the time we're able to do it, we like to help people. My son, who's three, says, "Mickey help too!" After he "helps," we thank him profusely,

114

and even applaud. Usually, he immediately does something else to "help" too. We all like to be recognized and appreciated. When we're toddlers, that's why we do it, right?

Because it makes us feel good...

When do people usually stop being so enthusiastic about helping out and serving others? Isn't it often when they feel it's under appreciated?

I don't know about you, but I just had a breakthrough as I type here. Wow!

I just thought about all the times when I hid out trying to avoid doing anything. And it occurs to me that I wasn't going to get any kind of heartfelt thanks. Or any kind of thanks. Just criticism if I didn't do something perfectly.

My mind also went to times when I was the critic and wondered why I didn't get enthusiasm and eager help.

I'll bet if you sat down, got quiet and got real honest with yourself, you would realize that one reason you often don't perform at your best, and look to help out more often is the lack of appreciation.

This is where the value of healthy self-esteem and confidence comes in to play. It must take over when the outside world isn't recognizing you for your contributions.

You must recognize you.

You must affirm your value and your ability constantly. This is what separates the winners from the losers...

The haves and have-nots.

The happy from the desperately depressed.

If you can't do something unless you get outside encouragement, then you're going to be sitting around a lot.

Serving others and being a "self starter" is what success is all about. I hear, "What should I do?" every day.

First you've got to get focused on other people. Helping others is why we were put here on earth, not to play and entertain ourselves all day. If you don't help anyone throughout the course of each day, you have no purpose. You don't have to have tremendous strength and capabilities to make yourself useful. Just the ability to care.

Even a sympathetic ear can be the biggest help sometimes.

When I train new salespeople, the first lesson is always about getting clear on why you're calling someone. It's to help THEM. They must love their customers so much that it comes out in every word, every action.

That's why you were put here. Make that the focus of your days and your hours. You'll get the appreciation you crave, if you do.

And if you don't?

Well, that's why we include affirmations in every letter. So YOU can give it to yourself, and so you can instruct yourself instead of waiting for someone else to tell you what to do!

TODAY'S WINNING BELIEFS

-- Service and I are one
-- My purpose is to serve others
-- I get everything I want when I am useful to others
-- The more people I help, the more I receive
-- I have the ability to help others how they need it most
-- Love stands behind all my actions

WHAT DO *YOU* STAND FOR?

TODAY'S EMPOWERING QUOTE

"The within is ceaselessly becoming the without. From the state of a man's heart doth proceed the conditions of his life; his thoughts blossom into deeds, and his deeds bear the fruitage of character and destiny."
        -James Allen (Author-"As a Man Thinketh")

TODAY'S EMPOWERING QUESTION

"What do I want people to say about me after I'm gone -- and even while I'm still here?"

TODAY'S FAST SESSION

I don't watch a lot of television. Watching other people live their fake lives is a tremendous waste of a real one, in my opinion.

I do, however, watch movies that have great lessons in them, like 'Rocky,' 'Rudy,' and 'Mr. Holland's Opus.' Stuff like that.

I first saw 'It's A Wonderful Life' in 1990. I cried a lot. It was then that I knew I wanted to be like George Bailey. I compared my life to his, and they didn't even remotely resemble one another.

I thought: If I die right now, how many people will really care? Have I done much for anyone beside myself?

It was then that I stepped up on the self-help books and tapes and seminars. I tend not to do things in small ways, so I became a sort of a fanatic. I figure that if you really want to become more, you have to learn how.

You can't give what you don't have, after all.

This is part of the path that led me to being able to talk to you every day.

Now, in your life, what is it that you'd like to stand for? Books like 'As a Man Thinketh' by James Allen teach about the power of thoughts. You see, we all are exactly what we think. It's no accident that we end up where we are in life.

I know, there are lots of situations like chance meetings, freak accidents, who your parents and family are, etc. that push us in certain directions. There's no refuting that circumstances play a significant part in what your history will ultimately be.

But regardless of what has happened to detour you, you still decide where you'll go and whom you become from where you currently are. Even if you are a world famous actor, business or political leader, or a successful professional in some other field (and there are many of all of those that read this letter every week), what is it that you want to stand for during this life?

I know a lot of people talk about actors that support this and that thing, and it makes them "sick." But think about it. Anyone who is absent of certain challenges (and it's challenges that make life worth living), feels empty. So they go looking for them. They don't want the meaning of their lives to be just the characters they played. That's not gratifying.

Only by helping other people and feeling a sense of purpose will you truly be happy during your time here.

Pick up whatever books you can, watch inspiring movies, listen to successful people.

Find some activities that make you feel alive.

If you're depressed every day, if you're filled with anxiety and panic, if you start things and don't finish them, then examine your thoughts. Are they all "self" centered? If that is what you hear when you listen to that little voice inside your head, you must set some goals. You absolutely have to find some purpose.

And for Heaven's sake, do just one thing at a time. Don't buy 10 books and try to read them all at once. This is not one more thing to get panicky about. Just get "other people" centered.

Start doing something for someone else beside yourself.

It really is that simple.

Don't look for the answer.

You're reading it now. Help someone else. Every hour. That could mean just doing your job as well as you can this hour. If you do, you're helping lots of people. Isn't that right?

You're helping your customers, your employer, co-workers, vendors, all those people's families and the service providers who serve all of them.

You see, you can't help someone else without having a tremendous effect on potentially thousands of others.

You can't possibly focus on being useful to the people around you without feeling incredible joy and satisfaction with yourself.

Is this starting to make sense yet? Good.

Think about whom you can help now. And if it's indirect, think about all the people whose lives will be impacted if you simply take your job a little more seriously.

I think you're about to have a few "Aha's."

TODAY'S WINNING BELIEFS

-- I am other person centered
-- I know that the quality of my life is the quality of my thoughts
-- I am a positive and optimistic person
-- I've released all selfish thoughts and ways

LIFE IS TOUGH—THE KEY IS HOW YOU RESPOND

TODAY'S EMPOWERING QUOTE

"Every experience that you have that doesn't
    kill you can make you stronger."
        -Unknown

TODAY'S EMPOWERING QUESTION

"What must I do or think to stay in the state of mind
    I need to be in to happily succeed today?"

TODAY'S FAST SESSION

People in the sales profession can rise to peaks of emotion if a call goes well. In the next minute, their mental state can be in the gutter, due to a bad call or missed appointment.

In truth, we all face those situations during the day, especially in dealing with other people who don't do what we want them to do.

Let's face it. We all have, potentially, hundreds of let downs every day... but we also have hundreds of possible opportunities to feel good, or at least keep our attitude and emotions even.

When your email is filled with Spam, when someone yells at you on the phone, when you drove for an hour and your appointment doesn't show up... you have a golden opportunity to work on your mind and to improve yourself and your prospects for the future.

Life is everything that's good... and not so good.

You can't change the fact that sooner or later, you're going to get a flat tire or the battery will die. One day, the phone is going to ring and the school nurse will tell you that you have to pick up your child because she's sick. Someone close to you is going to die without any warning.

Just the other day, we got an email from a guy who wanted a type of product we don't carry. He was in an irritated mood even before he got a response. He said something about don't be a "#%@^*" snob about the product. Before we even sent a response!

120

We told him that we didn't have what he wanted. He found it elsewhere and he emailed back and went on another tirade about how horrible we were. Thank God this guy found the self-help product he was looking for, I thought, because he's going to hurt a lot of people before he's through in this life... and THEY need intervention!

I personally emailed him back, and told him that we would be happy to send any future requests for this type of product to the same place he found it, if he would let me know where to send them.

Another tirade about how condescending I was and what poor service we provided. On and on he went.

Tell me...

Do you flip people off when they make errors on the road? Do you yell at people on the phone? When people do it to you do you have to go have a cigarette or a drink to calm down? Does your heart start pounding faster? Do you get flustered and become unable to think clearly?

Understand that it's all part of life... daily life.

When you wake up tomorrow, chances are excellent that someone is going to do something stupid on the road. Don't shake your fist at him. You'll feel even worse and less able to perform your daily duties. Plus, you'd be diverting his attention from the road again!!

Think about the consequences of YOUR actions.

I learned about the power of concentration and mental focus years ago, when I was selling face to face. I would chant a mantra for about 15 minutes before I arrived at each appointment. I chanted the same one before I started to make phone calls. My focus was complete. I could not be distracted. I learned, by failing to concentrate, that I would starve if I didn't keep my mind clear of all the crap that the day would no doubt rain down on me if I let it.

The net result was I made more calls than anyone in my industry and my closing ratio was the highest in the world... four times the average. If I had let those little things get me down and tick me off, then I wouldn't have been able to enjoy the success I had.

Those lessons are still with me today. Why? Because each minute of the day, I tried to remember today's empowering quote.

When bad things happen, there is always some kind of lesson in them.

Either you uncover the lesson or you don't. It's as simple as that. If you don't, then you'll continue to get P.O.'d at the most inane stuff, you'll carry on with your little grudges, you'll fight fire with fire, and your state of mind immediately after these mental episodes will prevent you from performing at your best and/or holding any peace in your mind.

Today, notice what happens around you. (It's OK to do this tomorrow, too.)

Ask yourself if it is normal.

Don't ask if it's desirable.

Just ask if it's normal, expected, typical, predictable, natural, common, and probable. If your answer is yes, then it doesn't make any sense to get upset about it, does it?

It's called life.

Then... find the lesson. Learn. And move forward more happily and better able to keep your focus and your mood high. You just turned a "problem" into an opportunity.

Your path has just changed.

Learn a lesson from everything that happens to you and from all that you witness, and you won't recognize yourself or your life a year from now.

TODAY'S WINNING BELIEFS

-- I see the chance to learn in every situation
-- Life is fun and interesting now
-- I am in control of my moods today
-- I accept the possible as the probable today
-- I've let go of all anxiety about today's outcomes
-- I am growing rapidly in my abilities now

RELEASE THE PAIN... AND GET ON WITH LIFE

TODAY'S EMPOWERING QUOTE

"When I left Charlie's place, I asked God to get all the badness, the sorrow, the hurt--all the anger--and leave it in the dust and to let there be a new world, a new life."
  -Reba McIntire

TODAY'S EMPOWERING QUESTION

"What would happen if I just let go of all the sorrow, pain and anger – just let it go?"

TODAY'S FAST SESSION

I recently read a short story about Reba McIntire's life. I gained a whole new appreciation for her.

If you're not familiar with her, she's sold more country music records than any woman in history.

Her first marriage was very painful. Just one example of the things she endured was her husband's demand that if they had any children, she'd have to quit singing because he wasn't going to change any diapers. Imagine a guy who's got a wife who makes tens of millions of dollars, and he wants her to quit because he won't help with the kids.

Schmuck...

He never made her feel like she did anything important.

But she never gave in to the treatment she got from him. Instead, after 11 years of marriage, she divorced him.

That was 1987.

Since then, she's done more in her industry than anyone before her.

You see, you don't have to give in to your challenges. Use them to make you stronger.

Look at the nay-sayers and tell them they're wrong. Use their criticism to feed your determination...

When someone tells you that you can't, double your efforts. They're probably wrong.

And if the worst thing happens, if you think you can't... be intelligent. Make sure you're not climbing a mountain that no one could scale. But if it's doable and if you have the resources, or if you can get them...

...Then get rid of the doubt. Say "I can do it."

Focus on your goal TODAY - RIGHT NOW, and get busy. Get very busy.

Life isn't going to slow down for you.

If it can be done, you can do it. But not by sitting on your behind.

I love it when I hear people complaining about how some famous person they read about is horrible.

"Not an environmentalist, not a supporter of this cause, they got a nose job, that's not their real hair color, what do they do with all their money, how could they divorce their wonderful spouse, what kind of hair-do is that, they don't compete fairly..."

Oh my God!

And all the while, they're sitting in the back yard stuffing themselves with that dessert they don't need, washing it down with that beer that won't erase the fact that they're a failure in just about every sense of the word.

Do you do this?

Then stop it and get busy making a life for yourself.

Do other people do it to you?

Then ignore them. They're not worth getting upset over. Are they?

Listen to people who've achieved what you want to achieve. Seek them out. If you don't know any, then find them. Read their books. Study what you need to learn.

Think about it. If everyone let criticism stop him or her, no one would do anything. Be like the people that let it fall right off their backs.

Let go of the pain... and accept no more of it. Be what you need to be when you need to be it.

You're steel. Arrows of criticism can't harm you.

You're wood. You won't sink under the weight of doubt.

You're passionate. Your new goals are too important to let anything get in your way.

And today is the day that you make great progress. Tomorrow is just a dream. Right Now is the only currency you've got...

...So wisely spend all your energy on getting where you are supposed to be going... today.

TODAY'S WINNING BELIEFS

-- I ignore my critics
-- I release all fear of making mistakes
-- I'm controlling my destiny today
-- I see my goals clearly and I'm going for them
-- I learned from yesterday, so I'm happy it all happened

MAKE EACH DAY COUNT

TODAY'S EMPOWERING QUOTE

"I wish that I knew what I know now, when I was younger.
I wish that I knew what I know now, when I was stronger."
  - Ronnie Lane/Ron Wood

TODAY'S EMPOWERING QUESTION

"What can I do today that I would be proud to
   look back on at the end of my life?"

TODAY'S FAST SESSION

As we mature, our minds and decision making abilities generally get better. Meaning that we typically don't make the same beginner mistakes that we made as youths.

I'm a sports fan. I see analogies to life in every sport and watch them in fascination, wondering about the backgrounds of the players and what makes one player a superstar when another, with equal and often greater physical ability, sits on the bench.

In sports, the body wears down just when the mind is at its peak in the sport. It reminds me of the scene in the movie, "It's a Wonderful Life" when a man yells at George Bailey, 'Youth is wasted on the wrong people!'

But in most areas of life, every day can be looked at as a learning opportunity. Maybe you won't have the energy in a few years that you have today, but you can still take advantage of today knowing that you'll still be able to enjoy the benefits of your experience... unlike an athlete who's considered old at 35 in their field.

Each stage of your life has doors and windows and even walls... that can be knocked down if necessary.

If you're a long time Your Day To Win reader, you know that I believe that you should live today as if it's your last, but...

If you don't accomplish what you wanted to, drop to your knees, thank God for the gift of today and... plan for tomorrow.

Don't live there. Just plan for it.

Pat Riley, the coach of the Miami Heat, wrote in his book, 'The Winner Within' that with his championship Lakers teams of the 80's, he implored his players, each game, to do just one percent better in every area of their games. There are a lot of areas, like passing, rebounds, steals, assists, scoring... you get the picture.

What this does is not make the task so daunting. Only one percent! But if you add that one percent in all those areas...

...you spell championship.

And they won a bunch of them. They didn't allow themselves to get down if they had a bad game. They planned for tomorrow... to improve.

This gave them positive anticipation.

I heard that in some restaurants that serve fresh fish, they put a predator in the tank with the fish. This keeps them lively and they stay fresher. Interesting.

People are the same way. If we just sit around and don't strrrettttch ourselves, we get stale; we lose our edge. And we're not as tasty. Just checking to see if you're paying attention!

Folks, life can be "long," but it's still too short to be sitting around "killing time." You're killing your life.

Breathe life into yourself instead and stop being scared of just one thing... just for today. Do what you're scared of and you'll look back afterwards and you'll see you grew right then.

That moment you did something you can be proud of...you stared that scary obstacle in the face.

Later you can think, "I didn't know what I was doing then, but I faked it so well that no one else knew I was full of it!! Haaaa!!"

Imaging that a few years from now, you're sitting around. You say to the person next to you, "I was watching TV about 6 years ago at home, boy what a night!"

Would you do that?

Go forward a few years and look back. What do you want to see?

Whatever your answer is, do it! Then do some more of it...
Today. C'mon!

Do it now while you're younger and stronger... than you'll be in a few more years.

TODAY'S WINNING BELIEFS

-- I actively look for new things to learn every day
-- I actively imagine the benefits of learning new things
-- I've released the fear of learning new information
-- I easily absorb and remember new information

YOUR QUESTIONS MAKE YOU... OR BREAK YOU

TODAY'S EMPOWERING QUOTE

"The smart ones ask when they don't know.
  And sometimes when they do."
    --Malcolm Forbes

TODAY'S EMPOWERING QUESTION

 "What would help me to _____?"

TODAY'S FAST SESSION

Questioning is one of the two main functions of the mind. The other being affirming old and new beliefs. What do I mean?

Well, all day long as information is pumped at you, you're evaluating it so you can decide which of it you deem necessary to focus on. You need to have a feeling about what everything coming at you means so you can take the most appropriate action or none at all.

Much of this questioning is unconscious. For example, if you're driving and a man steps in front of your car, you don't have to take a lot of time and say, "What does this mean and what should I do?" No, that should be automatic. As soon as you realize what's happening, you slam on the brakes or swerve, avoiding a collision.

And it's our level of awareness of what's around us that determines what we do...Our habitual questions, conscious and unconscious (literally automatic).

If you thought I was incorrect about the last series of events being automatic, you're right.

You get a gold star!

See, many people would "freeze up" and slam into the person. Others would miss the brake and hit the gas. Ooooh! Others would brake and keep the wheel straight. Some might swerve away from the man only to hit the oncoming traffic, or the other way... into other people.

It just depends on your awareness. And your conditioning. Ever see people who just back right out of their driveways into oncoming traffic without looking? It's amazing to watch.

No awareness of what's going on around them! Their minds are somewhere else completely.

The human mind has pictures and words flying in and out all the time, and it keeps most of us from being aware of what's going on around us. Many people are in a literal daze most of the time.

Let's separate you from the multitudes, shall we?

How? I'm glad you asked.

Without getting lost in the minutiae (I don't want to home in on driving skills), let's stay general and you can focus in on it yourself.

What separates the winners in most situations from the losers?

Most people's moment-by-moment questions just "fly in" to their heads all throughout the day... while many truly happy and successful people have a trained, practiced habit of asking empowering, course correcting questions all the time.

The sad truth, though, is that of those people, most of them came about this good mental habit by accident. They don't know how they got that way; the same way the larger group, the "negative" thinkers got their habitual thought patterns. The danger of this ignorance is that you can be good at some skills and simply horrible at others. So it's important to know how you succeed in one area of life so you can duplicate it in others.

Are you starting to see the life altering power of controlling your automatic questioning mechanism?

Good, because positive thinking is good, but you have to be able to do it automatically without "thinking" to be a true positive thinker and to able to reap the benefits.

A lot of people in the personal development field like to put their twist on how positive thinking doesn't work.

It does work...

But like anything else, if you don't practice it, you stop doing it. And since any kind of thinking, positive or not, is something that is going on every second of the day (except in our deepest levels of sleep), you really need to practice it for you to develop mastery.

So positive thinking, while great, can't keep you from getting sidetracked and backing out of your driveway into oncoming traffic. That comes from awareness and getting the right mental questions anchored into your nervous system.

How?

By practice. So don't think that I'm going to tell you that you can be a master of this in one day. One day goes by, you're still getting rotten results with people and projects and then you'd be even more cynical than before.

I'll give you an example of how our questioning dictates what results we get. This weekend, my step-daughter dropped a glass in the sink and glass went everywhere. The probability was that it was on the floor, too, since it was quite an explosion.

She had bare feet and was in no hurry to get some shoes on before the cleaning began. So I ASKED her if she thought some glass might have gotten on the floor. She said what you'd expect from a thirteen-year-old...

"I don't know."

You see, at thirteen, references for many things in life are limited. So questions like the ones I asked her don't pop in as easily or even at all.

The trouble is, hundreds of millions of people who are much older still fail to even think of asking these most basic of questions most of the time (yours truly included). If you aren't habitually (and eventually, unconsciously) asking the most empowering questions of yourself, you're going to be picking a lot of glass out of your feet... or just making the same mistakes over and over again...

...Living a life with little joy, peace or accomplishment.

Take heart. You can learn to do this, habitually. And with practice, it will get wired into your mind and body. You'll avoid making stupid mistakes at the simplest of tasks.

It's not easy, but it's simple to do. And there is a difference.

There are thousands of empowering questions you can use in your daily moments. Empowering questions don't only take the shape of the ones that you see at the top of my daily message.

They can be as simple as, "Could shards of glass have fallen onto the floor?" And, "How can I hold this so it won't fall?"

And please don't think this is too basic, in the scope of the challenges you face each day, to make a difference. Don't, Don't, Don't!

The awareness of this and then working at mastering it helped me become the highest paid person in the world in my field, and it can provide many other benefits for you.

At work, you can ask questions like, "What is he thinking right now?" If you don't, you can't anticipate the right thing to say NEXT! "Is it going to rain today?" is a question that many people don't ask and end up getting wet. Because if the answer is maybe, you can bring an umbrella. Not even being aware enough to ask the question, means higher cleaning bills, shoes that need to be replaced sooner, poor image to others...

...and a poor self image.

"I can't do anything right. Why am I so stupid?" become the questions that you come up with instead of ones that could turn your life around in a flash.

We've only covered the most elementary building blocks of question asking, but can't you feel a little of the power already? Hey, this helped take me from living on four wheels to standing on two feet.

Let's pick this up next time. There's more...

Lot's more.

TODAY'S WINNING BELIEFS

-- My habitual questions steer me in the right directions
-- I ask questions that give me options and alternatives
-- I pay attention to my questions and recognize their value
-- I ask "How?" and I get answers
-- My questions empower me to be effective and happy in all areas of life
-- I look at all consequences before I decide my actions
-- I'm aware of my immediate surroundings as appropriate
-- I ask questions that force me to get life changing answers

IT AIN'T OVER YET

TODAY'S EMPOWERING QUOTE

"The most rewarding things you do in life are often the ones that look like they cannot be done."
- Arnold Palmer

TODAY'S EMPOWERING QUESTION

"What can I do or say to fix this situation now?"

TODAY'S FAST SESSION

In the movie 'The Godfather,' there's a scene in it where Robert Duvall (Tom) is given some news that Marlon Brando (Godfather) isn't going to like at all. So as soon as he can walk out the door, he does... to go break the bad news.

The guy who told Tom the bad news wants to know what the hurry was. Tom says that Godfather likes to hear bad news right away.

Well, because Godfather got the information quickly, he was able to take immediate action and get his creative plan under way…

And as a result, he got his way.

Oftentimes, mistakes and bad outcomes can be fixed, but only if we act FAST.

In my business career, when there is a problem with an important issue, I want to know about it as fast as possible.

So I could worry longer?

No, so I could jump in my car and visit or pick up the phone within seconds. Not minutes. Seconds.

One time I did the craziest stunt to keep a client who said they never wanted to work with my book company again.

See, one of my employees didn't program the newest cash register with all our titles before it was packed for an event. So when the customers were lining up to pay for their books, none of their purchases were scanning properly.

So now each title had to be manually entered into the register... a painfully slow process when dozens of people are waiting and waiting, many not very quietly.

Well, my contact person wasn't pleased.

When the phone call came in a month later, telling us we were out, my office immediately called me on my cell phone, I went to the office, picked up all my sales awards, packed them into a large duffle bag and proceeded to this client's office...

...a two and a half hour drive away.

When I walked in the door, you should've seen her face.

Total shock.

She told me that the board made the decision, and that there was no sense in discussing it.

I made the case that if there were anyone in the world she could trust to fix this situation, never to allow this to happen again, it was me. That's when I began pulling the awards out, explaining what they were for. Not to impress her, but to show her it wasn't just talk.

These awards, I explained were the results of total commitment to her and others in positions similar to hers. I was recognized as the best, and that's what I promised her... the best from the best.

I kept the account.

They were worth over $25,000 in sales per year.

By immediate action, creativity, and by not accepting defeat, a lot of people won. She won. I won. And all those book lovers she was responsible for won big.

And more importantly, I learned, again, that "It ain't over 'til it's over."

So please, please... when all seems lost, and I know sometimes the situations we often find ourselves in seem hopeless, 90+% of the time it is not hopeless.

But 90% of the people quit.

I feel your frustration. No one is immune from life's crashing waves of defeat and torment. No one.

But the only time we can truly lose is when we quit.

Breakthroughs usually come when it looks the darkest.

And when you find yourself in no-win situations and consistently keep plugging away, you'll succeed so many times that you will learn this, too. "It ain't over 'til it's over."

So pick up the phone, get in your car, write that email, make that apology, do whatever you have to do to fix whatever isn't working.

Now. Yeah, right now.

You'll be so happy you did.

Even if things don't work out this time, you'll have put yourself in a position to win. Do that enough times and you'll be...

A winner in life.

TODAY'S WINNING BELIEFS

-- I always look for ways to come out on top
-- Victory is always close by
-- I always believe I will succeed no matter what
-- I am a winner
-- I create other winners
-- I am surrounding myself with winners

EMPOWERING QUESTIONS = WISDOM

TODAY'S EMPOWERING QUOTE

"I had six honest serving men-they taught me all I knew: Their names were Where and What and When and Why and How and Who."
--Rudyard Kipling

TODAY'S EMPOWERING QUESTION

"What kind of questions have I been asking myself in the last hour?"

TODAY'S FAST SESSION

Notice that Rudyard Kipling didn't say that those questions taught him quite a bit. He said they taught him all he knew.

And he knew quite a bit!

You are asking questions all day long just through the normal process of thinking...

And depending on the questions you ask consciously (which programs your unconscious mind to go on asking them in the future without your conscious knowledge), you either experience emotions and develop attitudes that support you in getting what you want in life, or you experience anxiety and worry.

If you are depressed and anxious and have thoughts of worry about what horrible thing is going to happen next, you must look to your thoughts. Watch them. Too much research exists to conclude anything but this...

If you focus your thoughts on empowering outcomes and ask yourself questions that give you answers that inspire you, then you'll find that your anxiety and panic attacks will reduce. And with enough practice, they can even go away. I don't care if you've had chronic depression for decades.

This works.

Your thoughts create chemicals- either depressants or stimulants. Studies prove that when rotten pictures are shown to people, their brains produce rotten chemicals on the spot...

The same ones that pharmaceutical companies make when they develop depressants. How do you think they developed these chemicals? They study depressed people!!!

Stimulants are made the same way. That's how many of these drugs are first discovered. Happy pictures, great questions, emotions of elation and joy.

Fast! Let's study the chemicals we were just able to produce in that brain!

We just get too many emails from people, who've been depressed and living in panic for years, that have been able to change their lives entirely by changing their questions and their affirmations (beliefs).

This daily letter alone has helped to transformed thousands. And all it does is change your focus for a while and urges you to continue your new focus... Because if you do something enough, it becomes a habit.

You can try to escape your problems by changing your environment, but... you take your thoughts with you!

Start asking yourself questions that empower. To make this stick, you'll have to write them down and read them throughout the day. Yes, even if you're rich and famous.

Questions like these:

How can I do a better job?
What is really cool about me?
What do I like about my job?
What's neat about my kids?
Who loves me and who do I love?
What's useful about this "problem?"
What can the next hour mean to me if I get this task done?

Each of these questions, and there are literally thousands more you can ask consciously, has answers. And the answers make you feel good. Why? Because they force you to focus on what's right. What's good.

Does it mean that your life suddenly becomes perfect? Of course not. But when you are looking in the right directions, you'll see just far enough to get encouraged. Even if your goal is only to not slit your wrist today.

Hey, you have to start somewhere, right?

Every day that you achieve your modest goal is confirmation that you can do more. And then more...

And when you follow that accomplishment up with the question, "How did I do that?" you get an empowering answer. An answer that teaches you how to do it again later.

This is why Rudyard Kipling could say the statement above with heartfelt conviction...

And why I'm optimistic for you today... All day. And every day.

Write questions down like the ones above in any area of life that is troubling you.

Read them often. A few times every day.

And you absolutely, positively CANNOT fail to make each day of your life more fun, no matter what outside stressors are working on you.

And isn't that how you want today and the rest of your life to be? (Now THAT was an empowering question!)

TODAY'S WINNING BELIEFS

-- My questions help me focus on what's right and good
-- I substitute rotten questions with empowering ones
-- I ask great questions and get great answers
-- My life is getting better each day because of my focus
-- I can create joy just by changing my questions
-- I'm successful because I have a disciplined mind
-- I'm great at turning problems into successful outcomes

HOW LUCKY AM I?

TODAY'S EMPOWERING QUOTE

"What leads to unhappiness is making pleasure the chief aim."
  --William Shenstone

TODAY'S EMPOWERING QUESTION

"How did I get so lucky to have the people that are in my life?"

TODAY'S FAST SESSION

Until I was 24 years old, I was the king of laziness. Pleasure was ALL I wanted. So certainly, I found what I thought was it. But I was unhappy most of the time. No matter where I was or who I was with, I wanted to be somewhere else and with someone else.

By then, I'd never dated anyone longer that about 3 weeks and I dated a fair amount. I always wanted someone better.

But no one ever explained to me that if I lived differently, enjoying each moment as much as possible, helping other people whenever I could, and by giving my absolute best at work, I would be able to get more pleasure in life than if I played all day, everyday.

I can tell you that since 1987, I have worked more hours than 99.9% of the world's population. Yet during that time, I have experienced more true joy than I ever knew existed in the world.

During my pleasure pursuits, I was miserable. I didn't like myself. I didn't trust many people, because I, myself, was untrustworthy. I figured all people were generally like me.

Think about the movie stars and rock stars that are so strung out that they kill themselves with drugs and alcohol. They have the false belief that everything has to be fun RIGHT NOW or it sucks.

The truth is your happiness has more to do with serving other people than you might be willing to consider at this moment.

Adjust your daily focus to how you can help others and your career will flourish, your relationships will blossom, your health will shine. And you will look back at the end of your life and be satisfied beyond measure.

Let's say that you don't even like half the people you live and work with. Nobody's perfect, but we are all pretty nice people at the root of it. If you force yourself to ask this question with total expectation of getting an answer, you will be shocked at how many good qualities that you can find about everyone you know or meet.

Take the next 24 hours and ask yourself, "What can I admire about _____?" concerning everyone you meet or spend time with, especially the people you don't necessarily like all that much.

This exercise, if done seriously, will allow you to see people for who they really are. You'll find out how really lucky you are. Those are the people in your life.

They may be there just to teach you valuable lessons...

Have you ever heard, "Let's make the most of it?"

Your life IS the people in it.

So to make the most of your life, make the most of those people and write down today's question...

And ask it often.

TODAY'S WINNING BELIEFS

-- I get pleasure from helping others
-- I notice the good in other people
-- I'm lucky to have the people in my life
-- I'm learning all I can from everyone I know
-- Others are teaching me now
-- I'm enjoying myself now

COUNT YOUR BLESSINGS INSTEAD OF SHEEP

TODAY'S EMPOWERING QUOTE

"Gratitude is not only the greatest of virtues,
  but the parent of all others."
        -Cicero

TODAY'S EMPOWERING QUESTION

"Comparing my life to the homeless person on the
  street, what do I feel grateful for?"

TODAY'S FAST SESSION

I felt I needed to ask a particularly pointed question today, by including the reference to the homeless person. Why?

Because most people who have a job, a home, a family, and a country that lets you live in freedom, for the most part don't appreciate it. You take it for granted. And comparing yourself to someone who would be grateful for 1/1000th of what you probably have puts things in better perspective...

...especially when you get angry at trivial stuff that doesn't really matter. :)

A perfect example...

I recently saw a movie starring Nicholas Cage and Meg Ryan, 'City of Angels.' Cage plays an angel, Seth, whose "job" is to take people who die onto the next place.

Ryan plays a cardiologist, Maggie, who loses a patient on the operating table. Seth takes Maggie's patient...

...and falls in "love" with her. First he learns what love is, then he falls. Ultimately, he decides to give up his place in eternity, to become human... and to die like all humans must.

Shortly after he goes through the painful process of becoming human, they have less than 24 hours together and she has a tragic fatal accident.

His emotional pain is beyond description.

He gave up eternal "life" for her and now he doesn't even have her.

Soon after, his best angel friend asked him if he knew this was going to happen, would he still have done it?

He said, "I would rather have had one breath of her hair, one kiss of her lips, one touch of her hand, than an eternity without it... One."

It was at that moment that I renewed my conviction that no matter how bad things could get, no matter what tragedy befalls me, I'm grateful for even the smallest of things.

But this feeling can be fleeting and of little value unless you actually take the time to acknowledge it.... Regularly.

To do that you must recognize what you have. If you don't, you'll regularly go on mourning the tiniest of inconsequential crap. And literally billions of people do exactly that every day.

Keep in mind the homeless person and Seth.

What can you be thankful for?

Does it HAVE to be your new car? Can't it be just a smile?

How about that dinner that was made for you last night? Did you shiver last night as you slept? Many did. Do you have a job? Marketable skills? A nice neighbor? New shoes? Any shoes?

What's all this about? What is gratitude?

It's simply a way for us to feel good any time we want... for free. And if we share it with others, it's a way for them to feel good, too... any time you want.

Can you see why Cicero has such an exalted opinion of gratitude?

Now take a minute and find out what you have to feel grateful for... And if it's someone else, tell him or her.

TODAY'S WINNING BELIEFS

-- I appreciate all that I have all the time
-- I am grateful for all my challenges

ANGELS ON EARTH

TODAY'S EMPOWERING QUOTE

"If you want others to be happy, practice compassion.
If you want to be happy, practice compassion."
                    -Dalai Lama

TODAY'S EMPOWERING QUESTION

"Who helped me when I needed it most desperately? How did it make me feel?"

TODAY'S FAST SESSION

The quick story below is possibly the most uplifting and motivating I have ever read in my life. At the end I have a message for you.

Do yourself a favor. Read this story when you can be by yourself, not when you have someone breathing down your back. Trust me. See you at the bottom.

...Don't major in the minors.

At a fundraising dinner for a school that serves learning-disabled children, the father of one of the school's students delivered a speech that would never be forgotten by all who attended.

After extolling the school and its dedicated staff, he offered a question. "Everything God does is done with perfection. Yet, my son, Shay, cannot learn things as other children do. He cannot understand things as other children do. Where is God's plan reflected in my son?"

The audience was stilled by the query.

The father continued. "I believe," the father answered, "that when God brings a child like Shay into the world, an opportunity to realize the Divine Plan presents itself. And it comes in the way people treat that child."

Then, he told the following story:

Shay and I walked past a park where some boys Shay knew were playing baseball. Shay asked, "Do you think they will let me play?" Shay's father knew that most boys would not want him on their team. But the father understood that if his son were allowed to play it would give him a much-needed sense of belonging.

Shay's father approached one of the boys on the field and asked if Shay could play. The boy looked around for guidance from his teammates. Getting none, he took matters into his own hands and said, "We are losing by six runs, and the game is in the eighth inning. I guess he can be on our team and we'll try to put him up to bat in the ninth inning."

In the bottom of the eighth inning, Shay's team scored a few runs but was still behind by three.

At the top of the ninth inning, Shay put on a glove and played in the outfield. Although no hits came his way, he was obviously ecstatic just to be on the field, grinning from ear to ear as his father waved to him from the stands.

In the bottom of the ninth inning, Shay's team scored again. Now, with two outs and the bases loaded, the potential winning run was on base.

Shay was scheduled to be the next at-bat.

Would the team actually let Shay bat at this juncture and give away their chance to win the game?

Surprisingly, Shay was given the bat. Everyone knew that a hit was all but impossible because Shay didn't even know how to hold the bat properly, much less connect with the ball. However, as Shay stepped up to the plate, the pitcher moved a few steps to lob the ball in softly so Shay could at least be able to make contact.

The first pitch came and Shay swung clumsily and missed.

The pitcher again took a few steps forward to toss the ball softly toward Shay. As the pitch came in, Shay swung at the ball and hit a slow ground ball to the pitcher. The pitcher picked up the soft grounder and could easily have thrown the ball to the first baseman. Shay would have been out and that would have ended the game.

Instead, the pitcher took the ball and threw it on a high arc to right field, far beyond reach of the first baseman. Everyone started yelling, "Shay, run to first. Run to first."

Never in his life had Shay ever made it to first base. He scampered down the baseline, wide-eyed and startled. Everyone yelled, "Run to second, run to second!"

By the time Shay was rounding first base, the right fielder had the ball. He could have thrown the ball to the second baseman for a tag. But the right fielder understood what the pitcher's intentions had been, so he threw the ball high and far over the third baseman's head.

Shay ran toward second base as the runners ahead of him deliriously circled the bases towards home.

As Shay reached second base, the opposing shortstop ran to him, turned him in the direction of third base, and shouted, "Run to third!"

As Shay rounded third, the boys from BOTH teams were screaming, "Shay! Run home!"

Shay ran home, stepped on home plate and was cheered as the hero, for hitting a "grand slam" and winning the game for his team.

"That day," said the father softly with tears now rolling down his face, "the boys from both teams helped bring a piece of the Divine Plan into this world."

And now, a footnote to the story. We all have thousands of opportunities a day to help realize God's plan. So many seemingly trivial interactions between two people present us with a choice: Do we pass along a spark of the Divine? Or do we pass up that opportunity, and leave the world a bit colder in the process?

I'm back.

Wasn't that incredible?

The first time I read it, I missed something important. I don't want you to miss it.

Shay had played baseball a number of times. Before that day, no one had gone out of their way to help him. He had never made it to first base before.

Shay may never completely be able to appreciate what happened that day, even though it was probably the thrill of his life.

The biggest thing that happened was that over 20 other kids got to experience what helping someone else can do for them. They got to feel the excitement that you can feel by putting yourself second, instead of first.

The world was made better just then... from the ripple effect it had on them, and now that this story is getting out.

And I too feel privileged to be able to share this story with you so that you can get closer to what may be the meaning of life.

I think it's to help ease the burden of it for others...and feel that joy.

TODAY'S WINNING BELIEFS

-- I help others every chance I get
-- I feel better helping someone than I do at any other time
-- I believe what goes around comes around
-- I become more and receive more every time I help someone

HOW CAN YOU LEAVE YOUR MARK IN THE WORLD?

TODAY'S EMPOWERING QUOTE

(Crying) "I need to try to be successful in business so I can take care of 700 families. I put my home phone number on our web site & I have women calling saying they don't know how they'll pay the mortgage. They don't know what they're going to do. I think the remaining staff is pulling together with the view that we want to make things happen for them. We need to find a way to take care of them. And I think it's going to be a different kind of drive than I've ever had before. It's not about my family. I can kiss my kids tonight. But other people don't get to kiss their kids tonight. And I just have to help them... There's only one reason to be in business, and that's to help 700 families."
> -Howard Lutkin (CEO-Cantor Fitzgerald, NYC)

TODAY'S EMPOWERING QUESTION

"What is my mission and purpose in life? Why am I here?"

TODAY'S FAST SESSION

So many people go through their lives without discovering it. Most don't really look for it. I'm talking about purpose.

Now don't get me wrong. I don't have any idea what "the" meaning of life is. But each of us has been given the unbelievable gift of being able to define our own... individually.

Howard Lutkin, whose 1,000 employee company was decimated by the attack on the World Trade Center, lived with true purpose before the attacks. He created a company where around 50 trillion dollars a year flowed through. Yes, I said trillion. The wives of a few employees called him to say that, if their husbands had to die, they're glad it was while they worked for him, because they loved going to work every day. And they loved working for him.

As he said in today's quote, he now has a different kind of drive. He loves his people. They're like his family. And he feels a strong responsibility towards the families of his fallen employees.

Like the fictional character George Bailey in the movie, "It's a Wonderful Life," Howard Lutkin inspires me to keep even more firmly in my sight my purpose and mission in this life.

And I share his tragic loss with you so that you can get a sense of what it's like to live for something much bigger than yourself. Unfortunately for Howard, he may never get over the feeling of responsibility he voiced over those tragic deaths.

But for you, before you take on a mission that is solely guilt ridden, do what you have to do (and I'll try to help) to find your purpose. Find something to spend your days or nights doing that will make a difference to someone. Something you love to do.

You don't have to run a multi-national company. You don't need to be the boss. If you're a teacher, for example, learn everything you can about teaching so that kids learn. Find the passion again. Whatever your profession is, look for reasons to excel. Stop hiding. Take risks.

Make some dust in the world. Let other people know you've been there. Stop worrying about what others think. Instead, make them want to join you. Take a break from the daily TV routine. Make some news yourself. Help someone... even if it's only with their homework. And do it regularly.

Missions aren't usually accomplished in a couple hours a month.

Isn't the one shot you've got on this earth worth a little more effort than the minimum required?

I'm hoping you'll say yes.

I get emails from all over the world with stories about how the anxiety and depression people have suffered with for years were reduced and literally evaporated when their lives took on a greater meaning to them... when their focus changed from their own problems (or perceived problems) to something bigger than themselves.

When their whole focus shifted from the inside to the outside, everything changed... everything.

Look inside. Pay attention to your every thought.

150

If you notice yourself thinking the Why me - Why them - This will never work - I hate ____ type thoughts all the time, then you're problem focused. If so, I'll bet you any amount of money that you experience a great deal of anxiety and fear in your everyday life.

Our world is far from being perfect. Hoping for it to be is completely fruitless and a waste of time.

We can only accept what is and do our best to live in it and, with the right amount of passion and drive, to help make a positive difference to others.

Right now, the world needs a lot more people working to make it more fun, safer, friendlier, more productive, cleaner, and more educated. Oh, yeah. I almost forgot...

We need a lot more love. Love makes all these things easy.

TODAY'S WINNING BELIEFS

-- I can make a positive difference in the world and I am
-- Every little bit helps and I'm willing to give my little bit
-- I'm focusing on the solutions to problems
-- I've replaced helplessness with asking, "What can I do?"

WHAT DO YOU WANT TO BE WHEN YOU GROW UP?!

TODAY'S EMPOWERING QUOTE

"Concentrate on finding your goal,
then concentrate on reaching it."
   -Col. Michael Friedsam

TODAY'S EMPOWERING QUESTION

"What would I like to be and do, more than anything else?"

TODAY'S FAST SESSION

The only way you are ever going to get what you want in life is if you KNOW what you want.

What do you want?

To be treated with kindness? To make a million? To get the girl or guy? To get rid of some awful habit that has complete control over you? To live at a normal weight?

How badly do you want it?

A movie about the early life of Homer Hickam is now on video. It's called 'October Sky.' As a teenager in 1957, he saw Sputnik, the Soviet satellite streaking across the sky, and from that day forward, he wanted to make rockets.

He learned that if he won a regional science fair, he could get a college scholarship and avoid working in the coal mine, where most everyone else in town worked.

First he had the stick, the pain of working in the mine. Then he found his carrot, working at NASA.

So he had an advantage that most other kids in the country didn't have... a very emotional reason WHY he had to succeed.

Homer and his 3 friends "The Rocket Boys," won not just the regional, but the NATIONAL Science Fair. Homer got his college scholarship and now trains astronauts for NASA.

This is the 2nd of Stephen Covey's '7 Habits of Highly Effective People.' - Starting with the end in mind.

Unless you know what you want, you can't achieve it.

"I want to stop falling apart at the thought of (taking some specific action)." "I want to stop smoking or overeating." "I want to get a promotion and a raise."

No matter what your ambition, the "end" you have in mind is also lined with markers along the way. They let you know if you're getting closer.

One big reason why 19 out of 20 people fail to reach ANY goal they set is that even if they are specific about what they want, the first time they mess up, they often say, "I knew I couldn't do it. I don't know why I even try."

And that is that. Bye-bye, goal. Hello self-image of a loser.

Your dreams aren't just going to be handed to you...

It takes many little actions to get there. Take it one hour at time. Make your goal not to give up for just one hour.

Big goal: To earn $40,000 a year. (Or plug your own number in.)

Intermediate goal: Buy and read a book on selling big ticket items, or building a down line, or sewing, or whatever the next logical step is on the way to your goal.

Make your goal reading (or other action) for an hour today...

Do the same tomorrow.

Jack Canfield (Chicken Soup for the Soul) told me that only 1 out of 7 people in the U.S. EVER goes into a book store and buys a book, IN THEIR ENTIRE LIVES!

That means that 6 out of 7 refuse to learn what they need to know to get what they want.

Take the next step today...

Give yourself hourly goals in the context of your larger dream. I think... no, I <u>know</u> that you'll start to get excited when you achieve your one hour goal today.

Then go out and achieve it again tomorrow.

Remember, when you mess up, and you will occasionally, it's no big deal. You didn't fail. You just delayed the attainment of the big goal. Just get up, dust yourself off and set a goal for the next hour.

Then pat yourself on the back when you achieve it.

I'm over here, cheering for you now. Woooooooo!!!

TODAY'S WINNING BELIEFS

-- I set hourly goals and I achieve them easily
-- I have dozens of written emotional reasons why I must achieve my goal and I read them daily
-- I've dissolved all reluctance to writing down my goals
-- I'm passionate about my goals
-- When I set a goal, I'll move heaven and earth to reach it

WE REAP WHAT WE SOW

TODAY'S EMPOWERING QUOTE

"My competitive spirit didn't stop because I became physically disabled. I never said, "Why me?" After my car accident, I still said, "Now, what's my purpose?"

    -Joseph Russell (Paralympian, Powerlifting)

TODAY'S EMPOWERING QUESTION

"Isn't it time I stopped feeling sorry for myself & got going?"

TODAY'S FAST SESSION

Many people don't realize how close athletics are to "real" life. A lot of people forget that a sport isn't just playing the game once or twice a week. The preparation before the performance is where the paycheck and/or glory are earned.

You too, won't get where you're going in life, whether it's losing the weight, stopping your most insidious habit or improving your financial health by waiting for the performance...

Every day is the practice. Every minute.

I used to be one of the people who blamed everyone else for my problems. I ALWAYS asked, "Why me?"

I had this dream of a dream life where I told everyone what to do and they did it. I wanted to play at the beach every day. I wanted to be friends with famous people. I wanted everyone to like me, but I didn't want to do anything for anyone. I wanted to be a starter on my school teams, but I didn't want to practice hard. I wanted to be rich, but didn't want to work hard, learn or take orders.

I am not making this up for effect... that's who I was to the core.

By the time I hit my mid-twenties, I was broke in every sense. But I've come to learn that there are no accidents in life. Everything has a purpose, even tragedy. Every experience tests us to see what we'll do with it.

My life and millions of other people's lives didn't get better until we realized that every benefit demands a payment... Just like a store that requires money for their goods, life demands that you put in effort and sacrifice for its rewards. There are no overnight success stories.

The good news is that usually, the sacrifice is only inside your own head. And this sacrifice doesn't take away FROM you. It actually adds TO you...

...Life gives you back exactly what you put out.

If you think a pill is going to take your depression and anxiety away, you're still hiding from the truth...

...The truth that few people care about the pain of others when it's self-inflicted. The attention you're getting is only pity. Not empathy.

When people like Joseph Russell take all the bad breaks they've been given and ignore them and continue on to find and live a life of purpose, you've got to ask yourself, "Am I not understanding ANY of what life's about?"

There are no victims here...

We're all only players. We all have a role. So let's find our roles and start joining the teams we'd like to be on.

Life is about learning...

Think about the average six-year-old. They know next to nothing. It's their role to learn how to communicate, to share, to read directions, to listen, to learn how to get a 15-minute job done in 15 minutes.

That never changes. After we leave our coaches and teachers and move away from Mom and Dad, why do we stop learning about the basics of life? School is not out. It's never out.

If you haven't already, let's make right now the minute that you decide to learn what it takes to right your ship. Get it into your head that things aren't going to get better until you start smiling, and realize that every single problem you have doesn't start with how you're talked to, what someone else did to you, where you live, where you work, who you're married to...

A problem begins when you see a situation and react improperly to it. The problem usually isn't the situation. The problem is your reaction TO the situation.

Shakespeare said, "Nothing is either good or bad, but thinking makes it so."

So if it's all an illusion, why not choose a happy illusion?

Now.

So smile, and focus on what benefits you'll get today if you bring enthusiasm and honest effort to the situations you'll encounter.

I know that's a hard reality. But the longer it takes you to face it, the longer your life will be less than you'd prefer.

TODAY'S WINNING BELIEFS

-- I take complete responsibility for my responses to situations
-- I respond positively to all situations, no matter what
-- Whatever happens to me, I live and renew my purpose in harmony
-- I am bigger than anything that can happen to me
-- I am willing to keep learning about life and what it takes to make it work

WATCH FOR POTHOLES, BUT KEEP YOUR GOAL IN FOCUS

TODAY'S EMPOWERING QUOTE

"Obstacles are those frightful things you see when you take your eyes off your goal."
  -Hannah More

TODAY'S EMPOWERING QUESTION

"What have I been paying attention to for the last hour?"

TODAY'S FAST SESSION

It is absolute genius to be aware of the obstacles in front of you whenever you start any kind of undertaking. If you don't, then you will be surprised when things go wrong. After a wreck, you'll likely be overheard to say things like, "It was a total shock. There's nothing I could've done about it."

And the other comical thing is that most people focus ONLY on the obstacles. They never get where they want to be because after they get started, hurdles appear. And suddenly the entire focus becomes the hurdles. The goal gets fuzzier and harder to see. "What are we doing this for?" is a common thought.

This might seem obvious as you read this, but as I've watched people for many years, I suggest that a main reason most people don't get where they originally steer their ship is that they have no clue where the rocks are... and once they see those rocks, they throw their compass away. They get so focused on the obstacles and turned around that it often is impossible to reach their original objective.

Last week, we were watching our seven-year-old Goddaughter, Mary Kate, for the day. In our back yard is a big wooden slide/swing set. At the top of the slide, there's a large wooden brace that helps reinforce the structure. Well, MK kept hitting her head on it before she slid down the slide. She must've hit her head 15 out of 20 times.

After a while, she'd smack her head and always follow it up with, "Ouch! I always hit my head on this!"

I suggested to her that she might try saying, "I keep my head away from the wood," and "My head feels good."

Notice I DIDN'T say, "I don't hit my head on the wood." That would force her mind to focus only on the obstacle, and not what she wanted, which was to keep her head away from it.

Now, I only mentioned this to her once.

Well, she started chanting it... over and over!

And in the next 40 or 50 trips up and down, she did not hit her head once.

That's the power of focus... and affirmation to help you keep your focus on the right actions and on the benefit.

Experience tells me that you can apply this in every area of life to get rapid results.

If you want to lose weight, create a few affirmations to help give you direction... and help you stay focused on your outcome and benefits. Repeat them over and over. A few times a day.

Remember, this is how your brain works…

It's not possible for you to hear something once and have it change your actions permanently... unless it's an incredibly emotional or traumatic experience.

You could repeat phrases like these...

"I love the texture and taste of vegetables."
"I stay away from processed non-foods."
"My body is becoming perfect in its proportions."

Of course there are many others...

Since every area of life has its high peaks and its low valleys, you can most certainly elevate your chances of achieving your outcomes in any or all of them by applying this simple little "secret."

Go back to any time in your life when you reached your outcome, even if that outcome was just peace... relaxation.

You probably knew what the obstacles were and you planned to overcome them. So you focused on your goal and when you were nearing a potential delay or "pothole," you saw it, navigated around it and moved on... without commotion.

You've no doubt done this thousands of times...

If you want to reach your outcomes in life and do so with little stress...

One of the keys to being successful at a skill set and enjoying the process of accomplishment in it is being able to get to the point where you can become unconsciously aware, without effort, of the obstacles to success and happily move around them without concern... again, without apparent effort.

That takes practice.

So practice!

TODAY'S WINNING BELIEFS

-- I keep my eyes on my goals
-- I successfully avoid obstacles because I plan for them
-- I quickly get back on track when delays happen
-- I focus on benefits, so my purpose is always in mind
-- My ability to concentrate grows stronger each day

WHAT AM I WAITING FOR?

TODAY'S EMPOWERING QUOTE

"When you are feeling fear of some project or idea or dream, ask yourself, 'What am I still curious enough about to override my fear?' Follow your curiosity like a delicious scent leading you to a kitchen. Let your curiosity peel back the dry, bitter skin of drudgery to find the sweet fruit of fun at the core. Focus on what you love rather than fixating on the feelings of discomfort that sometimes accompany desire."
   - Carol Lloyd

TODAY'S EMPOWERING QUESTION

"What the heck am I waiting for?"

TODAY'S FAST SESSION

I remember them all too well.

Sunday evenings...

I was eighteen. And for as long as I could remember, I dreaded Sunday evenings.

That was the time when I thought about all the homework and studying I hadn't done. I dreaded not being prepared.

But I still didn't prepare.

It would have only taken 1-3 hours.

But it just sat there. Untouched.

Man, I HAD to go out and party. It WAS the weekend after all.

And the chores. Well, no. I had tried like hell to avoid those, too. That's what the typical fights then were usually about.

What was wrong with me?

The laziest kid my 12th grade English teacher had EVER seen in his 20 years of teaching.

Nice label.

That didn't change for quite some time.

After I began to learn about self-image things got clearer.

Giving myself a reason for being alive melted a lot of fear.

Noticing how little actions can quickly lead to large accomplishments was exciting.

But that wasn't my focus for nearly 25 years.

MY focus was pleasure at all costs. Even if the cost was mental anguish at putting off the things that everyone else told me were important.

If only I had been conditioned to feel extraordinary joy at accomplishment - to shrink down the size of big jobs - to have some great role models that could have taught me what was truly important.

When I think now about all the accomplishments I've stacked up over the last 16 years, the joys I've felt, the inner peace I feel from knowing that I am becoming who I've dreamed about being, there is no effort too big and no job too demanding that it is not worth what it would take... if the only rewards were those.

You know, three to four minutes isn't enough to completely change a life. But stacked up, a lot of the right "few minutes" can be enough to change course and have a life of distinction.

It doesn't matter what your aim, there is nothing you can't do if you just begin.

Over the years, I've watched my sister in-law create some of the most beautiful quilts right before my eyes – even while a party is going on around her. She'll be talking, laughing, listening, telling stories, having a good time. And all the while, she's "multi-tasking" making her art.

To do great things, you've got to let go of the small things.

162

If you want to be more, then look at what you're hanging on to. Don't turn your head. Look at it. It will probably be painful.

Don't be afraid to look in the mirror.

To get out of whatever your current situation is, you have to know where you are. If you don't, you can't possibly know where to turn.

Honesty, especially with yourself, is one of the greatest virtues you can possess.

And if you are completely honest with yourself - if you have your eyes open - I know you'll see that no matter how large the goal or task or "problem," no matter how impossible you believe it to be, it's almost impossible to fail if you will just get started doing something...

It's the hardest thing to do.

But lean.

Roll.

Crawl.

Call for help.

Whatever you have to do.

Look at that task.

Shrink it.

Make it tiny.

Itsy bitsy.

It's definitely not going to hurt you.

Pay attention to the reward. Write down what you will get, and what you will start to become if you get this "horrible" thing done.

You WILL get something. THAT is what you must focus on.

You WILL become different IF you hang onto that image.

Feel it ahead of time. Over and over. Breathe deep. In and out.

And get started.

Soon it will be over, and you get to feel for real what you had just imagined.

TODAY'S WINNING BELIEFS

-- I'm getting started on important tasks today
-- I get a lot done because I begin
-- I enjoy starting and finishing challenging tasks
-- I can do whatever I set my mind to
-- I'm thrilled when I begin a big job
-- I feel incredibly alive at the beginning of a project
-- I'm a truly creative and imaginative person

HOW MANY OF <u>YOUR</u> PROBLEMS ARE TRULY PROBLEMS?

TODAY'S EMPOWERING QUOTE

"Joy is the life of man's life."
  -Benjamin Whichcote

TODAY'S EMPOWERING QUESTION

"How can I think about this situation so that I can enjoy it to the fullest?"

TODAY'S FAST SESSION

It's nearly impossible to be in a good mood all the time. No question about it.

People who are don't get to move about without supervision.

But it IS possible to take just about anything that could happen to you and USE it to feel good... happy, empowered, strong.

A woman I know used to look at the fact that her now ex-spouse did everything possible to sabotage her finishing college, and felt upset whenever she thought about it. It seemed to her that she would have been much farther along in her career, she'd probably live in a much nicer home, etc. if she had been able to finish college right after high school.

This was a constant source of despair. She felt that if she had not married him, her life would be so much better today.

I told her that I didn't believe in that; that I feel that there is a reason for everything... even though it often doesn't seem that way.

If you examine your own life, I think you'll see that those things that get you down often are, in truth, the source of some of your greatest joys and may have set the direction at some of the most important crossroads of your life.

In her case, as a result of her being married, she had moved to a different city, where she got a great job and flourished in it. She made a lot of great friends whom she loves deeply. She has a daughter that she wouldn't trade for the world. Plus, the move to the new city made it possible for her to ultimately meet and marry the man she calls her soul mate.

So, none of the great parts of her life would exist if it wasn't for her first marriage.

Although it wasn't the wisest thing to do at the time, it was now ridiculous to beat herself up for succumbing to the pressure her ex-husband applied all those years ago. I helped her to realize that it's BECAUSE of her decision to marry at a young age and not finish college immediately that gave her all the things that she enjoys most about her life.

She ultimately got her degree and joined the ranks of CPA, just as she would have if she stayed in college to begin with.

If she had done it differently, nothing that she holds so dear today would be in her life. Kind of like the movie, "It's A Wonderful Life," huh?

After I pointed that out, she realized that problems are not problems at all.

Problems, as we call them, are situations that either teach us to go forward more intelligently, or they're dead ends. But they can only be dead ends if we decide they'll be.

If we hold onto our old decisions, "bad" breaks, and situations that didn't work out for us in the short run, using them to remind us that we're just not meant to be happy, that we're not good enough, that we'll never get another chance...

...then that's exactly what our life's story will be.

Even when things are great, it's still possible to look back with regret, isn't it? How does it make you feel when you do that?

Like crap?

Then you just need perspective.

Look at all those situations that appear to have been tragedies. See what they meant to you in terms of people you met as a result. Career moves that worked out well. How about family, health, location, attitude, schooling and other learning? What about skills you now have that you may not have acquired if your "problem" never happened?

Do this for every "problem" you ever had that you think or even "know" stopped you or limited your life in some way.

I think... no, I know that you'll find otherwise.

There are no such things as problems.

Shakespeare said, "Nothing is either good or bad, but thinking makes it so." You see, there are certain indisputable principles of life, and this is one of them.

Just because you've managed to live for 20, 40 or even 80 years and this never occurred to you doesn't mean it's not true.

There is nothing more true. Nothing. Nothing. Nothing.

Once you start to instantly "feel" deep inside you that this thing that just happened to you is actually your next gift, your next chance to grow, to gain peace of mind, to finally understand that there IS such a thing as a problem-free life...

...that's when you'll stop living with wild mood swings. That is when you'll realize that you can reduce and even get off your happy pills because your mental focus isn't on problems any more. That's when you'll start doing things that used to make you nervous and scared and you won't be scared any more.

When you accept the unwanted hurdles that pop up daily as simply a part of your path and move over them like someone who's on the way somewhere, then every day will go a lot smoother and happier.

So do this...

Write down some rotten stuff that's happened to you in the last year or so. Then look for the silver lining in each one. Write down the good that came out of each one. If you can't, then you're not looking with intention of finding it... because it IS there.

Write them down and carry the list with you. Then, the next time you find yourself in an irritated mood, pull out your list and see what all your hurdles have actually done for you.

I bet you'll smile.

And isn't that better than fuming? You'd better say yes!

TODAY'S WINNING BELIEFS

-- I see all problems as valuable learning opportunities
-- No challenge I could face is bigger than my ability to beat it
-- I happily look forward to my next big challenge
-- I get enjoyment from everyone and everything in my life
-- I accept peace and joy in my life

NOW'S THE TIME

TODAY'S EMPOWERING QUOTE

"Whatever you want to do, do it now. There are only so many tomorrows."
  -Michael Landon

TODAY'S EMPOWERING QUESTION

"What would happen if I put that off until later?"

TODAY'S FAST SESSION

My parents were recently up north visiting from their home in Florida.

On their last night here, they stayed at my uncle's camp. So I drove an hour and a half into the mountains to see them one more time before they left.

Just as I was pulling into the little "one horse town" of Sherburne, I noticed that I was getting very low on gas, but I told myself that I'd be able to get some gas on the way back home.

Well, it was nearly 7 o'clock when I arrived, and we were having such a good time, that it was 1:30 in the morning before we knew it.

When I started the vehicle, the gauge was reading even lower than it did when I pulled in. I felt lucky that the camp was higher in elevation than the town, so I did a lot of coasting in neutral. Boy, was I happy to see the traffic light in town. A quick right and I'd be filling up...

But the gas station was closed.

Oh no.

I was running on fumes, and nothing was open - not even a bar!

Four miles to Earlville!? Uh. I'll never make it.

But with no choice, it was north to Earlville... at forty miles an hour to conserve gas. Man, it seemed all uphill! Where were the downhill areas?

Finally, mercifully I made it to Earlville... only to find that their gas station was closed, too.

I was sunk. What to do? What to do?

I was remembering the time twenty two years ago, when I used my mom's car and didn't put any gas in it before coming home. She ripped me a new one as she told me how she coasted into the gas station after the engine died. I'm not going to be so lucky this time.

Keep going north...

Oh, if I get out of this, I'll never let it get below a quarter tank again. I swear.

Twelve minutes and seven a-g-o-n-i-z-i-n-g miles later, I see Colgate University. Oh, thank God. There is no way that the gas station will be closed, not in a college town like Hamilton. Now if I can just make it to the gas station.

There it is!!

And the lights are on. Hooray!! Yippee!!

Oh. Thank you, God in Heaven. And yes, I coasted in, in neutral, just to make sure I made it all the way.

During the rest of the trip home, I felt lucky to have been given this lesson. Partly because I didn't lose anything in the process of learning... many lessons involve lots of pain. And mostly because it was a lesson that will most certainly serve me well in the weeks, months and years to come.

You don't put off things that should be done now.

I should have assumed that the mini-market would close. I didn't need to put it off. And I should have paid attention to the clock.

As I was praying for an open gas station, I was "shoulding" all over myself, and the good part was, I was listening.

It was my fault.

And the lesson was learned... again.

And in taking complete responsibility instead of cursing the store, I will have once again set a course in motion... to be paying attention to situations where my decisions affect outcomes.

No, you can't always plan for everything. And no, nobody's perfect.

But you *can* be intelligent. Stupidity is no excuse. Ignorance is definitely not bliss. It's loss. Pain. Possibly death.

Michael Landon was best known for his starring roles in Bonanza, Little House on the Prairie, and Highway to Heaven. He lived hard, worked hard, partied hard and put off eating healthy.

I'll never forget his final appearance with Johnny Carson's Tonight Show in 1991. He said that he had pancreatic cancer. For people not in the know, this is one of the most deadly cancers. Most people don't survive longer than a few months after diagnosis.

His wife had been pushing him to adopt a more vegetarian lifestyle for years. But he just put it off. There was always time to start eating right... right?

Not long before his Tonight Show appearance, in constant agony, facing death, he finally gave into her pressure. And he told Johnny that the pain from the cancer was out of this world. Simply terrible.

But, he said, from the day he started exclusively drinking the vegetable juices his wife prepared for him, the pain stopped completely. Just like that. So understandably, he was in good spirits on the show.

Unfortunately, it was too late.

The cancer had progressed too far - his body was too toxic for the pure, cleansing food to save him.

So the message today is this, whatever is pressing, whatever job has to be done or situation needs to be attended to, do it now.

Sounds simple right?

Well, it is.

Pull out your copy of First Things First - get your planner out - look at what is important in your life... and attend to it.

And you'll find that when you finally start paying attention to the big things, the important stuff, the important people, you'll feel... well, it's hard to put into words.

At worst it reduces the frequency of angry fights with others over your "forgetting" things. People WILL notice the difference in you.

And at best, you'll be setting in motion a habit that could transport you to the top of your profession. It can make you admired and respected by everyone you know. It can give you a peace of mind that few enjoy.

Ask constantly, "What COULD happen if I put this off?"

Join the few. It's not lonely there.

TODAY'S WINNING BELIEFS

-- I'm a "Do it now" person
-- I love being busy
-- I get the difficult tasks out of the way first
-- I do things that are good for me
-- I stay away from things that could hurt me
-- "Do it now" is my motto

HOW DO YOU EAT AN ELEPHANT?

TODAY'S EMPOWERING QUOTE

"The greatest things on earth have been done little by little."
--Thomas Guthrie

TODAY'S EMPOWERING QUESTION

"Is this a big, difficult job or just a bunch of small easy to do tasks rolled into one?"

TODAY'S FAST SESSION

I remember I used to get terribly excited every day when I was selling face to face. I asked myself the question above all day long. Once I started a new activity, I'd ask myself the question.

I'd get the answer, and then guess what?

Right. I kept going, and I had more enthusiasm than the moment before. No moping.

That habit is what allowed me to slaughter international sales records in 3 different industries. And because I made more sales CALLS than anyone else dreamed of making, I got really good at every aspect of my job. Simply a matter of practice making perfect... and of course learning from mistakes. But that's another topic all together.

It's terribly heartbreaking to talk to people and hear them say they just can't stop smoking, for example. They'll say it was a tough week and they needed to smoke or to do whatever their habit is.

But success in anything - from quitting a bad habit to gaining a good one, from obtaining a singular accomplishment or a string of them - requires many decisions and actions.

And they all come one-at-a-time.

You don't have a bad week. You have a weak moment. And then another one. Your life is made up of moments, not weeks. Have you ever noticed how, let's say... a basketball game can change momentum in 30 seconds or less? One team is in control and BOOM... 3 quick baskets by other team and they're in control.

It's all in the mind.

That's why it's SOOOOO important to make sure that your beliefs - your core-level beliefs - about yourself and about life are right. You've GOT to believe in your abilities. You CAN do whatever you want to do. You can. There can't be the slightest doubt. I don't doubt you and I don't even know you personally.

But I know this...

No matter who you are, where you came from, your physical limitations, your color, your age... it has nothing to do with what you want to do and your GOD-given ability to achieve it. It's true, you may have to work harder than others, but you can do much.

You might not ever pole vault over 19 feet, but within your physical abilities you can achieve a lot.

And I want you to get really clear about one thing. You need to keep your life in compartments of seconds and minutes, not days. Taking things "one day at a time" is one of the biggest causes of failure there is.

Emotions can change from one moment to the next.

One minute your resolve seems firm, and the next, after a particularly stressful meeting - bam! All your resolve is out the window.

When that cigarette, or whatever your habit is, is screaming for you, in that one moment you must do everything you can to block it out.   Do something.

Do anything...

One thing you can do is pull out your Victory Log and read it.

If you don't have one, make one. Mine has saved me on many occasions and led me to my greatest triumphs.

This is a great topic, so let's pick it up on the next session.

OK? OK.

TODAY'S WINNING BELIEFS

-- Big jobs are just a bunch of easy to do small tasks
-- I persevere in the face of all adversity
-- I see road blocks as stepping stones
-- Every moment provides me with opportunities to strengthen my belief in myself
-- I go after goals one task at a time, and then move on to the next one

REACH FOR THE STARS...
BUT KEEP YOUR HEAD OUT OF THE CLOUDS

TODAY'S EMPOWERING QUOTE

"The superior man makes the difficulty to be overcome his first interest; success comes only later."
--Confucius

TODAY'S EMPOWERING QUESTION

"Am I looking too far ahead to focus on the problem at hand?"

TODAY'S FAST SESSION

OK. Where were we?

Did you notice that?

Most people are thinking way too far ahead (or their head is somewhere else entirely) to focus on what they're supposed to be doing.

If you focus on the thing you should be, you'll do it well and you'll then be able to give the next task your full attention. Big companies have learned rather painfully that it's not possible to focus on too many things well.

When multi-billion dollar corporations buy other companies outside their field of expertise, even if they're billion dollar organizations, they often drive them into the ground. They wanted to conquer the world but found out that they better stick to what they know.

Remember the big W on the wall? You do have that W on your wall, don't you? Well, put an F next to it.

This stands for FOCUS.

A few years ago, I owned two companies at the same time. One was established but not wildly profitable. The new one needed all my time, since it was just getting started. They weren't related at all. Completely different industries.

Both suffered because they each needed a lot of attention...

If I had just focused on my primary goals, I would've been miles ahead. As it was, it cost me over $30,000 and 6 months of wasted effort.

Learning experience...

For you, use other people's experience to teach you those painful lessons - and notice what happens when you take your eye off the ball, too. Pay attention. Learn...

Stephen Covey uses the metaphor of the compass. It always points true north. Your internal compass needs to do the same thing. Operate on principles or those principles will operate on you. They won't change. You must change.

Success will come to you...

...if you're patient and if you put your mind on what is most important right now. I know, you want it now. Why should you have to work so hard?

Get used to it. That's life. We're here, we live and we're gone. You are governed under the same rules as everyone else.

Life is too fleeting to be willy-nilly all over the place.

FOCUS and you will reach your enormous potential.

TODAY'S WINNING BELIEFS

-- I enjoy staying focused on one thing at a time
-- I'm good at balancing many responsibilities
-- I am relaxed as I focus on my objectives
-- Focus and I are one

THEY CAN'T BEAT ME!

TODAY'S EMPOWERING QUOTE

"I don't like to lose, and that isn't so much because it is just a football game, but because defeat means the failure to reach your objective. I don't want a football player who doesn't take defeat to heart, who laughs it off with the thought, "Oh, well, there's another Saturday." The trouble in American life today, in business as well as in sports, is that too many people are afraid of competition. The result is that in some circles people have come to sneer at success if it costs hard work and training and sacrifice."
  -Knute Rockne

TODAY'S EMPOWERING QUESTION

"Whom can I have a (friendly) competition with to use as my motivator?"

TODAY'S FAST SESSION

So many people wilt under competition. So I don't want to propose that you use as an important source of motivation a mental activity that makes you perform worse in whatever area you'd like to improve.

What you find difficult today, though, with even a little "private" competition, you'll find to be easy.

What we're discussing is a way to give yourself a passion that can give you such drive to reach your objective, that it will not only get you there, but you'll actually love the process.

An example in my life is having been a very mediocre student in high school, and then flunking out of college. At that point, I kind of got the idea that I better start doing something well or I just might end up dead broke or just dead sooner than I'd like. So I enrolled in a local community college and began using my neighbor, who was an 'A' student his whole life, as my competitor. It was friendly, of course. And at that time, I was badly overmatched. I mean, he was a seasoned studier. He knew how to learn. I didn't.

Every day, I kept him in my sights. He usually beat me on tests and quizzes, but I won some occasionally...

...enough to keep me motivated.

In fact he drove me to achieve things that I had never done before. Enough to turn me into an 'A' student in a single semester. Not bad for someone who only ever got A's in Art and Gym.

That's the key. You can't pick someone, even in secret, that there's no way you'd ever measure up to. You at least have to be able to win occasionally. And someone you beat constantly won't stretch you.

You have to be able to imagine victory or else you won't try, long term. You'll get demoralized too easily.

Pick someone in a magazine, someone you used to know, who you work with. It doesn't matter. Pick someone that motivates you that you can reach.

If you want to lose weight, find someone who's a little slimmer than you. Make that an intermediary goal. Then, go for someone who's just a little further beyond when you arrive at your first guidepost.

Sure, aim for total success...

But don't swing for the fence every day. Little victories add up. Allow yourself to feel incredible satisfaction when you achieve your little benchmarks.

Every time I got a quiz or test within a few points, and especially if I beat my friendly rival, I literally glowed... like a star!

Those moments so revved me up that it completely redirected my life.

Now don't get me wrong. I was due for many more challenges in life... most of which I would not win for a long time.

But it was this process and those victories that gave me a taste of success that took a sustained effort to achieve.

I can't stress enough that the little victories along the way are every bit as important as the end goal. They keep you going when you have a setback.

If you want to quit smoking and you've quit for a week, don't let one slip up ruin all you've built. Every hour you go without a cigarette, where you didn't bite someone's head off, give yourself permission to feel an incredible sense of accomplishment... because it is. Call someone up on the phone. Go out to dinner. Celebrate in whatever appropriate way you can. Put a mark on the wall. Give yourself credit. Smile. You did it.

You must do this...

...because setbacks will come. And if you built up a series of successes AND RECOGNIZED THEM, you'll treat the setback as just a slight delay, a little detour. Without your private victory parties, setbacks can be made to look like a sheer rock cliff.

During the second year of my becoming a real student, I achieved something that found a permanent home in my victory log. On the Statistics final exam, I got the only perfect 100 ever recorded in that school.

Yes, I had beaten my rival...

...and it felt great!

TODAY'S WINNING BELIEFS

-- I turn my goals into a game that I enjoy winning
-- My competition keeps me sharp and exhilarated
-- I appreciate the value that competition has in my growth
-- I love winning
-- I see losing as just a temporary setback
-- Losing increases my determination to continue and win

REPEAT AFTER ME: "YES, I CAN!"

TODAY'S EMPOWERING QUOTE

"Self-trust is the first secret of success."
  -Ralph Waldo Emerson

TODAY'S EMPOWERING QUESTION

"Haven't I done many things I wasn't sure I'd be able to do when I started them?"

TODAY'S FAST SESSION

I was always perplexed by the question, "What came first, the chicken or the egg?" Does that have an answer? I don't know.

But an equally good one that does have an answer is, "What comes first, confidence or large achievements?"

The answer most definitely is confidence.

No. You don't need large accomplishments to gain confidence.

But what creates confidence and how can you get more of it so you can consistently achieve more and have fun doing it? And what is it that causes a loss of confidence?

It's easy to see in the world of sports the difference between confidence and doubt. Team A goes on a tear and destroys their opponent by an enormous amount of runs, baskets, goals, etc. But the next night, you've got the same two teams and this time it's Team B that administers the beating.

What's the difference? Players on the losing teams often say things like this:

- We just weren't focusing.
- Our emotions weren't in check.
- When they scored in the 3rd quarter, the wind went out of our sails.
- We just weren't taking good shots.
- Once the crowd got into the game, we got out of our rhythm.

Those things took their confidence away. They didn't trust themselves. So their performance for the ENTIRE game or large portions of it was sub-par.

The next day, different mind set... VERY different results. The focus was there now. They clearly visualized their outcomes. Momentum never left for long. Belief came back. They refused to be intimidated and wouldn't accept defeat.

I often use sports analogies because there is absolutely no difference between games and life... especially your life.

Every day, life demands that you perform. Whether it's just cleaning the house, raking or trying to enjoy yourself while you pack up and take a vacation with your family, your confidence level affects your performance and your enjoyment.

Confidence. What is it?

To me, confidence is just a feeling that you can do something.

It's the current knowledge that if challenge pops up, and they always do, you can overcome it. With this knowing comes the ability to perform at your best.

But as soon as the feelings wane, your positive expectancy drops and you start to focus on mistakes instead of your goals. You start to feel less capable, so you hesitate. When your confidence leaves you, you can't make decisions. And when you start to replay these unsupportive mental pictures, you literally couldn't buy a few minutes of success at any price.

This power was never more evident as when John Wooden and his legendary UCLA basketball teams won a record 88 games in a row. For nearly 4 years, they didn't lose a single game.

His teams won 7 consecutive national championships. In the next thousand years, it hardly seems possible that his records will be approached.

He knew that if he could gain momentum and hold it, the other team would mentally give up. Their pressure forced mistakes and caused the opponents to hesitate, to not want to make more mistakes.

But when your focus is on not making mistakes... you make mistakes!!!

So how do you gain confidence and keep it?

You must picture success before it happens. Your internal dialog must be that of expecting success... yes, even before you have success. How?

Well, how do you learn anything? By repetition, of course.

Look at your bookshelves. If there are more than a few self-help books, and you don't yet have the qualities taught inside the covers, then it's repetition that's missing.

Coke and Pepsi spend tens of millions of dollars each year to program you to buy their carbonated caramel water.

Why? Because repetition works.

They sell billions of dollars of their products simply because they communicate their message constantly. Do you remember the words of songs that you haven't heard in years?

I'll bet you do!

If you take control of your own mind just like big advertisers and communicate a positive message of belief and hope and of expecting to get what you want, and you do it with repetition, you know what?

You'll become confident.

At least you'll have hope, to start.

And confidence begins with hope. Without hope, a glimmer of optimism, you wouldn't even try.

If you haven't up until now, start really using this tool. If you do, just like a drill or a hammer makes building a structure a thousand times better and faster, you'll achieve more every single day... easier, better and with more joy than you ever thought possible.

TODAY'S WINNING BELIEFS

-- My confidence is soaring now
-- I respond to adversity with increased determination and belief in myself
-- I believe in myself completely
-- I am going to begin right now

GET MAD...THEN MAKE YOUR WORLD BETTER

TODAY'S EMPOWERING QUOTE

"Anger is a prelude to courage."
  -Eric Hoffer

TODAY'S EMPOWERING QUESTION

"What am I really dissatisfied about right now?"

TODAY'S FAST SESSION

I guess I better start right out by explaining the word 'Anger' as we'll be using it. By anger, I mean that you see something or something happens and it spurs in you a burning, all-encompassing desire to fix the problem.

The problem with most people is that they get angry at other people for taking advantage of their weaknesses. "You took my boyfriend." Hey, if your relationship was good, there wouldn't be a problem. The blame rests with you and/or your boyfriend, not anyone else.

A few years ago, I met Rudy Ruettiger. The movie 'Rudy' is based on his life. He told me that the thing that kept him going in the face of every adversity you can imagine was anger...

Anger at everyone that told him playing football for Notre Dame was crazy; for everyone that told him that he wasn't cut out for college; that he ought to work in the factory because it was safe; that he ought to forget his stupid dream.

The nay sayers motivated him. It made him angry when people knocked his dream.

If you've never seen the movie, I would recommend that you buy it and wear it out. And if you don't have any tissues, get some before you hit "play."

What do most people do when others rain on their parade? What do you do?

Inside, you probably laugh right along and say something like, "Yeah, it is kind of silly. That IS a little out of my league."

Why not get angry and do something about it, instead? Show them you can reach your dream.

Few people like to stand out. To be seen as different.

Well, anger is really just another way of describing one of the first elements that go into making a personal mission statement. I mean after all, what would a mission be if you weren't completely behind it emotionally? It wouldn't be a mission. It would be just a wish. And wishes don't usually come true.

Missions, though, usually ensure that dreams become realized.

But when you've got a mission, it sets your whole being into motion.

Great missions come about often when you just can't stand the way something is and you feel like you must change it.

"MADD" (Mothers Against Drunk Driving) came about because of anger. "America's Most Wanted" came about because of anger.

So many breakthroughs and achievements would never have happened unless someone got mad and said "I'm not going to take it any more!"

I did that years ago and went looking for tools to change the way I thought. It took a while, but I found them and altered them to create a technology that ultimately changed who I am and changed the lives of thousands around the world... all because of massive pain and dissatisfaction.

Here's what I want you to do...

Find something in your life that you're dissatisfied with and get yourself worked up. Ask yourself what your life will be like if this doesn't change. Feel the pain. Get angry. Don't blame others in this mental exercise. You're responsible for your own circumstances. Get that straight.

Feel the pain now. Compare those feelings to the feelings you'd have if you were just to fix the situation now. No matter what kind of effort it would take to fix. It might take years for you to get things the way you want

186

them. But compare the two futures. Get angry at the first future. Get scared. And get determined not to end up there.

Make it a must. You must change it. Feel it. If you've got to cry and scream and pound your fists, fine...if that's what it takes.

Look now at the better future you saw. How big is the gap? Would it be worth any effort that it might take? I think you'll find that it probably is.

Without dissatisfaction, and often anger, it's verrrry difficult to get and stay motivated. You must keep your dissatisfaction in your mind daily.

Use it as fuel for your motivation.

As long as you continue to take personal responsibility for your life, this can work miracles.

But as long as you keep blaming others for your problems, you'll continue to have them.

Get dissatisfied. It will help you feel courageous, even if last week you were hiding out.

TODAY'S WINNING BELIEFS

-- I use anger constructively to make things better
-- Courage and I are one
-- My abilities are boundless
-- My motivation and determination are both growing daily

BYE-BYE WEEDS!

TODAY'S EMPOWERING QUOTE

"What is the hardest task in the world? To think."
    -Emerson

TODAY'S EMPOWERING QUESTION

"When I did (some thing) right, how did I do it?"

TODAY'S FAST SESSION

No doubt, you have plenty of times that you can recall where you did something very well. You felt good. Your mood was positive. Your focus was on the task or game...and you were ON.

You said the right things. You hit the ball, made the shots, ran like the wind. Mistakes, if they happened at all, were brushed off and forgotten about. You were definitely in the ZONE and wanted the day to go on forever.

But it didn't...

The next day wasn't quite as good, possibly. And within a day or two or six, things were back to normal... average. Not good, not bad. Just vanilla.

Is this you?

If not, then congratulations. But even life's top performers don't regularly pull rabbits out of the hat in every area of their lives. It's too common for many people to be miracle workers at home or at work, but miserable failures at just about everything else.

Too often, in the area that works, it's more a factor of doing that one thing for so long that you get proficient at it. Repetition over the years has worn the grooves of mastery.

It happened over time, almost without your awareness. It just came because you did the same thing again and again. Through all your mistakes you learned how to get things done fast and easy.

It's too bad you didn't have a course to teach you how to get these same results in everything you do, no matter what it is... training that could help you regularly have this incredible feeling that nothing was above your capability.

But thoughts just kind of pop in and that's the way it's supposed to work, right? 'How could I control my thoughts?' you think. 'They just pop in. I feel a certain way because that's just who I am,' you say.

Wrong...

We get our beliefs if they SEEM accurate. A few mistakes and BOOM! We define ourselves as not good at something. It seems to make sense. If other people confirm our suspicions, then it must be true. Someone does something we don't like or doesn't look right and BOOM! we make instant judgments about them without a second's thought. If the first bite doesn't taste familiar, WHAM! Don't like it.

Most people get a belief about a thing and stay with that belief forever, whether it's true or not.

Where that can be the most detrimental is when it's a limiting belief about yourself and your worth.

Just because you made a particular mistake a number of times doesn't mean that you'll never be good at something.

Your mind doesn't have to be on autopilot. Thoughts don't have to just pop into your head. You can control your thoughts. And when you do start to take control of your mind, your emotions and actions can be similar to the greatest successes the world has ever known.

When I took the Silva Mind Method training course in the early 90's, I would get into my "alpha state" and repeat, over and over, statements that affirmed my success and ability. I told myself that there wasn't anything I couldn't do. I took all my limiting beliefs and put them on a mental screen and wiped them off one at a time.

Gone. Adios. Arrivederci. Au revoir.

Any belief that didn't support my new goals got cleaned away. And positive affirmations re-patterned new beliefs of ability, self-worth and confidence.

Keep in mind, I did this regularly. And I still do.

After all, your mind is thinking constantly. And it's impossible to tell yourself that you're a genius once and have it stick. Not when you follow it up with a very human mistake an hour later, and the first thing you're tempted to think is, 'See, I knew I was fooling myself! I am a dunce!'

Your current beliefs took time to take root and the new ones will also take time. Think of your mind as a field. You're planting seeds now. The new shoots will come up and produce fruit, but you've got to water and fertilize them. You've got to pull the weeds out constantly.

But what you'll have for your effort is some of the sweetest, juiciest crops of empowering and TRUE beliefs you could ever have. With these new beliefs will come powerful emotions and determination that will astound you. Sweet Success!

And the nice thing is, your new beliefs are always in season!

TODAY'S WINNING BELIEFS

-- I've released all limiting thoughts about my abilities
-- My thoughts are positively affirming now
-- I think about consequences before I act
-- My powers of visualization are increasing today
-- I use my past successes as templates for today

WHAT WOULD REALLY HAPPEN?

TODAY'S EMPOWERING QUOTE

"Every choice moves us closer to or farther away from something. Where are your choices taking your life? What do your behaviors demonstrate that you are saying yes or no to in life?"
- Eric Allenbaugh

TODAY'S EMPOWERING QUESTION

"The thing I'm doing right now... is it bringing me closer or farther away from my goal?"

TODAY'S FAST SESSION

What would happen if...?

Now THAT is a great question.

It's one that can lead you in creative directions when asked constantly.

It can also be used strategically to keep you on the right path - away from bad decisions.

This question is asked constantly in the design of software, buildings, automobiles... in fact it's probably the most asked question in the world.

What would happen if...?

But in our personal lives, in our every day decisions concerning our health, our career, our relationships, this question is often shelved, locked away, hidden from.

Most people are terrified of it.

Because when we ask it, if we're honest, we usually get the truth.

We get the "consequences" that we can't ignore.

That's why it's avoided like the plague.

More promising ideas have died quick, horrible deaths by avoiding this question than maybe any other reason.

What would happen if I ate that piece of chocolate cake?

What would happen if I cheated on my husband?

What would happen if we tested the new software for only two weeks instead of the usual four weeks?

What would happen if I tried to remember all my appointments this week without writing them down?

You see, if we don't ask, we can't fully consider the consequences. And when we don't think about what would happen as a result of our thoughts and actions, we can't be smart.

We lose opportunities by the boatload.

In the sports world, it's known as putting yourself in a position to win. Great managers know that if you can stay close, you have a chance.

Because if an unlucky bounce occurs, you've killed your chances to win if you'd made a bunch of dumb errors, unwise decisions or if a referee's call goes against you.

Achieving great victories, or simply getting any long-term project done on time, on budget and done correctly doesn't usually happen because of one great decision or one spectacular action.

It's done by making a lot of good decisions, which, added up, can be a great, great outcome.

People like "home runs," but success at anything isn't about having a great 30 seconds a week ago.

When a person loses 30 - 50 - 80 pounds or more, for example, it isn't because they said no to the cheesecake at the Christmas party.

It was literally thousands of individual decisions made each day guided by an overriding purpose, and great questions asked constantly.

When someone builds a company to a million, then tens of millions and hundreds of millions in sales, it's not only because they're so "smart" - many big companies have been built by people with less than average intelligence, average memory, less than average grades in school, no people skills.

But the ability to ask...

"Is this the best use of my time and resources?"
"What would happen if we changed this feature?"
"What would happen if we changed directions completely?"
"Is this product still going to be needed in the next year, two, twenty?"

...is the one of the single most critical abilities you can develop in yourself and in your team.

What could happen if I have one more drink? Could I get pulled over - get into an accident? What would happen then? How much would that cost in insurance, fines, attorneys and lost wages? What else could I lose? Do I want to risk all that?

Companies in the vinyl record pressing industry that didn't ask, "What is the next opportunity?" missed out on CDs and were gone almost overnight.

People who never consider all the consequences of eating "just one" brownie will always be looking for the "diet that works," hiding from the questions.

Asking forces you to see what you may not want to face.

But wouldn't it be better to have the answers?

Wouldn't it make it easier to reach your goals? More fun? Would success come faster?

Wouldn't you be happier -after weighing the negative consequences with the positive ones- making the decisions that will send you in the right directions? Wouldn't you find it easier to say no to the "tempting" but bad decisions if you focused on the ultimate consequences instead of turning away from them?

You know the answer!!

Don't you?

Man, I hope you feel more empowered now. You should...

Because the habit of asking empowering "what if" questions is one shared by successful people in all areas of life.

Make this a part of your every waking moment, and the opinion you hold of yourself will grow by multiples, due to your better decisions and better outcomes.

You'll probably gain one or two more productive hours every single day.

And you'll be less scared of life... able to smile even during the many important and impactful decisions you must make every hour of every day.

So, what else could happen if this became an "always on" unconscious habit?

TODAY'S WINNING BELIEFS

-- I have the courage to ask myself tough questions
-- I ask questions because I can live with the answers
-- I make good decisions because I get the facts I need
-- Opportunities are all around me and I am finding them
-- My decisions are getting better and better every day
-- I consider all factors when I make important decisions

LOVE IS THE ANSWER

TODAY'S EMPOWERING QUOTE

"Of all the earthly music, that which reaches farthest into
heaven is the beating of a truly loving heart."
   -Henry Ward Beecher

TODAY'S EMPOWERING QUESTION

"What can I remember, notice now or look forward to that makes
me happy and fills my heart with joy?"

TODAY'S FAST SESSION

Find your answer to today's question before you read any further. C'mon
now. Think...

As many of you know, my grandfather passed away a few months ago.
This weekend my family got together for a 50th wedding anniversary party
for my aunt and uncle. And today we spread Grandpa's ashes on my
uncle's property, in upstate New York, as he requested.

As I think about him, I just love him more and more.

And it makes me believe even more strongly that love is probably the
strongest power in the universe.

Isn't it true that those you would do the most for are those that you love the
most? We often go to great lengths to continue the work or fulfill the
wishes of the people we love, even after they pass on, don't we?

It's love, the devotion for something or someone other than ourselves that
makes us do this.

It's love and passion that drive us to do well the things that others struggle
with. It's often love that keeps us from giving up.

It's only love that could make you give your own life to save another's.

How much more would you treasure today if like no other day before, you
had on the tip of your tongue a compliment instead of a criticism... if your

mistakes and the mistakes of others were seen as chances to learn new distinctions and become smarter instead of as roadblocks to progress?

You can do that by increasing your ability to take extreme joy in doing your work, in solving problems and for other bringing happiness to other people today.

Would your missteps seem almost inconsequential if you loved the process of learning... learning to not make the mistake again?

Every experience we have is filtered by our emotions. We will act based on how our filters allow us to act. If the only things we notice about the people we encounter are their faults, their hair, their dress, then we can only treat them accordingly...

By prejudging, hating, feeling superior, being critical and indifferent we are keeping ourselves from enjoying our lives, because our lives are nothing more than the moments inside our own heads... what we think about.

Because we can't control most of the world outside ourselves, can we? To start enjoying your moments and days... and your life, you must do your utmost to allow joy and love in every second you can. How?

I believe it's by appreciating everything and everyone you encounter today. Your setbacks are actually lessons. So if you look on them that way--the right way--you'll accept them for what they are, you'll learn and move on happier and better equipped for next time.

Watch people. Try like crazy to notice something about each one that you can appreciate. Many of these things will be below the surface. You won't see them. You'll have to use your imagination!

Why are so many people sad, depressed, anxious, worried and angry?

Not enough love in their hearts. I'm convinced of it.

How can someone look at another person, and in an instant think all kinds of critical thoughts, yet make the argument that they have a big, loving heart?

Can't be done convincingly, can it?

When you view typical everyday occurrences with anger and frustration, you hurt yourself and those around you. Isn't that right?

You immediately lose the state of mind that allows you to think clearly and come up with solutions. But when you love each moment for what you can learn, no matter what the moment brings, it's very difficult to generate anger, worry or panic.

And it's possible to achieve. Don't think that I'm suggesting that I have this one conquered...

Far from it.

But the simple awareness of this power, or the lack of it in your life, can be enough to send you in a completely different direction. Pick up the book '14,000 things to be happy about.' I think you'll find that it's possible to find love and happiness in even the most mundane things.

Focus today. Put a big note on your monitor, or wherever you can see it often, reminding you to focus on what you can love about things and about people.

If you do this, today should be one to remember forever.

TODAY'S WINNING BELIEFS

-- I'm constantly focusing on what I love about my life, so I
   experience more of it
-- I've released prejudice, worry and false expectations from my life
-- I am filled with love for everything and everyone today
-- The more love I give, the more love I feel
-- People who meet me like me right away
-- It's easy for me to find things to admire about other people

IT'S WORTH MORE THAN A BUSHEL OF BRAINS

TODAY'S EMPOWERING QUOTE

"A handful of patience is worth more than a bushel of brains."
    -Dutch Proverb

TODAY'S EMPOWERING QUESTION

"What can I start on or continue today that will be worth a whole bunch to me later on?"

TODAY'S FAST SESSION

The lack of patience is ruining the world right now.

Instant gratification is not a reality. It's... an illusion.

You aren't going to be more popular by owning a particular pair of sneakers and you're not going to win the lottery. Do you personally know anyone who's ever won more than $2,000 in any of those government-run scams? If you do, they've put it all back into it and more... guaranteed.

The only thing you can truly count on is if you think the same kinds of thoughts as people who do what you want to do, then you'll take the same kinds of actions. If you do that, you'll get the same results...

...if you give it time and don't give up.

Perfect example: "I've tried everything and I can't lose this weight."

Sure, tried everything... for a few days. And if you didn't lose 10 pounds in the first two or three days, you quit.

And what's even worse, those who do lose weight successfully usually "forget" what it was that got them there. Then they slowly get back into the old habits within a week or, at most, a few months. So they "blossom" once again... and say, "I tried everything. Nothing works for me."

Am I talking about you?

Look you're not going to be the president of your company within the first year. Yes, it's true the company you work for doesn't always make the best decisions. But you've got to play the game and earn your promotions and higher salary. It's not always going to be fair.

Patience, my friend...

And persistence.

Life is not as short as it seems. You can't live tomorrow before today. You can only prepare for it.

You've got a lot to learn and plenty of time to learn it...if you look at today as valuable and get off your butt and learn your lessons well.

Don't be so fast to get ticked off at people that don't agree with you. Learn how to persuade instead. Ask questions. Get inside people's heads. Only then can you direct them... and yourself to where YOU want to go. Success comes in increments.

Remember the Internet boom where investment in dot-coms was all the rage? It was raining money.

I remember it too. I was the VP of Sales for a big dot-com.

That company doesn't exist any more.

Lack of patience and... unrealistic timetables. Investment firms forgot that it takes profits to keep companies stable, not ludicrous stock valuations.

For whatever goals you're working towards now (you better have some!), put a completion date on them. If that's what the date must be then commit to it. But if the date is soft, figure it's going to take longer.

What is the percentage of jobs you start that get done when you thought they would when you started? Hardly any?

But what's probably closer to the truth is that most truly meaningful goals are NEVER reached.

How come?

Typically it's because when the lust for instant gratification isn't satisfied, we pack our bags and we forget all about it.

The sad truth is that very few people value earning their success. Most just want it tossed into their laps. We want to be rich. We want to be popular. We want to get straight A's. Cool. Then learn from people who've attained long term success in that area, and do what they do.

There's no other way.

Bang your head against the wall. Splash cold water in your face. Do anything that will wake you up to this truth.

Any success takes effort... sustained effort.

But if you still insist on playing instant LOTTO, keep this in mind. Over 90% of those big jackpot winners lose all of it.

Rags to riches and back to rags.

Nine out of every ten.

Why? Because they didn't earn it. They never learned how to handle money. They thought money was the goal.

Keep in mind that it's who you become in life that matters, not what you get. If you become more, you'll get more...

And you'll be many times more likely to keep it.

TODAY'S WINNING BELIEFS

-- I am willing to work for the rewards in life
-- Patience and persistence are two of my greatest virtues
-- When I set goals I achieve them
-- Setbacks are merely delays, not denials
-- I'm learning what I need to know to succeed
-- I use proven, time-tested principles to get what I want
-- I take advice from people who've done what I want to do

SEEK TO UNDERSTAND

TODAY'S EMPOWERING QUOTE

"If you wish to please people, you must begin by understanding them."
  -Charles Reade

TODAY'S EMPOWERING QUESTION

"How can I learn about what's important to other people?"

TODAY'S FAST SESSION

An automobile manufacturer ran ads some months ago that focused on the fact that their car had the same features as another manufacturer's car that cost about $30,000 more.

The point of the ad was, of course, that nobody really NEEDS a luxury car. They want them... for THEIR own reasons. And car companies know this.

We all have our own specific wants. We want to be understood... to be heard. We want to believe we matter. Even people who don't do a stinking thing for another living soul have these desires.

So if you're in a profession where you have to lead others to your way of thinking or you're teaching others, you need to enter their minds. You must know where a person stands on an issue before you can direct them to the proper decision for them. You must learn about their needs or what their knowledge is about a specific subject before you can teach them anything.

In my sales career, I failed for a few YEARS because I just rattled my canned speech off, never really listening to what the other person was saying.

As a result, I went from brick and mortar to a one-room home that got 13 miles to the gallon. Not using your ears has consequences... for everyone.

OK, now. Let's play a game...

You have to give a gift to someone you've never met. You don't know their gender or even their nationality. If they like your gift, you get a million dollars. If they don't like it, you get your head blown off.

Feel a little pressure?

Okay. Game's changed. The person you must buy the gift for is your best friend in the world. You know everything about them. Same terms... Either a million dollars or you swim with the fishes.

Feels a little different doesn't it?

So how in the world can you get your point across to others when you don't know what their viewpoint is, what matters to them or what makes them tick?

In the hearing field, I found there were many different reasons that people had for wanting to improve their hearing. They may want to be a safer driver, have conversations in a car, hear the TV better, hear the phone ring, hear better on the phone, hear in crowds. The list is endless.

And there were just as many reasons why someone wanted to hold off. Too much money, cheaper somewhere else, never heard of us, only needs to hear in crowds, vanity. Equally long list.

How can you convince someone they need to hear better in crowds when they're only in a big group once every 4 months or so? Can't do it. I had to find out why THEY wanted to hear well. I was able to get so good at getting inside their heads that about 95% of my prospects chose me as their hearing instrument provider. Our industry average was about 25%...

All by asking questions thoughtfully and truly listening to the answers.

This doesn't only exist in selling products. This is every day life.

Do this...

Starting today, listen to conversations other people are having. Listen to your own. Notice whether or not you or others just jump in and try to convince people of things before first finding out their opinion or position. If so, you'll hear hesitation, doubt and rejection. If you pay close enough attention, you'll observe all of those.

We all do things for our own reasons, not for the reasons suggested by overzealous people as they tell us about vague "benefits" that aren't even important to us.

When I stopped reciting my memorized lists of features and benefits and started asking questions and began purposefully listening to the answers, I began helping many people to join the world of the hearing. My income skyrocketed, and I noticed that I learned something interesting and valuable from practically everyone I met.

If you can seek first to understand other people and what motivates them in every situation, you will be able to teach them, to lead them to the best decisions, and quite often to your way of thinking.

Tell me, why would that be important to you?

TODAY'S WINNING BELIEFS

-- I get my way because I give people what they want
-- The more I understand, the better I persuade
-- I lead others to my way of thinking by asking questions
-- I avoid conflict by understanding other people
-- I'm seen as agreeable even though I get my way

PICTURE THIS!

TODAY'S EMPOWERING QUOTE

"If you don't know where you're going, you'll end up somewhere else."
  -Yogi Berra

TODAY'S EMPOWERING QUESTION

"What do I look like reaching my goal?"

TODAY'S FAST SESSION

When the subject of goals comes up, I just get plain excited.

There is nothing like mapping out a plan, working like crazy and despite all obstacles, getting what you were after. Wow!! No matter what the goal is, even little daily goals, it's exciting. They build momentum and anticipation. Just like a road sign telling you that you've only got 3 miles to go. Cool!

In downtown Syracuse, NY, we have two towers that dwarf everything else in the city--The MONY Towers I and II. If you're from out of town and you want to get downtown, you don't even have to know the streets. You just keep following the two towers. And no matter how slow you go, you'll get there... eventually.

This is true of any goal you could possibly have. The most important thing is to be able to see what you're after. Or else, as Yogi said, you'll end up somewhere else.

If the goal doesn't exist yet, you only have to use your imagination. If it does; if others have already done what you want to do, watch tapes of them, talk with them. Read their books. If someone else has done it, surely you can too. Do whatever you must to keep the vision of you achieving your goal in your mind, especially if you're blazing trails.

This is vital, crucial, a must...

You must keep your goal in front of you all the time. The bigger, the more challenging the goal, the more important this is.

There are simply too many distractions, roadblocks, detours and temptations that can derail you on the way for you not to keep it in your sights all the time.

If you want to lose a bunch of weight, tape a picture of your head onto a picture of a person who has the body you want. Quitting smoking? Get a picture of lungs that are nice and pink and healthy. Get a picture of nice white teeth. Money? Pictures of your dream house, car, clothes. Grades? Copy your last report card and put straight A's in place of the other letters.

You're free to get as creative as you want.

See, hear and feel it as often as humanly possible.

Imagine how you'll feel, what other people will say to you, what you'll sound like when you talk. How will you walk? What will you think? Imagine it all.

If you can't see it, you most assuredly won't get it.

Think back to the times that you have wanted something and didn't get it:

Did you keep it in your mind constantly?
Did you visualize getting it?
Did you picture success regularly?

Or did you let every little diversionary thought and distraction get in your mind's way, and keep it from picturing you achieving your goal?

If the answer is the second one, then I hope you've stopped dead in your tracks right now.

This is an important moment. Right now is a turning point. If you can't imagine what it will be like to reach your goal; all the steps to get there and what it will be like once you're there, you're done. It's already over.

Not you though. Not this time. This time is for success. You are ready.

Be like Michelangelo, who just "released" the David from within the block of granite.

See it, feel it, hear it.

What is YOUR David?

TODAY'S WINNING BELIEFS

-- I keep my eyes on my goals at all times
-- I easily avoid obstacles because I plan for them ahead of time
-- I reach challenging goals because I just keep plugging away
-- I can because I think I can
-- Reaching goals is exciting; see it-do it, feel it-do it

SUCCESS LEAVES CLUES

TODAY'S EMPOWERING QUOTE

"He who seeks advice seldom errs."
  - Philippine proverb

TODAY'S EMPOWERING QUESTION

"Who would know - where should I look for the answer?

TODAY'S FAST SESSION

The old cliché "Success leaves clues" is possibly the most ignored pathway to achievement I know of.

Why?

In addition to not wanting to look unknowledgeable, I think, a big reason is because getting advice and answers often either costs money, which people don't want to invest, or time, which even fewer want to invest.

I say invest because whenever you "spend" time or money on learning, you've given yourself the chance to grow and become better now and in the future at whatever you invested your time or money in. And if you are better at something as a result of your "spending" then you've made a wise "investment."

The average person jumps head first into most situations without knowing a thing about what they're doing.

A great example of this is a story my uncle Dave told me this past weekend.

You see, he and a friend took a fishing trip to Canada a few weeks ago. Every guest in the lodge they were staying in was there for the same reason... great fishing.

Most of the guys there were fairly experienced fisherman.

And that was their biggest problem.

They were just going to go up there and catch more fish than they ever did before. Man, those fish were just going to jump in the boat. We'll just drop our line in and pull out the fish.

Right.

My uncle and his friend, also very experienced fishermen, took a slightly different view.

They'd never fished that area before.

So, for $150 [$75 apiece], they hired a guide for the first two entire days of their trip.

What they got was the experience of a 71-year-old man who'd been fishing in that area his entire life. He was an expert in that area. He showed them which lakes, where on each lake to fish, why, which lures, you name it.

Their results?

Well, consider this...

In a virtual fishing paradise, one guest in the lodge that week caught just 6 fish all week long.

My uncle, with the advice of the guide, caught 294 Walleyed Pike during the same week fishing the same lakes... more than any of the other guests.

He told everyone about the guide.

So did anyone else hire a guide that week? Nope. He told me that no one even asked him what he was doing to catch so much. I guess they all just thought he was getting lucky. Big egos.

This is a perfect parallel to how 97+% of all people treat all aspects of their lives.

I see it every day. Everywhere. In all settings. Obvious solutions to problems are just ignored.

If you want to reach an important goal in your life, if you want to beat your competitors, if you want to have great relationships...

If you want to excel at everything you do.

...Then you absolutely MUST get direction from someone who's been there before, wherever "there" might be.

Buy books and read them.

Ask experienced people for solutions and listen.

You might have already known 90% of the answer. So what you have to listen for and hold dear is the 10% you didn't know.

And use it.

I love going to amazon.com and reading the reviews people post for books. So many people give bad reviews because in their opinion, there was "nothing new." What they don't say is that all the "old" stuff, what now is generally accepted, they don't even use that.

There is nothing wrong with hearing the same old stuff. Because unless you use what you've heard or read, you don't really "know" it.

Most tasks look easy on the outside, and they are... IF you know what you're doing.

I wouldn't even dream, for instance, of trying to put something together or learning a new piece of software without having the instructions at my side. But most people ignore them. And their results show it.

Look, you may have an I.Q. in the stratosphere. But if you aren't constantly looking to learn what you MUST know to get your tasks done quickly and effectively in EVERY part of your life, then you are creating a destiny of almost doing a good job, of coming close to finding happiness but not quite getting there, of being known by everyone including yourself as undependable. And with that comes a poor self-image.

My purpose in writing this is for you to become more and more of a person who is passionate about learning what you MUST learn in order to set and reach the little and big benchmarks on the way to your dreams.

You just can't do it any other way. This isn't my opinion. It's an immutable principle of life. To deny this is to guarantee a high failure rate at many things you attempt.

You don't want that. I know it.

So do this...

Make a list of your To-Do's for the next week. Look at each item and ask yourself the question, "Am I really good at doing this?" If the answer is no, then before you start, write down all the things you need to know and do to prepare before you start. If you need some information, get it.

And get excited. Smile. Laugh. Because when you get that info, when you learn the thing you didn't know before and when you achieve your outcome easier and with more joy than you ever did before, you have expanded your knowledge, your capabilities and your value to yourself and others from that moment on.

Whenever you learn something new, no matter how small, you just taught yourself that you can achieve the largest of goals... the most amazing of accomplishments... because what are big accomplishments? Aren't they just many little ones all piled up?

It's funny, huh?

Success at just about anything is amazingly simple when you look behind the curtain. My uncle was a high school drop out. He didn't even go for weeks at a time.

But when he changed his view about learning, he got his GED, went to college at night, got his degree and ultimately became the highest paid civilian employee in Central New York in the NYS prison system.

In the process, he learned that learning is fun and that in every single experience he has, there is something he can take away from it to help him make smarter decisions in the future... like hiring a fishing guide when no one else would.

So, how many "fish" are YOU going to catch in the next week?

TODAY'S WINNING BELIEFS

-- I love learning
-- Every experience I have gives me new lessons for living
-- I have my eyes open to the learning opportunities all around me
-- I see the value in every lesson I learn
-- I learn something new from everyone I meet
-- I'm effective because I learn what I need to know to do the best job I can

RESOLVE

TODAY'S EMPOWERING QUOTE

"For the last nine days the world has seen for itself the state of our union, and it is strong... We will not tire, we will not falter and we will not fail."
  -George W. Bush, 43rd President of the United States

TODAY'S EMPOWERING QUESTION

 "Is my resolve sufficient to succeed in my next venture?"

TODAY'S FAST SESSION

Possibly the most important quality or skill you need to succeed at anything in life, whether it be getting in shape, excelling in your job, beating an illness or just plain being happy is a dogged commitment to doing it.

Ninety five percent of the time, people don't reach their aims because their resolve to get there was never very strong to begin with.

If you don't believe you'll get to your destination, how much effort will you ever be willing to put in? I mean, if you want to lose 20 pounds or 200 pounds and you've "tried" dozens of times only to ultimately quit trying, then what kind of effort will you be likely to put in this time?

Right. Not much.

The secret is your belief and your commitment.

How many times have you had some outcome that was an absolute must. You simply HAD TO GET IT DONE. The consequences of failing would be too great. At least in your mind, they were great. So...

You got it done! You worked all night. You rallied the troops. Your whole being was into it. There was simply no turning back. Failure was not an option...

And you succeeded.

Tell me, during those times when you rose to the challenge, was there much doubt about the ultimate outcome? Probably not, huh? You just knew that success was imminent, didn't you? Well, that's what happens when you're totally committed to a goal...

...AND when you're clear on exactly what you want.

To succeed at anything, keep your inner voice positive. Tell yourself you can... constantly. Every hour. At critical moments of decision.

Talking about belief and resolve: You've no doubt all heard the stories about people who exhibited amazing feats of superhuman strength and picked up a vehicle just enough to help rescue another person pinned underneath.

And what about those tireless rescue workers who simply won't let themselves stop until they find one more survivor. They have their outcome set and they're doing everything to achieve it.

Now, in our everyday lives, that kind of schedule is usually not required and definitely not healthy, but the principle is the same. Keep your eyes on the goal. Every minute. Every hour.

If you do, then you won't be wasting precious time on non-essential tasks. You'll keep yourself from feeling the agony of failure. Because if your resolve is strong, when you do meet those temporary setbacks, you'll see them as that...temporary.

When your determination is weak, each setback looks like the end.

So look at your next project, and the one after that, and even the one after that, and start talking yourself into doing what you must. Tell yourself that you're up to it. Make it a must.

Do that and I know I'll be hearing from you with one heck of a success story.

TODAY'S WINNING BELIEFS

-- When I commit to accomplishing a task, I do so with my whole heart
-- I am an achiever
-- My resolve to reach my goal is strong

YOU *CAN* CONTROL YOUR HABITS

TODAY'S EMPOWERING QUOTE

"We're worn into grooves by Time--by our habits. In the end,
these grooves are going to show whether we've been second rate or
champions, each in his way in dispatching the affairs of every day. By
choosing our habits, we determine the grooves into which Time will wear
us; and these are grooves that enrich our lives and make for ease of mind,
peace, happiness--achievement."
    -Frank B. Gilberth

TODAY'S EMPOWERING QUESTION

"What thoughts do I have that continuously drive me into taking the actions
that keep me down?"

TODAY'S FAST SESSION

You can't possibly make a positive change in your life if you don't know
how it is that you make the mistakes in the first place--the habits that
confine you to making the same mistakes over and over.

...And over.

I can appreciate how frustrating it is to be imprisoned to running the same
old patterns--only to get the same rotten results. I was a living, breathing
example of the power of bad habits.

No one type of person is immune to the power of habits. The other day I
was reading about some of the tightwad habits of a few famous, and
wealthy, people...

For example, Clarke Gable used to argue regularly with his grocer about
the price of jellybeans. John Rockefeller once gave his groundskeeper a $5
bonus...then docked it from his pay when the man took Christmas Day off.
Paul Volcker, Chairman of the Federal Reserve Board, used to pack a
suitcase full of dirty clothes and take it to his daughter's house so he didn't
have to pay to have it cleaned. Ty Cobb, the baseball great and early
investor in Coca-Cola, used to steal soap from hotels and locker room
showers and send them back to his home.

These are prime examples of the power of habit. Even after these people became wealthy, they still retained their old scripting.

Our habits of thought, especially the thoughts that we don't even CONSCIOUSLY think any more, control every action and emotion we have... even in our sleep.

So if you've been reading my newsletters for months, and even if you forward them all over the world, but you haven't once taken those affirmations at the bottom and attempted to incorporate them into your daily thoughts, you are missing out on one of the most powerful and life altering habits you have available to you; because it is impossible to change your action habits before you first make a thought habit change.

Reach up and scratch your ear. The only way you can do that is if you think about it first, either from a direct command like I just gave (which you had to think about) or by the thought, "My ear itches." So you take the action.

You can't take a single action unless you think about it first. The thought, "My ear itches" is an affirmation. If your ear lost all its feeling and went numb, a mosquito could suck it dry and you'd never get the thought, "My ear itches." So you wouldn't scratch it. The mosquito doesn't make you itch your ear. It's the thought, "I'm getting bitten." Numb ear means no thought.

For many decades, yogis have done demonstrations where they drink a toxic substance like turpentine yet it does nothing to them. They affirm in their minds that no matter what the liquid is, their body will react to it as if it's water. No cell in their body is harmed. No treatment is necessary.

You have a mind just like they do. Same structure. Same abilities. There is no difference. Well, there is one...

Your beliefs - your affirmations, are different.

You can only act based on what you believe... what you affirm is true. Affirmations like, "I'm too short, too tall, too this, too that, I can't do it, She would never like me, I'll never learn this, I'm going to die broke..."

...In fact any false belief you have isn't false at all if you believe it.

If you believe that you're going to own hundreds of rental properties, you'll learn what you need to know and you'll do what's required to make it happen.

Conversely, if you believe (affirm) that you'll need Social Security to survive and that you'll live hand to mouth forever, you won't try to save, you'll spend your money on junk, your time will be spent on recreation and you'll run the other away from setting meaningful goals.

Habits control all of us. Take control of your thoughts. Make it a daily habit of affirming powerful belief altering, action producing truths about you and about life, and it will literally force you to do and to enjoy (if you affirm to) the actions that will make your dreams come true.

Make a commitment now to be the one in twenty who gets what they really want in life; The one in twenty who takes information and actually does something with it; One in twenty who can take goal accomplishing actions because they convince themselves that it's fun...

And if you don't believe that... yet, then consider this.

Life is tough no matter who you are. What pain would you rather have, the pain of sacrifice and labor or the pain of regret and sorrow for the things you never did because you believed you couldn't and will never get the chance to do again?

Choose the first one... Please.

TODAY'S WINNING BELIEFS

-- I have the habits of the most successful people alive
-- My new habits lead me to successful outcomes
-- I am rising above all old limitations
-- I am an example of the power of belief and possibility
-- My habits make me successful
-- Good habits and I are one

WHAT ARE MINE DOING TO ME?

TODAY'S EMPOWERING QUOTE

""Why" and "How" are words so important that
they cannot be too often used."
--Napoleon Bonaparte

TODAY'S EMPOWERING QUESTION

"Are my internal questions helping me or hurting me?"

TODAY'S FAST SESSION

Two main activities our minds engage in consciously are affirming and questioning.

The problem is, most people use questions to make themselves feel guilty, depressed, get angry, and many other unsupportive emotions, limiting what they'd be willing to DO at any moment.

When you feel lousy, not confident, ugly, stupid, foggy, it's hard to get your best from yourself. And questioning, one of the primary activities of your mind, plays a big role in how you feel every minute of every day.

Here's an example:

The mind's question: "Why am I so fat?"
The mind's answer: "Because you eat too much. You feel like you are worthless and since that's the way it is, any attempt you engage in to lose weight, I (your subconscious) will thwart. You are not worth all the trouble of becoming thin. Why not just relax here on the couch, grab that terrific tasting chip dip you just bought and finish it?"

Isn't that pretty typical of some of the internal dialogs you have with yourself on a regular basis? Be honest.

With the use of anti-depressants on the rise, it must be a pretty common practice.

<Notice> If your questions & goals are unreasonable, you'll get answers that will keep you from reaching those goals. If you ask how you can lose

25 lbs. in a week, you'll get answers like starve myself, live on the treadmill, etc. And when you try to implement those answers, you'll get discouraged and tell everyone that no matter what you do you can't seem to lose the weight... or quit smoking, or go out in crowds, or whatever your silly dream was.

And you'll become a person that stops trying certain things. You could be great at some things, but in those other areas of life where your questions stink - forget it.

Questioning can just as easily work for you in the positive direction.

Example: What can I do to drop 25 lbs. within 4-6 months?
(Challenging, but very possible)

Your mind comes up with good answers to good questions. You could read food labels, join a health club, get a walking buddy or workout partner, buy some home exercise equipment (AND use it), get a good low-fat cookbook, stop eating fast food, like myself more, etc.

You don't have to implement all this at once. Do a few things. Succeed, then add a few more. Soon, you have a whole new set of habits. Your confidence will be higher. And you'll be on your way.

All because you used your mind to ask empowering questions instead of ones that only make you feel like a worthless failure. I know. I did that for over twenty years, and my life was a complete and utter chaotic mess.

Disempowering questions sound like this:

Why does this always happen to me?
When will I ever learn?
Why do I even bother?
If I don't study now, what's the worst that could happen?
Why can't someone else do this?
What is wrong with me?

Questions like these will chop you down in an instant and you'll never know why you can't achieve even the most simple goals...

And you'll continue to blame everyone but yourself for your failures.

Not you though, because you know better.

TODAY'S WINNING BELIEFS

-- I'm asking empowering questions throughout today
-- My questions make me feel strong and happy to be me
-- I ask great questions and get empowering answers
-- People are in awe by my ability to come up with solutions

HAVE YOU SMELLED ANY ROSES TODAY?

TODAY'S EMPOWERING QUOTE

"When we learn to give thanks, we are learning to concentrate
not on the bad things, but on the good things."
   -Amy Vanderbilt

TODAY'S EMPOWERING QUESTION

"What are five things I'm most grateful for today? Ten?"

TODAY'S FAST SESSION

It's so easy and it seems pretty natural, when things aren't going right, to get
angry and frustrated. It's common for people to shake their fists at the sky
and say, "Why me?!"

At these times, what's needed is a little perspective.

For me, right now, it's downright painful to even sit here and type, due to
these disks in my neck that may or may not be part of me for much longer.
There are so many 'What ifs?' that it's a bit daunting. What if I do nothing?
What is reasonable to expect from therapy? Surgery? What about mobility
afterwards? How about sports? Ever again? Precautions? Pain? Oh, the
pain! Paralysis? Loss of use of a limb? Gosh, I'm only 38!! This wasn't in
the plan!

And that's just what a lot of people do until they're 'paralyzed' with anxiety.

There is another way...

The desire must be to feel better mentally when it's not possible physically
or when outer circumstances aren't likely to change soon. Isn't that right? I
mean, you'd like to at least 'feel better' in your thoughts, right? It IS
possible.

So I literally can't think of a better thing to do than to put forth every ounce
of effort into gaining a perspective on things that will bring peace of mind.

Haven't we all known or heard of someone who has experienced
devastating circumstances, including radical deterioration to their health,

220

yet they 'managed' to stay 'positive?' They must be out of their right minds, huh? But the truth is that there are literally millions of people right now whose daily struggles make our own seem like a grain of sand in our shoe.

It's all about perspective...

Remember, things could be worse, right? You could be gone already. The pain could be triple. The loss could be total and permanent. The embarrassment could be worse... somehow. The scars could be worse. You could live in a refugee camp. You could be starving.

Remember, if you were born in a country with tremendous freedoms, you've got it a whole lot better than BILLIONS of others. Do you shiver in your sleep? Do you wonder where your next meal is coming from?

To go on with grace and a calming peace, I only need to think about all the things that ARE good... in comparison to what they could be... compared to what so many others are experiencing this very moment... compared to where I've been.

Take a minute or two or ten and write down a short list that you can pop in your wallet, pocket or purse. Put on it all the things you can think of that are good compared to what things used to be like. What's good compared to what others face? How's your country? Your neighborhood? Your schools? Your friends? Has anyone shoved a gun in your face in the last 24 hours?

No matter what can happen to you, keep in mind that it could be worse. Also, remember that you are bigger than any of it. You can go on with dignity and overcome all of it. One peaceful, smiling, serene and grateful minute at a time.

And there are plenty of role models who've experienced it all before you have, all around you to help you do it.

Isn't that rather comforting?

TODAY'S WINNING BELIEFS

-- I can overcome anything no matter what it is
-- I have the power to put things in the right perspective
-- I live with tremendous peace of mind
-- I accept all that happens to me with grace and calm
-- I am a clear thinker
-- People look to me for guidance and inspiration

BRING OUT THE BEST

TODAY'S EMPOWERING QUOTE

"For if the trumpet give an uncertain sound,
who shall prepare himself to the battle?"
-I Corinthians 14:8

TODAY'S EMPOWERING QUESTION

"Do I expect of myself all that I am capable?"

TODAY'S FAST SESSION

Harvard University researcher, Robert Rosenthal, did a study on a number of elementary school teachers. He went to the schools and informed the teachers that he was going to give their students a test that would identify academic potential...

But the test was a hoax.

Instead, he chose the students randomly and told the teachers that the students he identified were brilliant... that they were geniuses. These students would definitely excel, he told the teachers, if they were given support and guidance.

By the end of the school year, the majority of those students had improved their IQ scores and their grades had improved dramatically...

And some of those students happened to have been some of the worst students up until that point. These teachers were given no special training. All they knew was that they had some "stars" among them.

Rosenthal performed the same tests with college professors, and the results were just as dramatic.

This is known as the Pygmalion effect, so named after a story in Greek mythology. The Pygmalion effect is real. It's working every day, every minute... either for us or against us.

So here is the situation...

Here you are, with your career and your family and all the other things that make up your life. And you may excel in one or more areas. Maybe you're even the head of a large organization. But it doesn't matter if you're on the bottom or the top. This incredible force called negative expectation is no doubt working against you in some form in one or many areas of your life.

How?

Your past scripting, or past experience, has "taught" you that people you know are going to perform in expected ways. When you meet people, you'll place your imagined level of expectation on them based on their appearance, their vocabulary, what you've heard about them, their education level, their tone of voice... could be any number of things.

In an inordinate number of cases, the people in our lives will perform exactly as we expect them to... because we treat them how we see them.

You need to raise your expectations of the people you meet and know. Expect people to follow through. Expect them to excel. All people. Treat them in ways that show what you expect. Tell your "team" members that you think they're champions, that they can succeed, that you're committed to them and to their growth...and your own.

Ever hear of Marva Collins, arguably the greatest teacher in history? She treats ALL her students as if they could become the President some day.

After becoming disillusioned with the Chicago public school system she taught in for 14 years, she started her own school in her own home. Since then, she has taken kids labeled retarded and un-teachable. She's provided them with love, compassion and understanding. She has a firm belief that each student will learn. She absolutely will not let them fail. Failing is not an option.

What she has achieved is miraculous.

To learn more about Marva Collins, you can read her books. A movie about her life was made, starring Cicely Tyson. Her web site is http://www.marvacollins.com.

While we're helping bring out the best in others, what about you?

Don't think I forgot about you. This is really about you. You can't bring out the best in anybody if you don't even believe in YOUR own abilities. Take the empowering beliefs at the bottom of this letter. Read them every day with conviction and belief that you are the person you're affirming to be.

Expect more from yourself than mediocrity. Expect greatness.

And just as sure as the sun will rise tomorrow, you'll become that person. You'll persuade yourself to want to be even more. And in the process, you'll have what you truly want in this life, no matter what it is you desire.

After all, how do you think great teachers, mentors and coaches bring out the best in others?

They encourage, inspire, push, cheer lead, teach and love. Through the repetitive daily reading of the most empowering beliefs, you'll become your own best success coach.

And it's only then that you can begin to reach out and teach what you know... and change the world.

TODAY'S WINNING BELIEFS

-- I expect excellence of myself and those around me
-- I am a great coach and cheerleader to myself and others
-- People like to be around me because I bring out the best
   in them
-- I let go of all doubts about my own abilities
-- My abilities are growing stronger today
-- I expect to win

DO YOUR BEST AND YOU'LL WIN

TODAY'S EMPOWERING QUOTE

"Players fifty years ago wanted to win just as much as players today. Foot soldiers 1,000 years ago wanted to win the battle as much as combat troops today. The difference is that everybody worries about it more today because of the media and the attention they give to the question of who's winning and who's losing. Those are the wrong questions. The correct question is: Did I make my best effort? That's what matters. The rest of it just gets in the way."
 -John Wooden (10 NCAA basketball championships in 12 yrs)

TODAY'S EMPOWERING QUESTION

"Is my focus on winning and losing or on doing my best?"

TODAY'S FAST SESSION

I expect that most people reading that quote would disagree with Mr. Wooden initially. Why? Because so many people play "Lotto," cheat on their spouses, lie on their resumes, cook the books to make the stock price higher... all to try to short-cut the system.

John Wooden never talked to his teams about winning... only about doing their best.

And when you do your best, you often become THE best. Why? Because hardly anyone else is doing THEIR best.

I noticed that in my business career. I've risen to the top of four different industries now because I focus on doing the best job that I can possibly do.

To have one eye over your shoulder worried about things outside of your control does only one thing... it makes it impossible for you to do your best. With one eye off the road, you are going to crash sooner or later. Usually sooner.

My grandfather used an analogy with me to help me keep my mind where it should be. Of course I didn't do what he said to do for a long time, but here's what he told me. He said that no matter what I am doing, think of myself as on the top of a ball - balancing. I had to focus only on what I was doing or I'd fall off the ball. If I took my attention away from the ball, I was going to fall off.

Throughout this last season in the NBA, I watched all the team's statistics concerning their wins on "the road," games played in the opposing team's home field.

And I thought it was absolutely fascinating that, at the end of the season, out of 29 professional teams, only 5 had winning records on the road.

One of the main problems? The opposing fans rooting for the home team...

Interesting to note that of those same teams, 21 out of 29 had winning records in home games.

So when the game is on the line and that multi-millionaire superstar is taking a critical shot in the fourth quarter, chances are better that he'll make it at home but miss it on the road. Why? Because most of them aren't completely focusing on their task. Instead of the basket, they're thinking about the guy in the 4th row.

"Home field advantage" is at play in everyone's lives every day.

You see, when John Wooden was coaching in college, half of all their games were "away" games, but there was a period toward the end of his career where his teams won 88 games in a row. Nearly 4 full years without losing a single game.

You see, his players weren't thinking about winning –only of doing their best... every minute. Every play.

They were like machines programmed to do their job. If they were focusing on their job, the crowd couldn't affect them.

It sure helps to have a coach like that, but in life, you usually have to be your own coach. You simply can't rely on someone else to pump you up when you need it. Because quite often they'll let you down. You'll want some pep talk, and the person you call to make you feel better isn't there, or they aren't in a peppy mood themselves.

Bottom line is, you've got to control your own moods.

That's why I always have some kind of book with great thoughts near by, why I always have a tape playing in the car and why I always have a Think Right Now! CD playing throughout the night.

The world is a giant ball. Turning, turning, turning.

When we don't focus on where we're going, we fall.

The "crowds" are often hostile, but if we just pay attention to what we can do, to what our little job is and do it to the best of our ability, quite often we will come out on top.

Will you win awards right out of the shoot? Probably not.

Will you make a million in a year or two? Not likely.

Will you meet Mr. or Miss Right tonight? Does it really matter?

A better question is: With a different focus, will you get better at whatever it is that you're doing? In fact, will you quickly get better at nearly everything you do?

Absolutely.

Will you feel great about yourself as you are doing your best?

Yup... IF you pay attention to how you succeeded so you can repeat it, and IF you aren't worried about someone else's performance or what anyone says about you.

You see, all of life is a game. Whether you are in front of crowds or all alone, you will act based on what you are thinking about - on what you are paying attention to.

Do you think Tiger Woods routinely steps up to the ball thinking, "I'm going to hook this one. It's going in the trees."???

Not a chance.

Now, there is a chance it may go in the trees, but that is not where his focus is. And that is why it usually ends up right.

Every top performer in every field of endeavor focuses constantly on what they should be doing right now to get their desired outcome.

To allow others to control your focus, to lose sight of your goals for seconds, then minutes, then hours will cause you to fall down constantly.

Control your focus and you will be in control of your emotions, your actions and your life.

TODAY'S WINNING BELIEFS

-- I'm controlling my moods today
-- The only person who controls my focus is me
-- I'm doing my best today
-- No matter what I'm doing, I'm paying close attention

APPRECIATE THE PEOPLE AROUND YOU

TODAY'S EMPOWERING QUOTE

"Hay is more acceptable to an ass than gold."
-Latin Proverb

TODAY'S EMPOWERING QUESTION

"What is the most appropriate form of appreciation and/or
service I can provide to each person?"

TODAY'S FAST SESSION

Aren't you just amazed sometimes about how obvious it is that you or
someone around you fails to get recognized for accomplishments? It's easy
to see in others isn't it?

When it's someone else who should show the gratitude, it
RIDICULOUSLY OBVIOUS, isn't it?

But when it's US that should hand out some thanks and show that we feel
lucky to have the support and help we DO get, we quite often are just as
guilty of "forgetting" to do this as those we despise. Isn't that right?

I have watched some of the most incredible performers in the work arena
get literally forgotten when it comes to pats on the back. More
responsibility and longer hours are what they usually get. And less thanks.

Is it any wonder that it's tough to keep good employees? There's an
unfortunate tendency to believe that most people just know they're good, or
have done well, so we don't bother to tell them.

In the last few years, psychologists recently did a study about what
employees want in their jobs. And pay ranked something like number
seven in importance. That doesn't mean it wasn't important. Just that on a
day-to-day basis, that's not what we dwell on when it comes to job
satisfaction.

Feeling appreciated and a feeling of being in on things ranked at the top of
most lists.

If some of a company's computers worth several thousand dollars came up missing, they'd call the police and a full investigation would ensue. The company would want them back and would like to see the crooks behind bars.

But if a key employee were to leave suddenly, that person's bosses and the company owners would likely never get down to the root of why they just lost an asset worth possibly hundreds of thousands (or even millions) of dollars!

But I know why.

Most people don't want to take the time (or accept the possible guilt). Most of us simply don't understand the implications of not showing how much other people mean to us.

With great regret, I can say without hesitation that I have been very guilty of this. But the awareness of it is the first step towards having the power of appreciation help rather than hurt you.

If you say "I guess I should do more of that (yeah, right!)" then you are killing your chances of true and lasting success and happiness in business, career and personal matters.

None of us likes to be taken for granted. Many people have gone nearly insane because they don't feel appreciated. Think about times when you or someone you know got upset and/or acted in irrational ways. Aren't many of those times also times when you felt unappreciated, not necessary or that your opinion doesn't matter?

You see? It colors all your relationships--professional AND personal.

Cruising through your days just expecting that John is going to do what you need him to do because that's what he's always done in the past is crazy. Pretty soon John's going to be gone...

...and you won't even know why.

But now, at least, you'll have that seed of an idea why.

When you'd like a word of encouragement or a compliment of a job well done, even a little acknowledgement, and it doesn't come, notice how it feels. I hope it doesn't wreck your day, but just notice it. Feel it. Well, that's what others feel, too, when their deeds are ignored.

You could quickly become the most popular person in school, work, or just about anywhere else. Just start noticing small things. Pick them out and give a quick thanks to the person who was responsible.

Do this for a couple days or weeks and you'll see people instantly responding to you.

Try it out and watch everything change!!!

TODAY'S WINNING BELIEFS

-- I notice the little things that people do for me & others
-- I'm quick to say thank you for a job well done
-- I appreciate all the things people do for me
-- Other people like to be around me now
-- People like doing things for me now
-- I'm well liked by others
-- My opinion is important to others

SOLVE YOUR PROBLEMS BY THROWING THEM AWAY

TODAY'S EMPOWERING QUOTE

"I don't know who my grandfather was. I'm more concerned to know who his grandson will be."
   -Abraham Lincoln

TODAY'S EMPOWERING QUESTION

"Am I looking at yesterday as an excuse to fail or a reason to succeed?"

TODAY'S FAST SESSION

I don't know where I first heard this little mental technique, but it was just after I moved back from California to New York in 1987. Just one of the many little grains of sand thrown on the pile that I used to help me climb out of my hole. It has served me well over the years. When you get stuck and feel that there's no way out of a situation, try this.

Write down a "problem" you're embroiled in. Write how you feel about it. Write down all the reasons you can't succeed, why you feel powerless, why it's no use to even try...

Then take that paper, wad it up in a ball and throw it away. Upon my many arcing baskets I could usually be heard saying something like, "That is the biggest pile of horse crap I've ever seen!!"

After you do this, forget about it. Yup. Put it out of your mind completely. Start some other task right away. If you do this, something magical will happen. Your subconscious mind will go to work on it. You see, when you tell yourself out loud that your pity party is hooey, that your false excuses are just that, that you're not going to listen to the lies you've told yourself for so long, your mind, the one that God gave you to use for good and noble deeds, says, "All right!! Time to do what I was created to do!"

What you'll experience is, most times, nothing short of a miracle. Often, within a day or two, you'll be driving down the road, eating a snack or raking the leaves and suddenly you'll get a huge "A-ha!!" And the answer comes.

Life being life, we all get lots of opportunities to solve problems that seem insurmountable... sometimes daily. But by programming your subconscious mind in this way, you're teaching yourself to come up with answers quickly. Soon, all "problems" become nothing more than an easy decision or two from complete resolution.

Like any good habit, though, you need to be consistent. Don't do it once, solve a big problem, never to come back to your excellent technique. How many times have you watched a sporting event and your team's strength seems to be completely underutilized by the coaching staff calling the plays. Doesn't it shock you that these guys could be so stupid not to use their best chance to win? Don't be like that!

Grab a pen and a piece of paper... C'mon.

Soon you'll be making baskets from across the room with your little balls of paper... "Three seconds, two, one... the shot. It's good!!"

Problem solved.

TODAY'S WINNING BELIEFS

-- I find what works and I stick with it
-- Great answers come to me constantly from every direction

MAKE TODAY GREAT

TODAY'S EMPOWERING QUOTE

"It used to seem to me that my life went on too fast. So
I had to take it slowly just to make the good parts last."
   -Steve Winwood

TODAY'S EMPOWERING QUESTION

"What is really great or could be great about today?"

TODAY'S FAST SESSION

Happiness in life, or even for a day, doesn't mean that you run around like a chicken every day talking about how great you feel. And it doesn't just mean that you closed the big deal or your dinner reservation was accepted. Too many of us look at outside validation to prove to ourselves that things are good.

Trust me, when I was over $100,000 in debt with no earthly idea how it would be paid, if I had looked outside myself to try to feel good, guys in white coats would've been called in to take me away.

Immersing myself in subconscious mind re-patterning was essential. How do you go from being a person who always wished they were somewhere, anywhere else; someone who couldn't remember what they read for more than a few minutes, having to re-read stuff two and three times to get it; someone who just didn't care about anyone but themselves; who moved papers all over and said they worked a full, exhausting day?

So how can you get on the road to happiness?

-By completely accepting the fact that there are many things you must learn and that you can learn to be as effective and as happy as you dream of being

-By viewing criticism as a chance to learn... (at least in private)

-By trying to find something, anything, to be happy about... every single day

Even if you do nothing more than plant a big grin on your face all day, doctors have proven that chemicals are released by the brain that mimic those happy pills prescribed by the billions for depression. Actually, it's the pills that mimic the brain's natural function of producing euphoria.

Here's what I want you to do...

Write down today's question. And underneath it, write at least five things that you can think of that are, or could be, great about today.

Topics can include:
- Your health or someone else's
- The way you feel emotionally
- A bad habit that you've controlled recently
- Someone who has been noticing you- that you like, too
- Positive comments on your work
- Your new suit
- Big appointment coming up and you feel prepared! Or,
- You don't feel prepared but you have time to get ready
- Getting together with friends that you haven't seen in a while
- A new day to learn about yourself and what motivates you

You see, you can go on and on... and you'd better. It will only take a couple minutes, but will pay gigantic benefits to you.

There are literally hundreds of things that you can pay attention to that can make you feel good... at any moment in time. At EVERY moment!!

Don't confuse this type of mental focus as being Pollyanna. I'm not talking about putting rose-colored glasses on. I'm talking about a way to keep from worrying about things you can't control that probably won't happen anyway, about focusing on what's good instead of being depressed about things that are over and done.

Steve's quote about taking it slowly doesn't mean slowing down. It means being in the moment. Enjoying the good stuff as it's happening... Paying attention to the good things and being able to appreciate them, instead of only the "problems."

Depressed people DON'T focus on what's good or even what could be good... only on what's not right. I used to be one of the best "problem focused" people you will ever meet.

236

And as you will see very shortly, after you finish writing down all you can in response to today's question, you can immediately start enjoying each and every day at levels that seemed unattainable to you before.

Don't just read this and forget about it. Your happiness today and for the rest of your life depends on your ability to appreciate the fleeting moments that can give you some of the most wonderful memories you'll ever have...

I promise.

Now write down at least 5, and preferably 10-20 answers to today's question...and start smiling.

TODAY'S WINNING BELIEFS

-- All around me are things that make me smile
-- I appreciate the little things that people do for me
-- I enjoy the process of finding the good in other people
-- I respect the needs of others
-- I appreciate the differences in people
-- Life is good
-- I enjoy myself no matter what speed I'm moving

WILL YOUR CHANGES LAST THIS TIME?

TODAY'S EMPOWERING QUOTE

"He that never changes his opinions, never corrects his mistakes, will never be wiser on the morrow than he is today."
    --Tryon Edwards

TODAY'S EMPOWERING QUESTION

"What are some changes that I should make? How can I make them last?"

TODAY'S FAST SESSION

A few months ago, one of our cats, Rebecca, got out of the house for only the second time in eight years. Since she often spends time sleeping in hidden closet spaces, no one had seen her for a few hours and didn't think much of it.

But after hearing horrible noises outside late that night, my stepdaughter came and enlisted me to find out if Rebecca was outside.

Since she's white, I saw her instantly against the dark background of trees in the back yard. As I got closer, she looked like she had stuck her paw in an electrical socket. Her hair was standing straight up. After a few very nervous moments, I was allowed to get close enough to touch her and then, gently, bring her in the house.

The next day, the Vet shaved a couple spots to reveal some nasty bites from another cat. She was hurting really bad, but pretty soon, she was back to normal...

Well, almost.

Ever since, she has been the most lovey-dovey cat you have ever seen. Every time she's around, which is just about always now, she's rubbing up against us, purring, playing, and wanting to be petted... kind of like a dog except for the purring.

This is a cat that, while never mean, would never even let you pick her up for more than a few seconds. The only time she ever came really close was to meow for treats.

238

I think this new behavior is her way of saying, "Hey, all these years I never truly knew what you guys meant to me. I know now. And I'm not forgetting it."

She's literally like a different kitty. And she's NOT reverting back to her old ways.

When studying the behavior of people, we see that most sudden changes usually don't last because they haven't been "cemented in" through time and repetition. Typically, after a short period, old behaviors come right back strong as ever. Our OLD patterns, our MOST dominant programs... our true beliefs, come back to run our never-ending string of emotions and thus our moment-by-moment actions.

Rebecca's situation, though, was unique in that it was a HIGHLY emotional event. And those kinds of events tend to re-wire us without the requisite time and repetition before our new patterns can take over.

Since most of us have changes we want to make, and don't want to wait around for a high-intensity emotional event to occur, THAT is why it's so important, in the process of changing habits of thought and action, to repeat the ideas and visualize what you want constantly. Without it, change rarely comes or stays around for very long. Today, you never see athletes in any sport who don't do this daily.

That's why these newsletters are structured the way they are. Without making the continual effort to install action-producing, winning beliefs, there is no foundation for new behavior that will last beyond a few days or weeks.

It's vitally important to continuously implant the seeds of greatness on a daily basis...

Or nothing on the outside will change.

And it's SO easy to do.

Now, if you'll excuse me, I'm going to go play with my cat. She wants some attention.

TODAY'S WINNING BELIEFS

-- I enjoy repeating my most desired beliefs
-- Seeing myself reaching my goals is easy & automatic for me
-- I'm building upon my successes today
-- I feel myself changing and improving by the day
-- Adding new behaviors is so simple and easy for me

HOW COULD YOU BE ANYTHING BUT A SUCCESS?

TODAY'S EMPOWERING QUOTE

"To men pressed by their wants, all change is ever welcome."
  -Ben Jonson

TODAY'S EMPOWERING QUESTION

"Concerning my thoughts and actions now, am I using my past and present as an excuse for failure or as my motivation for success?"

TODAY'S FAST SESSION

A number of years ago I heard a powerful story about motivation. I don't remember where I heard it or even if it was true story or not, but it perfectly exemplifies the human ability to transcend circumstances.

My memory of it is fuzzy, so here's my version... with a twist.

A reporter decided to follow up on an incredible human interest story after hearing of two brothers, one a vicious, dangerous criminal to be locked up for the next ten years for his latest crime, and the other a highly respected university professor.

After the arrest of brother number one, he told the police about his brother, his closest living relative.

After the police discovered who brother number two was, a reporter was given the tip that this could be an interesting story.

Upon interviewing both men at length, the reporter learned that their father was a brutal man. He was a hard drinker. And his brand of teaching his boys "right from wrong" involved terrible verbal abuse no matter where they happened to be. When they "got out of line," he hit them with belts, his fists, sticks - whatever was handy.

They both told almost identical stories of extreme cruelty. Neither one was exempt from the old man's anger and drunken rage.

While the boys were 19 and 20 respectively, their father died of a massive heart attack. Shortly afterwards, the brothers had a falling out and never saw each other again - brother number one moved out of state and sort of fell off the face of the earth... living his life between jail terms.

Brother number two graduated from college and followed a designed path to living a rewarding life of service to his community, his church and his family.

The thing that practically knocked the reporter over was both brothers' identical answer to the same question.

After getting the background on both individuals, the question was, "How did you get here to this point in your life?"

The two answered the question with this same response...

"With a father like mine, how could I be any different?"

One used his father as an excuse, while the other used him as motivation - as training on what not to do.

You see, it's not what happens to you in life that dictates where you'll go and who you'll be. It's what you do with it.

I'll bet that, right now, you could sit down and list at least a dozen people who have risen up from hellish childhoods, or who are completely different than anyone else in their families in some significant way. You'll discover that, concerning the differences, there are completely different belief systems, different ways of "looking at" the situations, different motivations and reward systems.

So I'm being honest when I tell you there is no reason on the face of the earth why you can't achieve your next big goal. None. I don't care how many times you may have fallen on your face.

Do you want to reach some health milestone after repeated failures? Then decide to.

And stop with the excuses. You've been lying to yourself too long.

Do you need to learn something, to pass some test, to get a degree or license? Then get off your backside, shut off the TV and do it.

Do you see a failure when you look in the mirror? Do you know what to do, but just always decide not to do it? Then turn the volume of the criticism in your head down. Shut off the excuses. Write down on 3x5 cards statements like these:

-Good job, I really tried hard.
-I really have quite a talent there.
-I'm quite a handsome man/beautiful woman
-Boy, when I have a job to do I just tear right in and get it done.

...And read them often.

Write down empowering questions like these:

What is good about me? What could be?
What are the many benefits I will get by doing this or believing that?
Why do I want to achieve (some outcome)?
What is my best character trait?
How can I get (someone) to really truly admire and respect me?

There are thousands more.

And they all make you feel better and more capable.

With this reading as a habit, you will change how you see yourself.

What you're being exposed to now is what I discovered to be the inner differences between the winners and doers in life and the losers and watchers.

And if you think this doesn't work, you couldn't be more wrong.

Think about the two brothers and all the billions, dead and alive, who have risen above their circumstances and their old programming to be, do and have more than it appeared they ever would. You've experienced this. Now it's time to turn it up a notch. Grab yourself a huge goal.

Our Think Right Now! audios are based, in part, on this whole technology.

Go to our site and check out some of the changes people have made using them. It's downright scary.

When you change what goes in, you will change what comes out... IF it goes in regularly and in the right way.

Come on, make today something special.

Make today your day.

No more excuses.

Take your circumstances and all of your past failures and use them as motivation... as the reason for your imminent success.

Be like the professor.

With circumstances like yours, how could you be anything but a raging success?

TODAY'S WINNING BELIEFS

-- My success is guaranteed
-- I am motivated by my circumstances
-- I'm lucky to have had my past... it drives me
-- I am what I believe and I believe in me

CHIN UP! KEEP GOING!

TODAY'S EMPOWERING QUOTE

"Press on. Nothing in the world can take the place of persistence."
   --Ray Kroc

TODAY'S EMPOWERING QUESTION

"Am I even a little closer today to my goal than yesterday?"

TODAY'S FAST SESSION

For those of you who don't know Ray Kroc, he's the guy who took McDonald's from a little hamburger stand to the most successful restaurant chain in the world. He's long passed away and the systems that he set up still thrive and dominate today.

He developed and improved on systems of training, making the food, presentation, franchising, and advertising that made a moderately successful joint into a global phenomenon.

Systems and persistence.

Many people thought he was a crazed lunatic, concerning his fanaticism about consistency. But Ray understood that once a system, good or bad, is in place, it's nearly impossible to change it.

And that's how we all are as individuals, too. Once we get a habit, it becomes very hard to break...

Giving up too soon is the saddest thing in the world.

My wife told me a story the other day about a co-worker who has never hit the 'Help' button in any software program she's ever used...and she's used computers every day for years. She thinks it will take too long to find the answer, so she just doesn't even bother.

Don't laugh--you probably have a few of these yourself. Find them and snuff them out.

Do you look at potential goals and get overwhelmed by all the stuff you'd have to do to achieve it and thus never start anything? The right way is to write down all the benefits that you'll get--spiritually, physically, emotionally, socially... any benefit.

Look far into the future. Write 'em down.

This simple exercise will help you stay motivated to see it through.

If it takes months or even years to get what you want, keeping your eye on the ball will keep you going. If you don't even know why you're doing something, how can you possibly stay passionate about it?

You can't.

Have you given up on a goal recently, where if you attained it, your life would be dramatically improved?

Were you passionate about the goal?

Of course you weren't.

Passionate desire helps create persistence.

Persistence alone will often get you where you want to go. Without it, it doesn't matter how much you know, who you know, who you are, what you've done before, what you look like or how much money you have to throw at a problem.

Persistence, sheer persistence usually will win.   Determination will overcome even superior talent.

Even if you never reach the goal that you've worked so hard for, there is a pretty decent ancillary benefit...

Character.

Tomorrow's another day. Your day.

TODAY'S WINNING BELIEFS

-- I learn with each misstep and persist with commitment
-- I create systems in every thing I do and I save a lot of time
-- I become more with every job I put behind me
-- I always look for the benefit to me in a task

LOVE ONE ANOTHER

TODAY'S EMPOWERING QUOTE

"The tragedy of man is what dies inside himself while he still
lives."
   -Albert Schweitzer

TODAY'S EMPOWERING QUESTION

"How can I see, or what can I do about, this situation so that it can be a
true healing and a strengthening instead of a weakening or a tearing down?"

TODAY'S FAST SESSION

September 14, 2001

It is with a heavy heart that I write today's letter. No words or
encouragement can erase the circumstances and sadness of the last few
days.

This evil wants us all to hate one another, to mistrust and hurt each other
more. I have faith in us all to not let that happen.

A colleague mentioned to me how tough it must be to be a motivational
writer right now. I could only agree that I felt somewhat helpless in being
able to make much of a difference to anyone today.

But it later occurred to me that given the tens of thousands of subscribers to
Your Day to Win, I could help.

If you're reading this and you believe in the power of prayer, then please
pray that the events occurring around the U.S. and other countries in
retaliation against innocent people of Arab descent stop right now. That's
exactly what those evil cowards want. They will only be happy if we start
to unravel and end up at war with our neighbors. So please pray for that to
end. I'm convinced that prayer is the strongest force there is. So please
join with me to end the hostilities. We can't let them win.

You must know this about yourself... that you can still look at your
neighbors and see friends, no matter the color of their skin, their faith, or
their clothing. They didn't do this.

248

It's already time to trust again and to believe in the goodness of our planet's citizens. We are all hurting now. But we all must strengthen our resolve to continue and to find the good in life and in others.

And most importantly, please believe in your ability to carry on. No one thing is bigger than your ability to handle it. Know that. Believe it. It's true. The people who lost their lives NEED us to come out of this stronger, thus weakening the forces of evil that took them away and still threaten us from without and within.

The powerful beliefs below are for you to use to strengthen your ability and determination now to fight through and win over every adversity and struggle you're faced with.

Remember, you ARE what you believe. I believe that you and all of us CAN come together to give a positive meaning to Tuesday's tragic events... as hard as that may be to believe right now.

We all must believe.

TODAY'S WINNING BELIEFS

-- I have unlimited power to make a difference in the world
-- I see the world as a safe and wonderful place
-- I love my neighbors and they love me
-- I support and feel supported by all the world's people
-- I am sending and receiving unconditional love

DON'T YOU DARE QUIT!

TODAY'S EMPOWERING QUOTE

"When I was first diagnosed as HIV positive, I was really scared. I didn't know what it really was. But once I understood what I had to do, I wasn't afraid any more."
  -Earvin "Magic" Johnson

TODAY'S EMPOWERING QUESTION

"What information do I need in order to proceed ahead confidently without fear?"

TODAY'S FAST SESSION

Today's message is about hope.

When Magic Johnson was diagnosed with HIV, like many people in similar situations, he thought it was a death sentence...and that it wouldn't be long.

Many situations like that can cause a feeling of hopelessness. I know. We all know.

But when things look down, that's the time to start looking for answers. You simply must. When it appears like you have no way out, what do you have to lose by sucking it up and putting everything you have left into beating the odds? What?

Never count yourself out. It's almost ALWAYS too soon to count yourself out.

In doing the research for our program *I Am Healed Now!*, I was amazed to read study after study showing what the mind has done to heal the bodies of people who were left for dead. Doctors are often left scratching their heads when someone who isn't "supposed" to recover comes out of it. The word 'miracle' is often used.

Surely they are miracles, but these miracles often leave clues. Success at ANYTHING leaves tracks. God helps those who help themselves, right?

The body and mind are one. What the mind imagines (visualizes), the body carries out. And not just in healing itself.

Success in any venture is no different.

This is something you do all the time. You visualize thousands of times per day. You're so USED to visualizing everyday events so often that you may not realize that you're doing it, but you are. It could be something as simple as going to the kitchen to get an apple. You picture it and then you carry out what you pictured.

The key to ultra success is to visualize like you do all day long, but for the things that you want in life. Your goals. Your aims. Your dreams. This is where faith comes in too. This is where your already great visualization skills will help you succeed where you'd be tempted to think that you can't.

But most importantly, (and this is the most difficult part), when some verification comes that what you've visualized hasn't quite happened yet the way you want, you MUST NOT quit. You must keep going, and make your vision stronger than ever.

Winners don't quit. That's why they win.

If you've been a quitter until now, admit it and get off your backside. Stop feeling sorry for yourself and start up.

You're going to fall down dozens or even hundreds of times. That's life. But DON'T you quit... even if at first it appears hopeless.

When successful people in all areas of life are talked about, they are often called people of vision. They see what they want or they imagine the conversations before they succeed. They keep the vision and the discussions in their mind. That is what keeps them going in the face of defeat after defeat.

I get letters daily from people who say they lost hope. I say they lost hope LONG before they recognized it. Listen to your inner voice right from the beginning of tasks and journeys. Are you telling yourself it won't work? Do you tell yourself that you can't? Listen to yourself all day. Every minute.

251

This isn't only about health. It's not just about business. It's about your every moment.

If we were never to have another minute together, ever, and you were only to take this one last bit of info with you and you used it religiously, then you would have a skill that could carry you to heights that you can't even dream about right now.

This skill of awareness of your thoughts and pictures would not only give you success today, but prepare you for even greater successes tomorrow as well.

Join me. See what you want clearly. Keep the visions there. Visit them often, preferably when you're very relaxed with your eyes closed...

... And miracles will happen; every day

TODAY'S WINNING BELIEFS

-- Regardless of the situation, I keep my optimism
-- I learn what I need to know to get what I want
-- I keep my outcomes in sight and look at them often
-- When other people say 'impossible,' I look for solutions
-- I make miracles happen in my life every day

WHO ARE YOUR ROLE MODELS?

TODAY'S EMPOWERING QUOTE

"If each of us can be helped by science to live a hundred years, what will it profit us if our hates and fears, our loneliness and our remorse will not permit us to enjoy them?"
-David Neiswanger

TODAY'S EMPOWERING QUESTION

"What tiny step can I take today that will get me another degree closer to overcoming the fear that stops me?"

TODAY'S FAST SESSION

The strange thing about education is that you never know where you'll get it and what shape it will take.

I know that a lot of people have the mistaken belief that who your parents are and what happens to you during your first few years dictates what you can and can't become in life. I hope by now that, even if you haven't reached your potential, you've grabbed onto the belief that you CAN change anything about yourself you wish with the right attitudes and actions.

I know far too many people now who continue to teach me every day that growth can and should continue right up 'til the day we die.

I recently came across a study by psychologist Robert O'Connor on socially withdrawn pre-school children. He wanted to see if he could reverse the pattern of social isolation in children so that it wouldn't create persistent difficulties in social comfort and adjustment through adulthood.

He created a 23-minute video with 11 different scenes. Each one began by focusing on a solitary child who watched the other children participate in an activity. In each scene, the child joined the group to the enjoyment of all.

O'Connor then went to a number of pre-schools and selected the most severely withdrawn children and showed them his film.

The results were dramatic...

In each case, these children immediately began to interact to the same degree of sociability as the normal children in the group. And what was even more astonishing was that a follow-up 6 weeks later showed each of these children, who had viewed this single video only once, were now leading their schools in levels of social activity.

On the other side...

...the control group, the socially isolated children who didn't see the video, were as withdrawn as ever.

What this study and others like it strongly suggest is that when we have fears and barriers to achievements, it's important that we see other people similar to ourselves succeeding in spite of their difficulties. This teaches our brains that if they can do it, so can we.

Marketers have known this for years. But what I want for you is to be able to control your own thoughts, beliefs and actions as well as the commercials do.

I know this probably sounds like a broken record by now, but here I go again... Read the biographies of successful people. Read about the people who were born in the back rooms of shanties, people who couldn't afford shoes, yet rose up to levels of success that they alone believed they could achieve.

When you meet people who obviously have achieved some degree of accomplishment, ask them how they did it. Find out their beliefs. Tell them what you want to do. Almost without exception, you'll hear from these people that, while the effort was rarely easy, you've just got to believe that it's in you to achieve great things.

One thing I found out from all my mentors (even if they were only my mentors for 5 minutes) is that they like to be asked about their struggle to climb the mountain.

Ask people about their success and you'll likely have their attention for a good long time. Once you do, possibly your only challenge then is keeping the conversations from stretching into the night.

My point is this... Just like those children, who probably thought, 'Those kids could do it and so can I,' you can do whatever you want to achieve, too. And there's hardly anything as motivating as seeing a person who crawled from desperation and poverty to become a happy-to-be-alive success story.

Use the power of role modeling. It will never let you down.

TODAY'S WINNING BELIEFS

-- I learn by the mistakes and successes of others as well as my own
-- I enjoy stories about people who beat the odds
-- If others can overcome my same challenges, I can too
-- Every day teaches me more about my limitless potential
-- I seek to learn something from everyone I meet or read about

YES YOU CAN!

TODAY'S EMPOWERING QUOTE

"I've said many times, to myself, 'This is going to be no problem. I've done this before.'"
--Tiger Woods

TODAY'S EMPOWERING QUESTION
"What memory can I use in this situation that will give me a reference point for the right attitude towards a successful outcome?"

TODAY'S FAST SESSION

Man, what a great day this is going to be, huh?

Ready?

Say yes...

It's very well known that Tiger Woods uses a very specific kind of self talk. He talks himself into staying calm at times when others are literally trembling inside (outside, too!). He's not a wizard. He simply talks to himself in a way that encourages him. He says, "I can" and that type of talk opens up the door marked "memory of past success."

And you know what?

When you talk to yourself, you listen. No matter what you say, you're listening... and recording it in your memory.

And when you put thoughts into your mind, they CAN be rejected. However, if you do it often enough and they're the right thoughts, your mind - your subconscious mind - will ultimately bring you around to believing whatever you tell it.

How many times have you heard a thing—it could be anything--and your first reaction was one of complete disbelief:

You can earn your degree—*"I don't have the time"*

You can be a size 6 again—*"Yeah, right. I've had two kids and just can't lose that weight."*

You can be in really great shape—*"Who, me? I get out of breath climbing one flight of stairs."*

You can advance at work—*"I'm just a pee-on. No one notices me."*

Some things are just hard to believe at first...

...Until you've been exposed to those same thoughts over and over and over again. Advertisers know this--that's why the same commercials are run constantly.

Soon, after some repetition, you open up a little to the possibility.

"Could be..."

Then, perhaps your belief gets a little boost.

"Hmmmn, well, maybe I do have time to take one course at the community college at night."

"You know, I've just cut back on soda and I've lost 3 pounds!"

"Walking around the block with my neighbor is kind of fun, and I don't get as winded as I used to."

"I've been trying harder at my job and guess what—the boss paid me a very nice compliment on my work!"

At this point, a wonderful cycle has begun. As your belief gets stronger, you'll do a little more, then your belief gets stronger, then you'll do a little more, etc.

Positive, encouraging and optimistic self-talk is literally the software program that can flip your switch from lose to win in any area of life. It may not be "true" today. But with the right words and the right emotion - and with repetition - you simply must change. It's unavoidable. Your brain won't let you lie to yourself for too long before it says, "Ya know, I DO like getting up at 5:30 to exercise." Bingo!

This is a very important topic, so we'll have to pick it up later... very soon, in fact.

In the meantime, use some or all of these statements below to actually help to re-script your old worn out beliefs about yourself and help make you LIKE the process of changing your unsupportive, false and disempowering beliefs.

TODAY'S WINNING BELIEFS

-- I look forward to making my life even better
-- My subconscious mind remembers my successes and helps me repeat them
-- Daily success is good for me and I embrace it
-- I replay my successes in my mind regularly
-- I hold the memory of my successes close so I can access the feelings when I need them

DON'T BE A SLAVE TO GUILT

TODAY'S EMPOWERING QUOTE

"We cling to our bad feelings and beat ourselves with the past when what we should do is let go of it, like Peter did. Once you let go of guilt, then you go out and change the world."
  -James Carroll

TODAY'S EMPOWERING QUESTION

"What do I feel guilty about? Why? Isn't it about time I let it go?"

TODAY'S FAST SESSION

Whew! There are a lot of things to feel guilty about aren't there?

We could feel bad about our thoughts, our mistakes, our failures. We didn't try hard enough. We didn't make a decision soon enough and lost out on something we wanted. We invested too heavily in one company, and its stock bombed.

Something we said or did deeply hurt another person. We told an off-color joke. We were responsible to hundreds or even thousands of others and somehow, we let them down. It's endless.

And we die a thousand deaths over it.

It's true that our thoughts, words and actions can have negative consequences.

Fortunately, it's these consequences, thought out beforehand, that keep us from doing many things that WOULD hurt others as well as ourselves.

But we can't foresee EVERY bad result coming down the pike. To err is human, as they say.

Knowing that, though, doesn't always (and for some people, it never does) make it feel any better when we make a blunder. Soooo, we get the guilt... which can be very useful.

But it's when we get overrun with guilt that we just get paralyzed, unable to forgive ourselves for this "heinous" act we performed.

As James Carroll said, St. Peter was able to forgive himself for denying Jesus and move on to take actions that changed the course of the world in a positive way. If he had forever thought himself horrible and unable to make amends, our world could be very different today.

We're all exactly the same as Peter.

So many people make a mistake or say something in a fit of rage, and forever after define themselves by it.

We say that we ARE stupid, or we ARE a bad person, a lazy person, a selfish person. Guilt literally can put us behind bars in the sense that it takes away our freedom to choose our future actions.

We too often don't want to risk these mistakes again, so we stay quiet. We don't voice our ideas, in case they wouldn't work out... Because if they didn't work, not only would we feel stupid, but we would feel overly responsible for the consequences.

Yes, guilt and shame can be a vicious circle that can literally shackle our potential.

But because it's invisible, we usually don't see it. We just think we're being wise... that we're protecting ourselves.

Have you ever wondered how people who are in the spotlight or who have been successful in business deal with their impactful decisions that turn out badly?

Well, the trouble with being well known is that your mistakes and blunders are also well known.

So how do these people treat their gaffs?

They put them in a perspective that minimizes them. And as long as this perspective allows them to learn to not repeat the same mistakes over and over, they can go on and continue to be a top performer in their field... which can benefit themselves and others.

260

What would happen if a popular actress had a movie flop and decided she was the cause? She may never want to risk that kind of failure again. She may start making incredibly bad career decisions... decisions that could potentially affect the flow of hundreds of millions of dollars.

If you are responsible for someone else's tremendous pain or bad situation, how do you go on and achieve a high degree of success, happiness or wealth without feeling guilty?

You don't. Feel the guilt. And learn from it.

But when you've learned what you need, give the guilt a shape, pop it in a jar, seal it up and throw it away.

Forgive yourself.

All our products are filled with statements about letting go of guilt and past hurts because unless you do, there is no risking, no effort, no accomplishment...

...And in the event that you do accomplish much, without self-forgiveness there is little joy in what you've done. You just feel guilty about it.

There are too many good books on the subject for me to steer you toward any one in particular, but do some study on it. Learn about how guilt is affecting you...

...Because you can be certain of one thing. Guilt is negatively affecting your daily decisions to some degree.

And the extent to which you can lessen it is the exact measure of additional accomplishment and joy you will have in your life.

Many people will NEVER forgive you for your actions. That's why YOU have to.

Right now, think of something great that you experienced in the last ten years that you had absolutely no concept of before you experienced it. Remember what it was like during the experience? Stunning. Exhilarating. You were awe struck.

Well, when you can let go of the things you've done and move on with a clean slate, you will feel something that is possibly ten times greater than what you experienced back then.

TODAY'S WINNING BELIEFS

-- I am a good person
-- I deserve happiness
-- I feel forgiven

SCHOOL IS NEVER OUT

TODAY'S EMPOWERING QUOTE

"Phil Jackson knows how to coach me. He gets me angry.
When I get angry, I dominate. It's perfect."
   -Shaquille O'Neal

TODAY'S EMPOWERING QUESTION

"Who else can I learn important skills and lessons from now?"

TODAY'S FAST SESSION

In today's quote, Shaquille O'Neal, the All-Star center with the Los Angeles Lakers, underscores an incredibly important point. And that is this...

No matter what your individual accomplishments are, no matter how good you think you are at something, you can still get better. Sometimes a LOT better.

Shaq was already named as one of the 50 greatest players of all time.

When he wants a basket or a rebound, he won't be denied.

But the problem is that while he has always had the physical skills to be great, his decisions haven't always been the greatest.

One problem was, his mind was often somewhere else besides the game. When that happens, he might get his points but his team would lose... even though he may have scored 40 or 50.

Another one is, for years he was basically a one-man show. His teammates were not made better because Shaq was playing. Result? Seven years... no championships.

What the addition of Phil Jackson as coach has meant, besides back-to-back championships, is Shaq now plays a more team oriented game... the kind that makes everyone better. He now has his head in the game more. He's less selfish. He's a better listener... more teachable.

Because no matter how good you are at some task or profession, you can't possibly push yourself or motivate yourself as well as a coach or teacher can do it for you.

It's interesting that Shaq made this statement, because recently he was extremely angry at Phil for pushing him too hard.

But he's to be admired, because he again realized that championships are the goal.

It's often hard to take orders from people, especially when you don't agree with them.

But keep in mind that it's almost unheard of to self-teach your way to excellence through high school, college or a business career. Guidance is the most valuable thing about institutions of learning and business. Deadlines are usually better enforced by someone other than ourselves.

Willpower, quite often, is anything but powerful.

This is why self-help info products and gadgets don't usually produce the change in people that they want. An exercise bike can't force you to get on it. You have to do that by yourself.

When I talk about seeing each day as a day to learn, much of that learning must come from simple observation.

Watch people.

Listen to those who get a lot done. Listen to their words. Ask about what motivates them. Ask them about how they get over their problems and how they 'use' them to carry on.

Yes. I said USE their problems.

Most people have challenges and they are seen as problems, excuses, valid reasons to fail.

Effective people see them as motivation.

How?

By realizing that EVERYONE has challenges.

Just because you have some tragedy doesn't mean you're cursed. It means you have to get over it. It means that when you do get over it, you will go on with valuable experience that will help you in the future.

You have been given another mental tool.

If you see challenges and tragedies as legitimate excuses to hide, to quit, to fail...

...then you don't get the valuable experience. You will be less, not more, in the future.

You'll be less able to handle it again, when life hands you another big challenge... and another.

And life will. You can count on it.

So don't beg for life to be different than this. Because it won't change.

And that's good.

See this as one of the great mysteries unveiled for you and you'll be richer and happier by multiples.

See it as unwelcome news and you'll continue to hide, to quit, to fail.

TODAY'S WINNING BELIEFS

-- I see each day's new challenges as the way toward high achievement
-- I overcome all challenges that come my way
-- I learn something valuable from everyone I meet
-- I'm now achieving my potential
-- I am getting better at everything I do
-- I believe I can learn anything

CELEBRATE YOUR LITTLE VICTORIES TOO

TODAY'S EMPOWERING QUOTE

"One great difference between a wise man and a fool is, the
former only wishes for what he may possibly obtain; the latter desires
impossibilities."
    --Democritus

TODAY'S EMPOWERING QUESTION

"What can I do today that will get me closer to my larger ambition?"

TODAY'S FAST SESSION

It is your right as a living human being to set a goal, be able to work for it
and achieve it.

One reason most people don't reach their ambitions is that they fail to set
small milestone goals; weekly, daily, hourly.

To use the baseball analogy, you can score a lot of runs by doing nothing
except hitting singles. A home run gets the biggest applause, but you can't
reach your outcomes by only swinging for the fence.

I was able to rise up from years of failure by giving myself daily and hourly
goals.

Sexy? Hardly.

Always fun? Not really.

But they were effective. Partly because every day I could look back and
see that I had accomplished the tasks I had set forth for the day... which, by
the way, tied in to my bigger goals.

Now that's sexy.

You simply can't reach a big goal without lots of little tasks that take you
down the road to reaching it.

If you just internalize this one thing, you'll be able to conquer bad habits that heretofore have beaten you bloody.

If you want to stop smoking or overeating, for example, quit for an hour. If you accomplish that, you have something for your Victory Log. Then do another hour.

Of course, it CAN be more complicated than that.

Maybe you don't feel particularly worthy to join the ranks of the non-smokers and thin people of the world. That's a self-image issue. But if you want to get to it the fastest way, set a goal each hour.

If you do that, you can achieve 16 goals per day in your waking hours and get on a tremendous roll. If you've never gotten that kind of momentum going, it's a high I can't fully describe. You've got to experience it yourself. I smoked for nearly 20 years, nearly 10 of those at about a pack and a half a day. And it's a minute by minute fight until you win, not a daily fight.

Set some small, more easily achievable goals and see how easy it is compared to looking at some big unimaginable mountain you want to climb.

Remember, break things down in bite-sized chunks and you can do anything you want...

Anything.

TODAY'S WINNING BELIEFS

-- I see my issues around my desires completely now
-- I set attainable goals and I achieve them
-- My ambition is growing daily
-- I set daily goals and I achieve them

RESOLUTIONS

TODAY'S EMPOWERING QUOTE

"When nothing seems to help, I look at a stonecutter hammering away at his rock, perhaps 100 times without as much as a crack showing in it. Yet, at the 101st blow it will split in two, and I know it was not that last blow that did it, but all that had gone before."
  -Jacob A. Riis

TODAY'S EMPOWERING QUESTION

"Can't I keep going for just one more day, one more hour, one more minute?"

TODAY'S FAST SESSION

Resolutions...

That's what new years are for, aren't they? New beginnings.

"This is the year that I'm going to get in shape, quit the bad habit, start my new business, get better grades..."

And by January 14th, what usually has occurred?

Complete withdrawal of the New Year's Day resolution. Back to the old ways.

Let's see what does resolution, or resolve really mean?

Webster's defines it as this:

Resolve - To form a purpose; to make a decision; especially, to determine after reflection; as, to resolve on a better course of life.

Hmmm.

I notice that it doesn't say, "To try something out for a while."

No. To resolve is to form a purpose. To achieve something as part of a bigger plan.

So it would seem to me that to achieve anything worthwhile, even crucial, you would need to keep in mind the 'Big Picture.'

You must continually ask yourself why you're doing this thing. You need to know why you're giving up all that luscious chocolate, or the television, or the gambling.

It must go back to the word "Purpose." Isn't that true?

No purpose means no resolve. A BIG purpose makes it easier to stay the course.

I mean if there are no big, emotion-stirring benefits at the end AND along the way, why would you put forth any effort?

You wouldn't...

And that's why so many New Year's Day resolutions are quickly forgotten.

Let's make a switch. What do you say?

In fact, not just now, but when we want anything big, whether it be some material thing, health goals, relationship goals, let's focus on some new stuff.

Namely, what's truly in it for you?

If you have no reasons, ones that you can really get behind and defend when that little voice tells you that it's OK to slip, you'll give in every time.

You must keep your eye on the benefits. They need to be good.

What are the emotional benefits? Write them down. How will you feel when you reach your goal? If it's a long-term goal, how will you feel as you're progressing? Imagine it often.

This could be crucial in keeping your resolve.

How will your relationships be affected if you reach your goal? Imagine it.

Would anyone else like to see you succeed? How would it benefit them? Would you like that?

Any career benefits? Would it mean more money? How much? Prestige? New office? How does this feel?

Any physical benefits? Less pain? Smaller dress size? How would it make you feel?

Write down ALL the benefits, even if it takes you days or weeks to think of them all. Carry this list with you and read it often.

Think back now: Have you made any big resolutions to stop some long-term bad habit or to start a new long-term good habit?

Have you ever stuck with them?

So don't just read this and forget about it. This is a formula for life success that you're being given. And more than an idea that can only affect a small inconsequential part of your life, this is HUGE!

This kind of habit, skill and "resolve" generating activity can affect every single part of your life... forever.

And it will help develop your character.

The dictionary calls character "A description of a person's attributes, traits, or abilities."

What are yours right now?

Well, I'll tell you, if you can stick to even one important resolution or goal, right to the end, because of constantly keeping your focus on the benefits, then your personal attributes, traits and abilities will all grow in direct proportion to your commitment to keep those benefits firmly in front of you in vivid, living color.

You CAN do it. I know you can.

Happy New Year!

Let's make this year your best year ever!

TODAY'S WINNING BELIEFS

-- I am a goal achiever, through and through
-- When I commit to something I stick with it
-- I keep focused on the benefits of reaching my goals
-- Benefits are what compel me and drive me toward my goals

IMAGINE THAT!

TODAY'S EMPOWERING QUOTE

"Something almost magical happens when people break through the obstacles that hold them back and discover what is truly inside them."
   -Brian Biro (from Beyond Success)

TODAY'S EMPOWERING QUESTION

 "What can I achieve today if I make just a little shift in my belief about what is possible?"

TODAY'S FAST SESSION

Brian Biro, the former coach of a national swim team, was about to coach his last meet.

One of his young swimmers was a girl named Allison, who despite good natural speed, always "died" at the end of races. Finally, after years of just missing the Junior Olympics before she moved up in age brackets, she made the final spot (by one hundredth of a second) on the team for her only event, the 100 meter butterfly... seeded last out of 64 other girls.

She was just happy to be there and felt absolutely no pressure. So in warm-ups with no undue expectations, she turned in her best 25-meter time ever.

Brian got an idea...

When he told her what her time was, she was bubbling over with enthusiasm. He asked her to remember how she felt as she was swimming... to remember how high on the water she felt. This got her in an incredible state of excitement. She couldn't wait for her race.

They had it all set up. She was to get into the same excited mental state she was in at the beginning of her recent sprint. Then, to give her the strength at the end of the race so she would finish strong, at the 75-meter mark, Brian was going to be waiting. He would yell, "NOW!" When she heard it, she was to pretend that she had just dived into the water in her most recent personal record-breaking sprint.

In her race, Allison exploded off the gates.

By the 25-meter mark, this last seeded swimmer, had opened up a one-length lead on her competitors. Approaching the 75-meter mark the lead was two lengths.

By now, all her teammates had joined the coach beside the pool, screaming wildly, cheering her on. When she reached 75 meters, Brian dropped his hand and 100 voices screamed in unison, "NOW!!!!!"

She poured it on.

When she finally touched the wall, she looked around. There were no other swimmers nearby. She thought she had finished last and that everyone had gotten out of the pool!!

Actually, she had won the race by a giant margin, dropping 10 full seconds off her personal best. 10 seconds in a 100-meter race!

With tears in his eyes, Allison's father asked Brian, "What did you do to her?" Brian said, "SHE did it."

That day, he had changed his coaching with Allison. In his frustration with her habit of sputtering at the end of races, he had started his own habit of saying, "One of these days, you're not going to die."

That day he changed, by helping her focus on what she wanted instead of what she didn't want.

When we fail to get what we want in most situations, it's often because we're focusing on not failing.

Sports psychologists have been training athletes for decades now in imagining the perfect performance. Mental rehearsal. And world records have continued to fall in every category of human physical performance.

Focus on what you want...

See it over and over. Get in the right state and you can achieve almost anything. The words will just come to you. You'll magically feel wonderful... precisely when you have to. The right actions will come easily. They'll be fun. You'll achieve your personal best.

And you'll get what you want when you want it more predictably... After all, when you do this a few times and you start winning more consistently, you'll want to continue this mental habit forever, right?

TODAY'S WINNING BELIEFS

-- I easily imagine myself doing my best
-- My mental success rehearsal is so real I can feel it
-- I pay attention to my thoughts and keep the positive
-- I quickly turn pictures of failure into success
-- I am setting new records of personal achievement now

IF YOU GET A SECOND CHANCE

TODAY'S EMPOWERING QUOTE

"If you ever get a second chance at life, you've got to go all the way."
  - Lance Armstrong (5 time winner of the Tour de France)

TODAY'S EMPOWERING QUESTION

"What must I do to increase my determination and improve?"

TODAY'S FAST SESSION

It's now official.

Lance Armstrong has won the Tour de France for a record tying fifth time.

The most difficult, grueling sporting event in the world.

He survived 2,100 miles over two mountain ranges in 20 days, the stomach flu, dehydration, crashes & near crashes as well as the weather to do the unthinkable. Three weeks and over 83 hours of pushing himself past exhaustion. I can't even imagine what that must take physically and mentally to run that race.

To most people, it's just two words, "bike race," that don't mean too much.

But in life you've got to grab inspiration wherever you can.

To me, his record setting performance is just one more push to make this lifetime a masterpiece. One more confirmation that with determination, anything can be achieved. Absolutely anything.

Here's a guy who in 1996 was diagnosed with an advanced form of testicular cancer that had spread to his abdomen, lungs and brain.

Because of its spread, he was given only a 50-50 chance of survival.

But he had aggressive surgery and chemo treatments that alone would've killed the average person, and was pronounced cancer free in 1997. Then began the arduous road back to health.

A few months ago, I was watching a 1997 video of him training after his surgery. He had no hair and you could see the U-shaped scar on top of his head where they went in to remove part of the cancer. He said training was difficult... he would get wiped out after only an hour and a half on the bike.

An hour and a half, and he got wiped out!

Most people are ready to quit after 2 minutes.

After the treatment and surgery, he was no different than anyone else... actually much worse off physically than practically anyone alive.

But he had Lance Armstrong's mind...

...the mind that made him the best cyclist in the world.

You see, that is what separates the winners from the losers in life.

Everyone who knows of Lance knows of him as a winner, but in his first Tours he didn't do so well.

Here's how he did in his previous Tour races:

'93 - Did not finish
'94 - Did not finish
'95 - 36th
'96 - Did not finish
'97 - Did not enter
'98 - Did not enter
'99 - 1st
'00 - 1st
'01 - 1st
'02 - 1st
'03 - 1st

He didn't even finish 3 times. See? We're talking about a grueling race!

But success in life is about how many times you pick yourself up, not how many times you fail.

Since I was "this" close to using another quote today, I'll include it. Here it is: "A winner must first know what losing's like." Billionaire publisher Malcolm Forbes said that. So he knew something about winning, I'd say.

You see, so many people I work with are just so scared of losing that they just won't get involved in life and risk falling down... of looking foolish... of losing what little they have.

But you must.

The good stuff is on the other side of failure. You just can't get there without it.

It hurts, sure it does.

Those months I spent in the van hurt worse than I can go into right now. And lots of risk went into getting out and creating an actual life. And without failure there is no success.

None.

I've been reading the press coverage of this year's Tour extensively, and I read a quote of one of Lance's fans saying that this is the most excited she's ever been in her life.

And I thought about how sad that is.

Someone else's achievement, someone they've never met - and it's the most thrilling event in their life.

Look, I don't care if it's the World Cup, the Super Bowl or little green men landing on Earth, the most thrilling moment in your life should be from something YOU achieve.

And there is inspiration all around every day. You just have to open your eyes. It's constant and never ending.

Tell yourself that you are prepared to look stupid a dozen times today. And when you accomplish the first one, find out what you can learn from it. After your twelfth stupid action, you should have learned twelve new lessons that hopefully made you smarter and better prepared for tomorrow.

Are you getting this?

That's how you use failure... to learn.

Lance did.

He failed and failed and failed.

But because he used his failure to learn...

...he got smarter and smarter and smarter.

Without the failure, he wouldn't be so dominant today.

Without the cancer, he may not have gotten so mentally strong so as to be so unbeatable.

Unless this is an unconscious habit of yours already, do this:

Every single time you mess something up, miss a deadline, miss a sale, lose a race or a game, get angry when you shouldn't or any other kind of screw up, write it down and ask yourself today's empowering question.

You will have answers.

Act on those answers, and you'll grow so fast, learn so much and improve your life skill so completely that you'll look back on your life a year from now and shake your head in amazement.

And don't mourn all the years you didn't do this.

Just get excited. Let go of the failures. Use them to learn and let them go.

OK? OK!

TODAY'S WINNING BELIEFS

-- I use failure to inspire me to improve
-- I am determined to win in life beginning with today
-- I am a champion in all I do
-- I see myself as a winner and I do the things winners do
-- Failure is simply a part of my education process
-- I'm going to win today. I know it

DREAM... AND MAKE IT COME TRUE

TODAY'S EMPOWERING QUOTE

"Far away in the sunshine are my highest inspirations. I may not reach them, but I can look up and see the beauty, believe in them and try to follow where they lead."
   -Louisa May Alcott

TODAY'S EMPOWERING QUESTION

"What can I fantasize about achieving in my life beyond the ordinary?"

TODAY'S FAST SESSION

It was back in '84 or '85, I think.

The new cars had just come out, and one of the new safety features was a change in the rear taillights. Now, instead of just two backlights, there was an additional one in the rear window. This is so that drivers can tell that the automobile in front of them is stopping even if they can't see the lower lights, for any reason.

To me, it was an indicator of wealth.

You see, I was broke, broke, broke.

The way I saw it was, if you could afford a new car--the kind with the new headlight in the rear window—you had made it.

I'd project myself years into the future... as I was surely buying my next old junker. If it had one of those lights, I'd have reached the highest level of success that I could hope for.

I couldn't even imagine anything more than that.

My images of the future were of struggle and hardship.

I would hear imaginary conversations all going wrong. Nothing ever worked out in my mind.

So I never even considered taking any kind of actions that would transport me to a better life. I never tried hard at anything.

It wasn't until I started using affirmations that things began to change. After I made my first audio, my life really started to morph into something completely different.

Now, I know that many people have trouble with affirmations. "I can't do affirmations," is a common belief. That's wrong, because you naturally affirm all day long with every thought you have.

The problem is that you just don't do it CORRECTLY.

I couldn't imagine being successful in a sales career. So naturally my first attempt was with sales and career affirmations. Soon my sales skills (and income) grew by leaps and bounds.

I can't stress enough that to succeed at anything, whether it be career, health, relationships, finances or education, you've got to see what you want. You absolutely must be able to imagine yourself having your goal... You must AFFIRM that you already have it, that you're worthy of it, that you can have it.

See the enjoyment of it. Feel it.

Imagine yourself holding hands with someone. Imagine looking in your bank account and seeing all the zeroes... after another number, of course. See yourself getting the A's and enjoying the process of the studying... of the learning.

Notice how it feels.

See the mistakes that are bound to happen as falling off you like rain. Mistakes will still happen. And you have to see them as temporary... as fixable.

Most people visualize and imagine success, but when things don't go right, they quit... and exclaim that it doesn't work for them.

WRONG!

It DOES work.

But if there are 7 steps to success at something and you take the first six, suffer a setback and give up, then you don't get the success.

That's not a horrible thing if you will just wake up, splash some cold water on your face and admit that whatever temporary setback you had was your fault on some level. Then start your visualizing again.

And if you blame others for your failures, you're doomed. Done. Finished...

...until you wake up.

I believe it's never too late to wake up.

But the longer you're asleep to the fact that, no matter how many areas of life you may have under control, the part of your life that just doesn't work is a reflection of decisions you make, the longer you will fail in that one area.

Sure, there may be other factors that ARE out of your hands.

But you can't blame them. Or you'll continue to fail.

Accept responsibility. Keep your vision alive. And sooner or later, you'll reach it.

TODAY'S WINNING BELIEFS

-- I imagine how my successes will make me feel
-- I enjoy imagining a bright future for myself
-- My images of success are getting clearer now
-- I hold the images of success in my mind for long periods
-- I enjoy taking the steps to make my images come true

STOP WHINING AND START SHINING

TODAY'S EMPOWERING QUOTE

"You can overcome anything if you don't bellyache."
-Bernard M. Baruch

TODAY'S EMPOWERING QUESTION

"Don't I see my solutions easier and faster when I'm calm and relaxed?"

TODAY'S FAST SESSION

One of my subscribers sent me a story that deserves re-telling. So here goes.

One day a farmer's donkey fell down into a well. The animal cried piteously for hours as the farmer tried to figure out what to do.

Finally he decided the animal was very old and the well needed to be covered up anyway. And since it just wasn't worth it to retrieve the donkey, he invited all his neighbors to come over and help him.

They all grabbed shovels and began to shovel dirt into the well.

At first, the donkey realized what was happening and cried horribly. Then, to everyone's amazement, he quieted down.

A few shovel loads later, the farmer finally looked down the well and was astonished at what he saw.

With every shovel of dirt that hit his back, the donkey was doing something amazing. He would shake it off and take a step up.

As the farmer's neighbors continued to shovel dirt on top of the animal, he would shake it off and take a step up.

Pretty soon, everyone was amazed as the donkey stepped up over he edge of the well and trotted off!

Hmmm.

Let me ask you a question...

Today are you likely to get some dirt thrown on you?

How about tomorrow?

And the next day?

Well, that realization will either get you depressed, or you'll feel like you just got the everlasting key to happiness.

Gosh, I hope you choose the second reaction.

Because I'll let you in on a little secret...

There is a solution to every problem. And as each one is on the way to getting fixed, it may be painful.

As soon as that donkey stopped bellyaching, he realized what his answer was.

There is no way, when we are upset, that we can think clearly enough to come up with the answers to the challenges we are faced with.

And why do people get upset when they have oh-so-predictable challenges? Because most folks refuse to believe the basic tenet of life, which is...

EVERYBODY HAS PROBLEMS, EVERYDAY!!!

"That can't be!! John is always in a good mood!! He doesn't have the kind of problems like I do!!! He couldn't possibly!!!"

Look, in a few minutes someone just might burst through your door and tell you of some huuuuge "problem" that just happened.

So instead of crying, do this...

Get the facts. Write down all the options. Weigh the consequences with the potential results of each option.

And make a decision!!!

Just do that.

Wait 'til later to cry.

Because your tears later will have a greater likelihood of being tears of joy over a successful effort that fixed that rotten "problem" than it would be if the tears came earlier.

And remember, life isn't out to get you.

Just keep cool.

And shake it off.

TODAY'S WINNING BELIEFS

-- I learn something new from every challenge I face
-- I am becoming more optimistic every day now
-- I love being alive
-- I'm good at finding the silver lining in every obstacle
-- Life is good

YOU SHOW REAL CLASS WHEN YOU DO THIS...

TODAY'S EMPOWERING QUOTE

"I will utter what I believe today, if it
should contradict all I said yesterday."
  -Wendell Phillips

TODAY'S EMPOWERING QUESTION

"What would I think of (Joe) if he came in right now and told
me he was wrong about the thing he fought so hard for earlier?"

TODAY'S FAST SESSION

I don't know about you, but today's question just blows me away.

Let's say that your employee or co-worker failed to do something very
important. And for whatever reason, let's also say that you happened not to
be in the most resourceful state of mind. In fact you were in a downright
rotten mood.

Now, when you're feeling like this, you don't always act the way you want
to act, right?

Little things can get you going. Possibility?

You're not as forgiving when you feel like this.

You're simply not in the mood for failure or excuses.

Instead, you want to assert your authority, tell 'em what you think. You're
ready for a fight. If you hear any crap, you can't be held liable for what you
do or say. Bring em on!

You call the perpetrator into the room to read them the riot act. You ask
why such and such wasn't done. You tell 'em how important it was. Your
voice starts to get shaky.

"Please just argue with me," you think.

And what do they do?

They agree with you.

Yup.

They start in. "You're absolutely right. I should've done that. There is absolutely no excuse, so I won't give you one. I could've done it, but I didn't. It's my fault totally."

So what do you say?

"Well, it's not all that bad..."

Can you believe it?

They took all the joy out of it for you. You couldn't possibly rip them the new one you had planned.

You must be seen as benevolent now. Merciful. Certainly not the three-headed monster that you'd be if you kept thrashing at them.

I probably shouldn't admit this, but when I was in direct sales in the late 80's and early 90's, I spent a lot of time driving between appointments... and I did my share of speeding. I scheduled myself tight and was in a hurry everywhere I went.

In a space of about 3 years, I got pulled over for speeding 12 times. And I swear to you, I talked my way out of every one of those situations. Of course #13 was unlucky for me, but still... 12 times in a row!

I did it by doing what we're talking about here. I admitted my error... told them that I wasn't in any kind of a hurry and that I wasn't paying attention. I was in the wrong. I deserved a ticket.

So they let me go!

It just wasn't any fun for them. We usually ended up laughing together. One of those times I was going 35 miles per hour over the speed limit. Imagine that!

And yes, I've changed my ways and don't do that any more.

Now obviously, you don't want to be making the same mistake over and over. However, there are often situations where mistakes and setbacks are built into the job by nature.

If you constantly argue and debate and deny and point the finger somewhere else... well, who likes to hear that?

Do you?

When you pull this, you can almost guarantee a fight.

When people do it to you, YOU don't like it.

So don't you do it... Because when you do, you look just as dumb as the people who do it to you. And you will get no mercy.

If you mess up, admit it sincerely... and try not to repeat it.

But if you do it again, admit it again. And learn again.

And you CANNOT say things like "ALLRIGHT, I MADE A MISTAKE!" in an angry, sarcastic tone said obviously just to shut the other person up. You know what it means when others are doing that and so do they. Mean it.

This is a small change, but it has GIGANTIC implications in your life. Because you're probably making little mistakes and inaccuracies all day long. It's called being human.

Admit yours (but don't ever call yourself stupid) and do your best not to repeat them and you'll gain the respect and admiration of all the people in your life...

...Including yourself.

TODAY'S WINNING BELIEFS

-- I respect myself enough to admit my mistakes
-- I'm taking responsibility for my actions
-- I'm helping others become more responsible today
-- I'm able to handle all my duties effectively now
-- I'm honest and sincere with myself and others

IT'S OFFICIAL: NOTHING IS IMPOSSIBLE

TODAY'S EMPOWERING QUOTE

"A lot of people didn't believe in us, but our players believed in themselves and that's all that matters."
  -Bill Belichick, head coach, New England Patriots

TODAY'S EMPOWERING QUESTION

> "Have others been counting me out? Have I?
>   Why have we all been wrong?"

TODAY'S FAST SESSION

It's now official.

NOTHING is impossible.

The second largest underdog in Super Bowl history has won.

David slew Goliath.

All the doubters were wrong... including me.

All week long, every time I got into a conversation about the upcoming game, I expressed how I felt that the Rams were just too good, spouting off facts and statistics, marveling at all those high-powered weapons they possessed...

...forgetting all about desire.

The burning kind.

That is one thing most everyone, including yours truly forgot about.

Look at yourself for a second...

It's easy to count yourself out, isn't it, when no one believes in you?

Isn't it hard to go on when all you see is insurmountable problems?

The Patriots refused to look at how impossible their task seemed.

Instead they looked at their strengths. They focused on what they had, not what they didn't. They had that burning desire.

Adam Vinatieri, the Patriot kicker who ended any final doubt with a 48-yard field goal as time expired, said his sleep the night before the game was filled with dreams about that exact moment, should it occur.

He said after the game, "I must have seen that kick 200 times the night before in my sleep. It always ended good."

If you're not a football fan, that's OK. This isn't about football.

But if you've got a big challenge ahead of you and you have lots of doubts about the outcome, do this...

...Read this past Sunday's newspaper. The same one where all the experts said that there was no way the Rams would lose.

This is important, because you must understand how futile the task seemed, how invincible the Rams seemed, how the Patriots didn't deserve to be there. One journalist even predicted that the Rams would score over 100 points.

It supposedly was that hopeless.

So I ask you to read this because you must know that when things look bleak for you and for people on your team, you must not give up...

...No matter how seemingly impossible the task.

To flip your switch from lose to win, you must be a possibility thinker. And the only way to do that is to constantly be reminded in as many ways as possible that nothing is impossible.

Ignite that burning desire.

Moods and shifts and cycles and tides and momentum threaten us every single day. They can take away our beliefs and our convictions.

Try this habit out. In your local paper's sports section, save the stories of underdogs beating heavily favored opposition.

Re-read them regularly.

And set your goals.

Whenever you make a mistake, a wrong decision, or when someone counts you out, pull the stories out and reaffirm a new belief...

NOTHING IS IMPOSSIBLE!

Even for you.

TODAY'S WINNING BELIEFS

-- Anything is possible for my team and me
-- My faith in myself is strong
-- I trust in my ability to get up from any and all defeats
-- I am all I've got and I am enough

DO UNTO OTHERS...

TODAY'S EMPOWERING QUOTE

"Kindness it is that brings forth kindness always."
  -Sophocles (447 B.C.)

TODAY'S EMPOWERING QUESTION

"Could I gain greater cooperation right now by showing genuine kindness and respect than by demanding it?"

TODAY'S FAST SESSION

A couple days ago, I was watching 'Santa Claus is Coming To Town' with my three year old son, and I noticed an important principle of life playing out.

In the story, the village dictator (the Burgermeister) had outlawed toys because he had fallen on a toy and broken his leg. No child was to play with any toys or they would be locked up.

Well, Kris Kringle (a.k.a. Santa Claus) was delivering toys to all the kids, so he was branded an outlaw. Public Enemy #1.

When Kris confessed to giving the town's children a bunch of toys, he was to be arrested. In a flash of quick thinking, he presented the Burgermeister with a toy--a yo-yo.

For a moment, the Burgermeister began playing with the yo-yo, reminiscing about his youth, until he was reminded that he was breaking his own law. This gave Kris an opening to escape...

...into the forest, which was the home of The Winter Warlock, who captured Kris.

Again, Kris gave him a toy--a choo-choo train. This kind act melted the heart of the warlock, who let Kris go.

Isn't this how it usually happens in your life?

If you aren't the type, yet, who can inspire the cooperation of others because your kindness makes people want to help you and be around you, then it's time to try it out...

...And even get good at it.

But before you do, think back. And look around.

Who gets the admiration and support of others? Who do people work harder for? Is it the one who brings in the doughnuts for co-workers occasionally, the one who asks respectfully or the one who rants and raves that nothing gets done?

Who would you work harder for?

To make this easier to see, imagine how you would like to be asked (not told) to do something.

Isn't it easier to take when you're asked to drop what you're doing, if the person says something like this?:

"I know you're busy and this looks important, however I need to ask you a big favor. Could you...?" Or,

"I wonder if I could ask you to take a few minutes to help me with this...?" Or,

"I know you've got a lot to do, and I don't want you to get behind on account of me, but I have to ask you to..."

Man, wouldn't you like to hear that?

What do you hear from the people who make your blood boil?
Things like:

"Get in here, I need your help!"
"You're working OT today, so cancel any plans you have."
"Get doing your homework now!"
"I need a ride and I have to be there in 15 minutes."

Boy, that makes me want to blow a gasket. How about you?

Also, this can be extended to times when we make mistakes. Let's say someone made a big boo-boo. Of course, they get called on it. The boss, co-worker, spouse, whoever it may be loses their temper. They don't care why the mistake was made.

What do most people do? They deny responsibility, of course!

Aaarrrgh!

Mistakes are not death sentences. They're truly chances to see where your weaknesses are... golden opportunities to identify what you need to work on to make your health, your business, your relationships and your finances better.

But what do most of us do?

"It wasn't me!! The copier was broken. They didn't return my call. I was stuck in traffic." Etc.

Try this. When you make a big blunder, whether you're alone or if someone else catches it, immediately admit it...

...Immediately. Gracefully.

This takes the wind out of the sails of the person who wants to pounce you. If you admit a mistake before it's even noticed by others, they'll likely react in a way that's only about 10-20% as strong as they would if you deny it or blame your circumstances for the error.

And...

Try not to repeat it. And smile. Because you can do this.

TODAY'S WINNING BELIEFS

-- When I want to feel good, I make someone else feel good
-- I treat others how they want to be treated
-- My relationships are getting better today
-- I like people and they like me back
-- I learn from mistakes and avoid them in the future.

LIVE YOUR PASSION

TODAY'S EMPOWERING QUOTE

"I would be banging pillows, thinking I needed eight hours of
sleep. It bothered me for a long time until I found a doctor
who told me to find something I liked to do and consider it a
blessing. I like football."
   -Jon Gruden (Head Coach of the Tampa Bay Buccaneers)

TODAY'S EMPOWERING QUESTION

"What do I love doing that is beneficial to me and other
people?"

TODAY'S FAST SESSION

Before I start, I want to make it clear that Coach Gruden's quote is NOT
used today to tell people who have trouble sleeping, and whose quality of
life is compromised by it, that they should consider it a blessing.

What it DOES mean is that with all the spare time that most of us have
available, the choices that are too often made are very unproductive and kill
any chances of success and happiness.

Many people don't have the luxury of a spare minute. But when it comes to
true spare time, do you spend it playing video games, watching TV or
sitting in a bar somewhere hiding out from life?

If so, we've uncovered one MAJOR cause of feelings of failure. True,
wasting time can also be a symptom as well as a cause, but nevertheless,
different choices can and should be made.

Jon Gruden chose to take his extra 3-4 hours per day and turn himself into
one of the greatest offensive minds in the game of football. At 34 years
old, he became the coach of a professional team. Many of his players were
older than he was. A few years ago at 36, he was asked for I.D. just to buy
a beer at an Oakland A's game.

Top players all over the league would take pay cuts just to play for this
"kid"... because he's a winner. He pushes his players to play with desire
and passion.

We all like to be associated with winners.

So what's it take to be a winner?

A great place to start is looking at the lives of successful people. Go to the library and skim the stories about the lives of the famous. You'll find that they didn't become known because they sit around. They're not just lucky. They're not famous because of their glimmering smile.

This is true even of 'super' models. There are tens of thousands of women as beautiful as they are. But in addition to their looks, the ones you see on all the magazine covers are there because they've worked hard for it.

After you've become thoroughly convinced that success has little to do with luck, the second thing you need to do is look at the thing you love to do the most. I don't care if you're hooked up to oxygen tanks all day; you have something you like to do.

So get on the net, join a club and get involved.

You don't have to be as unbalanced as Jon Gruden. Keep your life together.

But above all else, get involved in the thing that lights your fire. Without a passion in life, there is no spark.

Every day, I get emails from around the world thanking me for my work. They come in because I have a blazing fire of passion for what I do. I love it. I feel like one of the luckiest people on the face of the earth.

But I work extremely hard at it.

Success in one area of life doesn't mean that everything is perfect. When you are in the midst of chaos all the time, you've got to keep up. You've got to strike a balance.

But as things are changing all around you at warp speeds, keep one eye on the part of it that you love. THAT part, despite whatever isn't perfect, will keep your hopes alive, your moods right and give you faith and energy to work on the things that aren't yet how you'd like them.

And it all starts with a passion.

TODAY'S WINNING BELIEFS

-- I watch successful people & learn all I can from them
-- I make the best of every situation in my life
-- I naturally look on the bright side of things
-- I see all weaknesses as challenges that I CAN overcome

THE EXTRA MILE

TODAY'S EMPOWERING QUOTE

"There is no joy in getting by on your job - doing as little as you can.
There is a LOT of pleasure in doing more than you have to. 'And
whosoever shall compel you to go a mile, go with him twain,' says the
Bible, wisely."
   -Norman Carlisle

TODAY'S EMPOWERING QUESTION

"How will I be changed by doing my best at this task?
What will I think of myself?"

TODAY'S FAST SESSION

When we were doing the research for our audio program, Financial
Abundance Now!, I was stunned by a few bits of information researchers
Thomas Stanley and William Danko had published in their 2 million copy
best seller, 'The Millionaire Next Door'.

Among their many remarkable insights gained by interviewing first
generation millionaires (not inherited) for 20 years was that even though
Russian households in America account for only 1.1% of all households,
5.8% of all households in America with a net worth of one million dollars
or more were of Russian ancestry.

So Russians in America are 5 times more likely to become wealthy in
America than the average American household.

It's a prosperity mindset. And that translates into action and wise financial
decisions.

Interestingly, in America, 80% of all wealthy households are first
generation rich. Only 20% are second generation or beyond.

What does this mean?

Well, one thing it means, according to Stanley and Danko, is that by the
2nd and 3rd generations most of the wealth is usually gone. Pfffft! Spent.

298

See, if the kids are born here, the society orients them not to the value of hard work, or of sacrificing for the good of their family, not with teaching values of thrift. We're conditioned here to be good consumers... to spend it.

All of it.

Hey, man. When the economy is in the doldrums and you're in serious danger of losing your job, SPEND! Don't get another job. Help the economy and spend all your spare time spending all your money! Put other people to work serving you... 'Cause you deserve a break today!

That's no joke.

Honestly, this session wasn't supposed to be about finances. The actual topic revolves around the Empowering Quote and Question. The subject is interchangeable. It can be about money, relationships, career, health or spirituality... you plug in your own topic.

Finances just provide an interesting backdrop to how the typical person in America views tasks - any task besides leisure pursuits.

Not to say we don't put in long hours. Studies show we "work" longer than ever before. But our performance as it compares to what we're capable of doing is, well... it sucks.

The average person hates doing things that could actually give them a better life - things that could give them true freedom of choice.

Listen... the floor you've got to refinish, the walls that you're painting, the book you have to read and the test on those chapters are the greatest gift you could ever be given.

I remember how I used to avoid labor of any kind.

My habitual inner thoughts were,

'How come I have to do this?'
'Gosh, they're picky. It's good enough.'
'Why can't someone else do this? He hates me.'
'I'm too good for this.'
'Oh, I can't wait until this is over.'
'I can't do that. It's too hard.'

'I'll never get this done.'
'What can I spend this money on?'
'The boss is gone. Let's take a break.'
'I'll do it tomorrow when it's cooler outside.'

And I woke up each day dumber than the day before.

Man, your tasks are a part of life. If you shirk your responsibilities, other people may get hurt, but think of it this way. You might "get out of" doing something, but you are hurting yourself more than anyone else.

I was the laziest person alive. Many people told me that. I was forced to live in a van because of it. I was drugged out, drunk and stupid for years, yet with some neat technology, turned it all around and now have choices than 99.999% of all living people don't have.

Why?

Because I began to believe that responsibilities were a blessing instead of a curse.

Dirty floor? Wow! Cleaning it will be more practice at being like people I admire... 'do it now' people.

Build a garage? Cool. Think of the space we'll have after it's done. I'll have acquired some great skills, too.

Tearing down, moving and re-installing thirteen office cubicles? Ooh, lots of work. But we'll be so much more productive when it's done. Tons of benefits. Awesome!

What will I think of myself if I do the best job I'm capable of? What will I think of myself if I put in a halfway effort?

You see, when you do less than your best on a regular basis, you see who you are. You can't hide from yourself. Deep inside we all know what top performance looks like - what it feels like inside.

And I'm telling you that your tasks aren't punishment from the gods. They're valuable practice for when it really matters. Every thing you do, no matter how small, creates your character. Your self-image is built from how well or how poorly you do the jobs in your life.

Your gorgeous blond hair doesn't improve your self-image. Your actions do.

When you leave the kitchen table a mess every day, you're creating a destiny. If you start lots of stuff, but finish little, you're watching. You may be ignoring it consciously, but your subconscious mind knows and one more grain of sand is put on the "Loser" side of the scale in your mind.

Get angry a lot? Ever wonder why? It's not because of what others have done to you. It's often from watching people in your same station in life gaining characteristics and opportunities you wish you had but never made work.

It's impossible to act like a loser, to perform poorly at even unimportant tasks and feel like a winner.

The truth is, there are no unimportant tasks. None. Every one is practice for the next one, training to help prepare you for more challenging, more rewarding opportunities. Practice bad habits day in and day out, and you cannot perform well or make correct decisions when you need to.

Every little short cut you take - Every time you lie to someone to cover up a mistake - Every time you take something that isn't yours, YOU are watching. No, you may not get "caught" by someone else. But you caught you.

And that is a whole lot worse.

Ever start to achieve success in some arena of life only to sabotage it? Try to quit a habit but always go back to it? Does this happen over and over?

It's probably because you've caught yourself failing so often, that when you do start to succeed, since you now don't see yourself as a success, your mind literally forces the failure oriented behaviors.

I know today's session was a bit of a pummeling. But the best coaches and leaders who ever lived don't pull punches. You must assess yourself honestly and understand the implications of every action you take, or you will consistently be in spots you can't get out of. Success in life comes from knowing how to duplicate success from one area of life in another area. Master success in one area and you've created the ability to do it in many other parts. You just need to know the core formulas.

We talked about some critical areas just now. Pay attention to them. It's vital to your life. Success and happiness are not mysterious.

It can be predictable. Ask any Russian American.

TODAY'S WINNING BELIEFS

-- I'm doing what is best for me and those important to me today
-- I see myself as a winner and do the things winners do
-- I love solving difficult challenges
-- I am disciplined... that is why I'm successful
-- My willpower is growing every day
-- My tasks in life are my most valuable blessings

ALWAYS DO YOUR PART--YOU'LL NEVER REGRET IT

TODAY'S EMPOWERING QUOTE

"I've never known a man worth his salt who in the long run,
deep down in his heart, didn't appreciate the grind, the
discipline... I firmly believe that any man's finest hour--this
greatest fulfillment to all he holds dear-- is that moment
when he has worked his heart out in a good cause and lies
exhausted on the field of battle victorious."
   --Vince Lombardi

TODAY'S EMPOWERING QUESTION

"Why should I try hard today?"

TODAY'S FAST SESSION

Well I can't hope to say it any better than that master motivator above, but
I'll just add a few feelings about what he said.

Raising children allows us to see the feelings that most adults have when
asked to do something difficult, but who, with years of practice as adults,
hide the fact that we're bummed out about having to do it. Boy, you can
see the physiology of a child change immediately, can't you? They can't
believe their rotten misfortune at having to do this task. We adults hide it
better...sometimes.

And I'll bet you grumble sometimes too. I know I do. Yes, yes. Don't be
shocked. We ALL do it to varying degrees, don't we?

But as is one of the major themes throughout your daily messages, life's not
about just playing and doing selfish things that makes it valuable; it's the
giving and the sacrifice that puts your mark on this world. Soon you'll be
gone. There won't be any more "You" to worry about.

Those of you who still drive while you're wasted won't like this story.

A few years ago, my wife and I were coming home from seeing a movie,
and we got behind a person who was completely bombed out of their mind.
Stopping in the middle of a busy 3-lane highway, swerving all over, barely

missing dozens of cars... who all just drove by, getting where they were going.

It was about 12:00 on a Saturday night, by the way. It happened to be Prom night for a lot of local high schools.

I couldn't bear the thought of seeing the next day's headlines about a group of teenagers killed by a drunk driver.

I followed this person for about four miles and saw 35-40 very close calls with other cars. The 911 operator was on the cell phone with me the whole time until the cops showed up. The person didn't even pull over until he/she drove another quarter mile, driving about 5 miles per hour with the police car right behind them, lights a blazing!

Now, I had other things I wanted to do at that time (like getting some sleep!), but someone probably would've gotten killed without me following back a ways with my flashers on, warning other motorists to be careful as they approached this lunatic at 65-70 MPH, with him/her doing 0-40.

I never got a thank you from anyone, but I saw it as my duty, even if it wasn't in the plans.

My wife was scared as heck throughout the whole thing. I sounded like a basketball play-by-play announcer while on the phone with the 911 operator. "Oh, just missed them! But he'll have another chance in a second. Ooooh!"

Quite a show.

I guess the message today is, do your part. Sacrifice. Help someone else that needs it. Put your shoulder down and work. It's good practice for the times when you'll REALLY need all the determination you can muster. Try as hard as you can at every moment.

Soon enough you'll be where you dream of being. You won't get home any sooner just because you're thinking about it constantly.

Thanks, Vince. You were right...

TODAY'S WINNING BELIEFS

-- Today I'm putting my best effort in everything I do
-- I enjoy my work, no matter what I'm doing
-- I see my obligations as life's cost of admission - and
   I'm happy to pay it
-- I enjoy the thrill of victory after a job well done

FALL DOWN –GET UP, FALL DOWN –GET UP

TODAY'S EMPOWERING QUOTE

"Perseverance is failing 19 times and succeeding the 20th."
-J. Andrews

TODAY'S EMPOWERING QUESTION

"Isn't there something else I can try to get the job done?"

TODAY'S FAST SESSION

Awesome message today!!!!

It seems like at every turn, we get confirmation that some thing that we're working on or something that we want to happen isn't going to go quite like we planned. I mean, doesn't it seem like no matter what you're doing-homework, yard work, packing for a trip, fixing a broken 'something-or-other,' that it takes longer than you planned or might not work at all?

And doesn't it get you really upset to invest a whole lot of time into something and watch it all go 'Poof!' before your eyes?

Many of us have been conditioned to believe that easy is best. We're surrounded by examples of this everywhere:

- Why buy the walk-behind mower when you can get a riding one?
- Stand up to change channels? Just use the remote!
- Why chop, slice and cook fresh food when ready-to-cook and frozen is available?
- Exercise to lose fat? I'll just get liposuction someday.
- Adopt healthy eating habits? No way—I'll just pop this diet pill or magic herb to lose weight.
- Go to counseling or take other self-help measures to feel upbeat? It's easier just to pop an anti-depressant everyday.

Now don't get me wrong, there may be instances where these "conveniences" could be necessary. Someone may need to use a riding mower if they have leg problems and cannot walk to mow the lawn. Someone may be helped by an anti-depressant in conjunction with therapy following the death of a loved one.

306

But for the most part, the conveniences that surround our lives are the result of, and help perpetuate, the "easy is best" mindset. If it's tough, requires hard work or takes a long time, many people run and hide!

It doesn't help at all, does it, that the images we see on television show problems getting solved in 30 seconds, or at worst 60 minutes? So when our own problems take days, weeks and years to solve, it's too tempting to give up. Call it quits...

...long before we should.

It's sad, but many of us, (and I was a part of this group until my mid twenties), "learn" that things don't go our way, usually. We believe that nothing is easy. And since "easy is best," why bother?

In short, we settle.

Eating right, for example, would require discipline. Can't have that. It's not easy or fun. So we "settle" for being not that fat and indulge in fast food.

Concentrating and studying would earn A's and B's, but it means ignoring all the fun things we could be doing right now. So, we "settle" for just passing grades instead.

Having a vice like a drink or smoke comforts us when we do try something and fail...like we knew we would.

But it doesn't matter what age you are--you can start now to begin learning how rewarding and exhilarating it can be to shoot for something big.

Here's how.

Give yourself guideposts along the way. If your goal has 20 steps, write down what each of them are. When you reach each one, it's time for a little celebration.

How likely would you be to give up and quit after you reached a guidepost and it's time to celebrate? Not very, huh?

Let's say you wanted to run 3 miles per day, 5 days per week. Look at the existing patterns—can't even walk 50 feet without being out of breath. OK.

One guidepost could be to go for a 20-minute stroll without getting out of breath. After doing this for a week, you notice you're no longer getting winded. It's time to celebrate!

Smile. Write down how you feel right now. Ask yourself how you did it. Write down the answer. And smile some more. Laugh if you want!

So you go a little longer now—30 minutes. Once you have that down, you maybe pick up the pace from a stroll to a brisk stride. Then you extend your time to 40 minutes. And so on. One guidepost after another...

And let's say that you've done well for two whole months, and then you try to jog instead of walk and get all out of breath, sore and tired. Did you fail?

Listen: Making mistakes ISN'T failure. Failure is quitting. So did you fail? No. With a qualifier. You can't fail if you continue trying, and if you attempt to learn something from your setback. In this case, you just tried to do too much too soon.

When I started climbing out of the hole I'd dug for myself in life, it seemed like I "failed" even more than before. I fell down a lot. After all, I was used to failing... really failing.

And it hurt. Really bad sometimes.

But the big difference was that I quit quitting. I started learning what I was doing wrong and corrected it. And failing some more. And learning. And succeeding. And failing and learning and succeeding again.

And I'm telling you that the procedure that I just shared with you is an often used formula of success in all areas of life. Millions of people have done this. Millions are doing it today to change their lives right now.

You can, too.

Pick a goal. Doesn't matter what it is. Apply the formula. And when you're tempted to quit, look back at the guideposts that you've passed. Smile. Cry. And get excited...

...Because you're on the right path.

TODAY'S WINNING BELIEFS

-- I get back up and keep trying after a setback
-- I learn from every non-success
-- When I succeed, I ask how I did it and learn from it
-- At every setback, I ask why it happened and learn from it
-- All my goals give me the chance to succeed many times at many stages

WHEN YOU LOOK FOR THE FUN, YOU'LL FIND IT

TODAY'S EMPOWERING QUOTE

"Experience shows that success is due less to ability than to zeal. The winner is he who gives himself to his work, body and soul."
    -Charles Buxton

TODAY'S EMPOWERING QUESTION

"What do I really love about what I'm doing right now?
What could I love about it?"

TODAY'S FAST SESSION

For years, I chased money. I thought if I could just earn a lot of money, I'd be happy.

Boy, was I wrong!

All I did was work harder and harder and never truly got paid enough for what I was putting in. So not only did I not have the amount of money that I really wanted, but I was miserable to boot!

Sure, I put on the happy face and used all the mental techniques to get top performance out of myself. But when the day's over, you've got to be happy doing what you're doing.

If you're a student, you've got little choice. Go to class and study!

But look to do something after graduation that you'll love! If you do what you love, you'll find a way to make your mark.

Recently, I saw Larry King interview Steve Irwin, better known as "The Crocodile Hunter." I think he's a little bit "crazy," but one thing stands out about this guy...

He LOVES what he does!

His mother and father were both into animal conservation, so he had little choice about his surroundings as a kid. But he loved it and got really good at it.

310

None of his friends where he moved to believed that he hunted crocodiles. So he bought one of the first video cameras on the market, and filmed himself wrestling with these crocs. It's AMAZING to watch him do it.

A producer got a hold of one of these tapes and immediately thought, "This guy's crazy! People will love it!" He was right, and since then, Steve's life has never been the same. His show now plays in over 60 countries.

Steve blew me away. And it's not just animals that flip his switch. No matter what the subject, he is interested, inquisitive, excited and gets all he can out of every experience of life.

Do you know what the difference between Steve Irwin and most every other person alive?

Two things...

One, he loves what he does.

If he were just chasing money, we probably never would've heard of him... because he wouldn't have stayed in animal conservancy. His fame and wealth grew out of his passion for his career.

Two, no matter what he's doing, he's asking better questions than most people ask all day.

He's always asking, 'What's interesting about this?' 'How do they do that?' 'How can I make this more fun?' 'How can we do it better or more efficiently?' 'What can we do now that will make this job less boring?'

You see, he has to do a lot of boring work... sitting around observing, writing technical papers, etc. So it's not all fun and games. But he habitually asks questions that most other people don't ask...

Every single minute of the day.

How can you make today more fun? How can you make your work easier today, while actually maintaining high quality and/or speed? How can you remember the information more completely?

Keep asking those questions and more like it, and no matter what you do for a living, you'll be happy and successful.

TODAY'S WINNING BELIEFS

-- I'm doing what I love and I love what I do
-- I make my job interesting and fun
-- I ask myself empowering questions all day, every day
-- I look for the fun in everything and I find it
-- Laughing is high on my list of priorities

LEMONS + RIGHT ATTITUDE = LEMONADE

TODAY'S EMPOWERING QUOTE

"Adversity introduces a man to himself."
   -Unknown

TODAY'S EMPOWERING QUESTION

"Who can help? What can I do? Can a tool help? What's the worst that could happen? Can I live with that? Is it possible to put a smile on?"

TODAY'S FAST SESSION

Lots of empowering questions today, huh?

Well, in many situations you've got to keep firing these kinds of questions at yourself and keep your possibility hat on so real answers can come to you.

The first step in getting through any trying situation is to first realize that you can... if you don't break down.

If you don't have the core belief that you can get through this next thing, then it won't be possible for you to ask these types of questions...

...Just as if the ability itself to even think of asking these questions is locked in a vault. Tell yourself that you believe.

That's why so many millions (billions) of people lock up and never come up with answers when they need them. They don't ask the right questions. Why? They don't believe there is an answer, and if there is, they don't think they can come up with it.

I happen to live in Syracuse, NY...the snowiest major city in the US. In March of 1993, a storm roared up the east coast. Rain, snow, high winds. Not good. In Syracuse, 43" of snow fell in just under 48 hours. Add bone-chilling winds and you've got a real "party"...

...which is just what we were preparing for that day.

About 40 people (business associates and friends) were supposed to come over. We had the food. The drinks. My wife loves to entertain, so she spent the previous 24 hours buying the stuff and cooking and making phone calls. It was going to be a party to end all parties.

Well, I'm coming from business in Albany, two hours away, flying down the NYS Thruway listening to the weather reports. People are all over the road. Off to the right. Off to the left. The DJ's saying that any minute they could close the roads...

...I'm flying. I got a party to go to. And a driveway to clean!

They closed the Thruway within 5 minutes of my exiting.

My wife was getting really bummed out. It didn't look good. In fact, if you watched the news, it was a absolute horror show.

What to do?

I got on the phone. Calling everyone. "Hey! Party's still on! Bring your sleeping bags and pajamas! Lots of food. Plenty to drink..."

...nothing. No one can make it. The plows have stopped plowing. A state of emergency is declared by the governor.

What to do? We're not eating all this food!

Call the neighbors! They can walk. Well, they can trudge! Yeah! There's the answer I've been looking for!

Soon, we had a bunch of people over eating and laughing and having a ball! And that was the idea in the first place.

I have a question for you...

How many times, when you have a situation where things don't look good at all, do you stop asking the barrage of questions that bring you the positive answers that will solve it. Do you ask any?

Or do you ask questions like, "How am I going to explain this to..." or "Who or what can I blame?"

During that storm, aside from when I was shoveling snow, I kept a smile on because there are few things in life that are worth getting worked up about.

Now go forth today and make yourself proud!

Ask yourself to come up with answers. And keep asking until you get them. Find the lesson that is hiding -wanting to be found- inside each adversity.

Rarely do champions in any sport end their seasons undefeated. But they still get crowned Kings and Queens because they learn from their mistakes and defeats. They ask, "What should I do next time?"

The ones that don't, go home... confused?

By the way, after Syracuse was pounded with more snow than any other US city during that unbelievable east coast massacre, the Sunday newspaper (that arrived on Monday) had this headline:

WE'RE SNOW KING!

TODAY'S WINNING BELIEFS

-- I see problems as learning opportunities
-- I focus on solutions and I find them
-- I take responsibility for my moods
-- My attitude is in great hands with me
-- I always find the lesson in each adversity

REPEAT AFTER ME: "I'M AWESOME!"

TODAY'S EMPOWERING QUOTE

"I began to understand that self-esteem isn't everything; it's just that there's nothing without it."
 -Gloria Steinem

TODAY'S EMPOWERING QUESTION

 "What are five things that are good about me?"

TODAY'S FAST SESSION

A number of years ago, an eastern university conducted a study on self-image and some of the ways it can affect a person's actions.

The women in a large neighborhood were targeted for a direct mailing. Letters were addressed to them. The letters were kind of a celebration. They were just a generic "thank you for being so wonderful in all you do"-type letter. Thanks for being so generous where you're needed, for being a good Mom, neighbor, wife, employee in a world where they're being pulled in lots of directions. "We salute you!"

Hundreds of letters went out...

...to <u>half</u> the women in the neighborhood. The other half got nothing.

Then, a week later, a national charity (not related or affiliated with the university that did the study) sent volunteers into the neighborhood to solicit donations for their cause.

Can you guess?

The women who received mailings saluting them for their generosity and other qualities gave over 60% more often, and when they did give, they donated over 50% more money than the women who received no mailing.

The conclusion the researchers came to was that the image they now had of themselves which they had to live up to was one of being generous with their time, skills and financial resources.

316

Think about it. Only one letter. And a week later, they were still glowing in their new self-image.

It must have been one heck of a letter!!

We all WANT to feel good about ourselves. But not many people, including ourselves, are coming up and telling us how wonderful we are.

It makes me think of the Budweiser slogan, "For all you do, this Bud's for you!" Do you think they came up with that by accident? Heck no. They want us all to feel we "deserve" to have a Bud, that we're good enough. Keep your eyes on commercials and how they try to make you feel smart and then tie that feeling into their products.

So how can you use this interesting study to your benefit? Glad you asked.

What you need to do is become your own letter writer.

The minority who become the most, enjoy life the most and who produce the most and get rewarded the most, don't sit around waiting for other people to tell them how smart, handsome, polite or what a hard worker they are.

They tell themselves this stuff.

Just before I created my first 3x5 cards and my first tapes, I was almost dead in every sense of the word. And within days, I started to feel the feelings and take the actions that would spin me around and send me in the direction I'm still moving in today.

Go back and look at previous day's sessions. Check out those affirming beliefs at the end of each letter.

Make them who you are by reading them at least three times per day. Choose only 10-15 at a time and stick with the ones you are reading until they have changed your attitudes and actions. I promise you they will. If you have gotten through this whole book, read it consistently, not all in one day, and still you have not overcome some major hurdles, I'm going to tell you why.

It's because you've treated this just like all those other self-help books you have in boxes or sold in your last garage sale. I'm asking you for 5-10 minutes a day. That's all it will take.

The only way for you to stop stuffing your mouth full of junk food, to start that exercise program, to stop any and all of your bad habits and to program your body's intelligence to start fighting whatever diseases are fighting you, is to change the image you have of yourself. You've got to.

Start today.

You ARE awesome.

Tell that to yourself every single day and it will grow to be truer every single day.

TODAY'S WINNING BELIEFS

-- My self-image is that of a winner
-- I am what I need to be when I need to be it
-- I play an important role in the lives of many
-- My energy is growing every day

HOW TO REACH THE TOP STARTING FROM ANYWHERE

TODAY'S EMPOWERING QUOTE

'Twenty years ago, when I went blind, it was tough to even find the bathroom. Now that I've climbed Mount Everest, well, I guess I've come a long way.'
  -Erik Weihenmayer

TODAY'S EMPOWERING QUESTION

What limitations have I been clinging to that I should and will throw right out the window, never to look back at again?

TODAY'S FAST SESSION

Erik Weihenmayer went completely blind when he was 13....

Since then he's climbed the world's tallest mountains, run marathons and jumped out of planes, among his many pursuits.

Erik's story is about having the 'vision' to dream big; the courage to reach for near impossible goals; and the grit, determination, and ingenuity to transform his life into 'something miraculous.'

If you want to learn more about Erik, his book, 'Touch the Top of the World' can be found just about anywhere.

OK. So if a blind guy can climb the world's tallest mountain...

How do those excuses sound that you keep coming up with about why you can't do that paltry little project that's been sticking its tongue out at you for months now.

People like Erik only have one thing that separates them from most everyone else; the attitude that life is to be lived; that accomplishments require some risk, and that the risks themselves can make life juicy and fun.

Now, it's probably not required that you risk life and limb to achieve most of your goals, is it?

You want some juice, don't you? Accomplishment? Real excitement?

Then set a big goal. A REALLY big goal. But whatever it is, it's got to stretch you. It's got to be something that you really want... something that would really change your life.

Write down all the steps it will take. Who do you have to call? Where do you have to go? Does it require special training? Do you need tools or supplies?

What sacrifices do you have to make?

Sitting on the couch for another 10 minutes might be pretty 'comfortable.' Taking one more unimportant phone call might be more 'fun' in the moment.

But at the end of the day when you look in the mirror... the only way THAT'S going to be fun is if you cut short the unimportant phone calls, got off the comfortable couch, stopped hiding out and took some major steps toward a big goal... every day. If you do that consistently, you'll start to really be proud of who you're becoming.

Those 'sacrifices,' if you'll look at them aren't sacrifices at all.

Happiness comes from what you become, not what you get. If you become more, you'll get more automatically. It's one of those cosmic universal laws.

Erik Weihenmayer, in achieving his goals, has become more. Now he gets paid huge sums to talk to thousands of people every year about the thrill of working to reach your wildest dreams. He gets to write about it.

90% of the people who attempt to climb to the peak of Mount Everest fail. Many die. Erik 'looked' past the risk and 'focused' instead on the reward, and went after it passionately.

So even though he's blind, he wouldn't trade his life for anyone else's. His life is his life, so he's enjoying every bit of it.

When Erik was about 15 minutes from the top of the world's tallest mountain, so close to his goal, he started to cry... but his tears were freezing, making it difficult to breath in his mask.

So he had to put off crying with his blind eyes for another 15 minutes...

...until he actually reached the top of the world.

TODAY'S WINNING BELIEFS

-- I am working hard to reach my biggest goal now
-- I learn something valuable every day in pursuing my goal
-- I am becoming more today than I was yesterday
-- I love reaching for and achieving challenging goals
-- I can do it... I know I can

Congratulations. You can and you did!

I love you,

Mike